Historians

Also by Daniel Snowman

America Since 1920 (1968)

Eleanor Roosevelt (1970)

Kissing Cousins: An Interpretation of British and American Culture, 1945–1975 (1977, published in USA as *Britain and America: An Interpretation of their Culture*)

If I Had Been ... Ten Historical Fantasies (editor, 1979)

The Amadeus Quartet. The Men and the Music (1981)

The World of Plácido Domingo (1985)

Beyond the Tunnel of History: the 1989 BBC Reith Lectures (with Jacques Darras, 1990)

Pole Positions: The Polar Regions and the Future of the Planet (1993)

Plácido Domingo Tales From the Opera (1994)

Fins de Siècle: How Centuries End, 1400–2000 (editor, with Asa Briggs, 1996)

PastMasters: The Best of 'History Today' (editor, 2001)

The Hitler Emigrés: The Cultural Impact on Britain of Refugees from Nazism (2002)

Historians

DANIEL SNOWMAN

First published 2007 by
PALGRAVE MACMILLAN
Houndmills, Basingstoke, Hampshire RG21 6XS and
175 Fifth Avenue, New York, N.Y. 10010
Companies and representatives throughout the world

PALGRAVE MACMILLAN is the global academic imprint of the
Palgrave Macmillan division of St. Martin's Press, LLC and of
Palgrave Macmillan Ltd.
Macmillan® is a registered trademark in the United States,
United Kingdom and other countries. Palgrave is a registered
trademark in the European Union and other countries.

ISBN-13: 978–1–4039–8805–8 hardback
ISBN-10: 1–4039–8805–6 hardback

This book is printed on paper suitable for recycling and
made from fully managed and sustained forest sources.

A catalogue record for this book is available from the British Library.

A catalogue record for this book is available from the Library of
Congress.

10   9   8   7   6   5   4   3   2   1
16 15 14 13 12 11 10 09 08 07

Printed and bound in Great Britain by
Antony Rowe Ltd, Chippenham and Eastbourne

Contents

Introduction: Historians Today

Historians are Very Important People (for reasons I'll come to in a moment). Some of them, anyway. In these essays, I have written about some of the best and most important among them. The essays were originally published from October 1998 until October 2005, more or less quarterly, in the pages of *History Today*. From the outset, and in close consultation with *HT*'s editor Peter Furtado, I decided to concentrate on historians of proven excellence who were still publishing and whose work had reached a wide audience and raised issues beyond the purely scholarly. In each case, I tried to read everything I could that had been published by the historian concerned and we would then usually have lunch together followed by a lengthy interview which I would record. The essays are reproduced in the order in which they originally appeared. All – especially those published longest ago – have required updates and the historians themselves have each been invited to provide this in the form of a CV and bibliography and (if they wished), an epilogue. Each was also invited to correct any errors of fact that might have crept into my original essay (and, as you will see, one or two have also chosen to rectify what they view as errors of judgement on my part). For all the variety of talent represented in these pages, there are notable absences. I would like to have included a wider range of expertise (there is little Ancient or Asian history here and not enough North or South American). And there are of course many historians whom I haven't been able to write about but whose work would warrant inclusion. Next time, perhaps. I particularly regret the absence of two late friends: Raphael Samuel, whom I first met in about 1970, a genial Socrates figure whose immense influence was generated primarily through personal contact and example and only latterly through his published work; and Roy Porter, a scintillating supernova of talent, charm and productivity, with whom I had been discussing a possible date shortly before he burned himself out at age 55.

Most of those included are people whose work I was already acquainted with and admired, and many I knew personally: Asa Briggs and Peter Burke were colleagues at Sussex, while several had broadcast for me during my years at the BBC. Some had achieved considerable fame, especially on TV, though it was their work as historians not their celebrity that I wanted to write about. When I phoned Simon Schama to discuss our forthcoming meeting, he expressed delight that, for the first time in years, an interviewer wanted to talk about his researches into Dutch and French history rather than his blockbuster TV series about Britain.

One of the historians in the collection remarked to me recently that over the previous few years I had probably read more books on a wider range of subjects than any other historian he knew. I can't quite believe that. But I have certainly been immensely enriched as I have worked my way through books about warfare ancient and modern, empires and imperialisms, social and economic history, art and popular culture, food, gifts, witchcraft, plague, banditry, maps, the media, impostors and the nature of history itself. I have spent weeks at a time intellectually immured in medieval England, Early Modern France and Germany, Tudor, Stuart and Hanoverian Britain, revolutionary France and Russia, post-Civil War America, Poland, Ireland, and Wilhelmine, Weimar and Nazi Germany, as well as some of the further reaches of time and place.

On re-reading the resulting essays, I find they provide an interesting snapshot of history and historians at century's turn. All the major issues in current historiography are here. These historians, indeed, are among the leading figures who have helped set the agenda. Thus, social history owes an immeasurable debt to Asa Briggs and Eric Hobsbawm, and cultural and women's history to the work of Natalie Zemon Davis. Davis has also led the way in the imaginative reconstruction of the past, and has helped pioneer cross-cultural history – an approach that has yielded rich fruit in recent works by David Cannadine and Linda Colley. Some, such as Norman Davies and Jeremy Black, have broadened their purview still further and attempted to incorporate the history of entire continents. Geoffrey Hosking, one of the few historians of Russia to take seriously its religious and regional past, has been vindicated in recent years with the revival in the former Soviet Union of cultural nationalism and religious observation. Another Russian expert, Orlando Figes, has – like Lisa Jardine – made notable efforts to bring the arts and sciences in from the historiographical peripheries, while Lyndal Roper and Theodore Zeldin (again, like Natalie Davis) have attempted to comprehend the psychology of those they have written about. Peter Burke and John Brewer have been formative influences in our understanding of the reception and dissemination of culture and its artefacts, while Richard Evans has helped lead the fight against excessive postmodernism. There may be no out-and-out postmodernists among this collection; but if you are interested in 'counterfactual' history, you can read about one of its most persuasive practitioners, Niall Ferguson. Old-fashioned virtues are on display here, too. Is the much-vaunted 'return of narrative history' reflected in the work of these historians? Few can pen a good story better than Schama, while well-researched, well-crafted biographies by Antonia Fraser, Ian Kershaw, David Starkey, Roy Foster and Peter Stansky demonstrate that a long-tested genre is far from exhausted. Some historians have led me, like Watson following Holmes, into the forensic minutiae of specialist investigation; others took a larger view – none more so than

Felipe Fernández-Armesto who taught me how to adopt a galactic view of our little global story.

As I encountered my procession of historians, it was illuminating to discover how each, when faced with a large and daunting project or an initially inchoate mass of data, would find a way of drawing upon particular talents and techniques in the struggle to coordinate, shape, pare and share the relevant material. The works they have published are as varied as the people themselves, and I have found myself reading, and writing about, long books, short books, books that describe and books that analyse, books brimming with personality and colour and others stuffed with statistical analysis. Some are chronological, others primarily thematic, some picture-packed, others unillustrated. One historian, like the potter turning his clay this way and that, forever refining it upon the wheel, favours extended metaphor; another goes for the literal. Most were affable and communicative, generously prepared to reveal much about themselves as well as about their work. I have not only learned a lot of history; I have also learned about the wide variety of ways in which it can be approached, researched and written.

*   *   *

I have also been led to think about the current significance of history and historians. I began by saying that historians were important people. Let me explain why I think this is so.

History is everywhere, or so it seemed as we entered our new millennium. On television, Henry VIII and Hitler, Pyramids and Puritans, antique roadshows, costume dramas, *Timewatch* and *Time Team* jostled to fill the airwaves and garner large audiences on a plethora of terrestrial and specialized channels. Visitor numbers to museums, galleries and heritage sites burgeoned while a raft of new historical magazines sprouted. In the bookshops, sales of biographies and war books almost rivalled those on how to enhance your corporate, coital or culinary competence, and the 'qualipop' press mined new gold with daily stories purporting to show how recently discovered historical documents threw new (often contentious) light upon historical personalities, artefacts and events. Family and local history flourished, while monarchs and emperors, presidents, popes and premiers were pressed to 'apologize' for the actions of their predecessors several generations or even centuries before. The past may be a foreign country; but history, it seemed, was inescapable.

Or was it? Was the succession of sensational press stories new gold or fools' gold? Was the demand for historical apology a serious attempt to come to terms with the past or a form of crude (and often financially fuelled) gesture politics? Did radio and TV programmes, or the opening up of 'Heritage' sites, provide a genuine sense of continuity between past and present or an anaesthetized theme park, fun to experience but nothing to do with us? Our age, many argue, is one that lives in an immediate present, obsessed with the 'new', the fashionable, with little awareness of the ways our living present derives from its continuity with all that has preceded it. When Britain marked the great calendrical transition from one millennium to the next, it contrived to do so with a vast domed exhibition that avoided all mention of life in these islands over previous centuries. When the Mayor of London invited suggestions regarding the Trafalgar Square statuary, he made a point of displaying his ignorance about – and indifference towards – the statues already there. Interest, it seemed, was focused on the immediate present. The point was not lost on historians. 'Most young men and women' (wrote a disgruntled Eric Hobsbawm) 'grow up in a sort of permanent present lacking any organic relation to the public past of the times they live in.' Eric Foner ended his book on the history of American freedom noting that Americans 'have sometimes believed they enjoy the greatest freedom of all – freedom from history', a chimera, Foner warned, for no people can escape being bound, to some extent, by their past. We live, said David Cannadine (in his 1999 inaugural lecture as Director of the Institute of Historical Research), in 'a society which is increasingly amnesiac and ahistorical'.

So, is an interest in history in the ascendant? Or, *par contra*, do we live in an age singularly bereft of historical awareness? Could both be true? Perhaps there is no mystery and we are simply talking about different groups of people: those who are more interested in history and those who are less so. Evidence from book sales, TV audience and heritage visitor research and the like suggests that people expressing an interest in the past tend to be older, better educated and wealthier than the average. Since the population of Britain and most Western societies contains more and more elderly people with disposable time and income than ever before, an overall increase in what we might call the 'consumption' of history would seem almost inevitable. Against that, however, is the fact that it is the younger generation, not the 'oldies' with time and money on their hands, who are most at home with that miraculous modern gateway to local and family history, the computer, while cheap travel enables even youngsters with limited resources to visit such hitherto remote exotica as Angkor Wat and Machu Picchu. The historical re-enactment societies that have sprouted like hydra heads succeed in recruiting plenty of young enthusiasts keen to learn what it was like living as a Roman or a Roundhead. Yet these are the same youngsters who, in other aspects of their lives, are preoccupied with the transient and the fashionable. While there is a plethora of 'popular' history around, in other words, we also seem to live in an age in which many who express an interest in it nonetheless seem to live their normal lives in a bubble of immediate present and imminent future.

Why, in such a world, would people be so keen to revisit the past, to consume it, to 'experience' it? What can history

mean to those who so avidly commodify and consume it?
It would seem the current 'history wave' might be telling us
more about ourselves than it does about the past. What are
the messages behind today's portrayals of the past that people
seek, or receive, from the ways it is purveyed and consumed?
The answers to that question will place the purveyors of history
– the historians – in a new light.

*   *   *

There is nothing novel in people being interested in earlier times.
There was a burst of 'historicism' in the decades following the
French Revolutionary wars, for example, when 'Gothic' and
neoclassical buildings sprang up across Europe and America,
while Victoria and Albert posed for Landseer as medievals and
Italian composers placed their latest operas in Tudor or Stuart
England. What's new, perhaps, is the sheer scale of today's
engagement with the legacy of the past. By the late 1990s,
when I started writing the essays in this book, people were
beginning to take note of the emerging history wave, dubbing
it 'the new rock and roll' and 'the new gardening' (and even
'the new sex'). Let's not overstate the case. History isn't any of
those things, and has probably never been quite that popular!
But there's no doubt: history 'sells' – not just to a cultured elite
but, nowadays, to a mass market.

An interest in the past can answer many needs. For some,
history seems to provide an imaginative escape from the 'here
and now' to the 'there and then': a kind of tourism of the mind.
The past is, indeed, a little like a foreign country where they
do things differently. Everyone can recognize the pleasure in
browsing through the tourist brochures. Similar restorative
powers reside in a book or television programme about larger-
than-life characters caught up in exciting events in exotic times
and places. What better, after a busy day at the office and a
debilitating fight with the rush-hour crowds, than to settle

down to an evening with the Pharaohs, the mistresses of Louis XIV or the epic battles of World War II? The sheer romance and drama of history is part of its attraction.

So is its apparent capacity to provide ballast from the past to vindicate the present. We visit magnificently preserved sites and come out feeling good about our 'heritage' or our 'traditions'. To British eyes, a book or TV programme about Elizabeth I, Nelson or Churchill might confirm views about national intrepidity in the face of an invasive continent, much as Americans might find an absorbing account of Jefferson or Lincoln reinforcing their views about the integrity of the present-day USA. We all look to the past to help explain, or affirm, aspects of the present. Indeed, one can hardly make sense of the present at all without at least some effort to understand how things came to be the way they are. Every sectarian or nationalist cause has its litany of historical wrongs to be righted: Serbs and Croats, Greeks and Turks, Israelis and Palestinians, Indian Muslims and Hindus, Irish Protestants and Catholics – all have appealed to history to help boost their cause, to justify the present or to reinforce the dream of an alternative future.

In recent years, the political use of the past as a weapon with which to demand a supposedly improved present and future has taken on new forms, in particular the widespread demand that leaders 'apologize' for supposed wrongs in the past. Thus, governments in Australia and North America have been pressed by indigenous and ethnic minorities to apologize for earlier oppression, those in Germany and Japan for their countries' atrocities in World War II, the British for the Irish famine or Amritsar massacre, the Vatican for the Crusades, Inquisition and Catholic anti-Semitism.

If history is a favourite refuge for those seeking justification, compensation or vindication, it can also provide a seductive home-away-from-home for those in search of nostalgia. Which of us hasn't succumbed to the golden glow of times faintly but warmly remembered on hearing a song from our childhood or leafing through an old photo album or sheaf of old newspapers? Nostalgia has potency beyond personal memory. We may not have been raised in a medieval castle or fought for Cromwell, Bonaparte or Robert E. Lee. But anyone with a little historical imagination and a good book can relish the vicarious experience. 'Experience', indeed, is the favoured word nowadays of many historical museums and exhibitions which, like TV reconstructions of times past, are designed to give the person of today a feel for the texture of life in an earlier era.

We cannot literally 'experience' the past, of course. In reality, we are distanced from it, immunized from its deleterious effects, able to savour even its most appalling moments from a position of safety. We are similarly distanced, too, from its beauties. Of course, millions nowadays read about the world's most magnificent historic buildings, see them on television and are invited to vote for which dilapidated historic buildings they would most like to 'save'. Huge numbers visit legions of art-filled palaces and chapels once erected and occupied by the elite and now open to the wider public. You and I can stand where once only monarchs and emperors stood, see paintings and hear music that in former times only they and their entourage would have been able to enjoy. Yet the way we share these aristocratic glories from the past keeps us firmly at arm's length from the experience of those for whom they were originally created. Many great historic houses and palaces have, in effect, become art museums in which visitors – or television cameras – are led along corridors, past one carefully roped-off bedroom or reception chamber after another, and invited to glance up at a priceless tapestry, an elaborate candelabra, an elegantly-carved secretaire, a superbly painted ceiling, before moving on to the next room. Nothing must be touched, no spinet played, no chair or sofa sat upon. The artwork may be magnificent. But it is easy to forget that people used to live here.

Thus, the historical 'experience' becomes anaesthetized, prettified, a degree of clinical safety built into the way we view the past and its denizens. Our predecessors, even the mighty popes and princes we see pictured on palace walls, seem vulnerable to our gaze. We know more and more about them and the times in which they lived as we seek them out, discuss them, argue about them, visit their homes, look at their clothes, read their private letters, gaze on their beds, tables and tombs. But they know nothing of us and our times. History is one-way traffic. The present can investigate the past, not the other way round. There is perhaps a subtle message of reassurance in all this. The objects of the past, its barbarisms no less than its beauties, are available for our inspection whenever we want, while we ourselves remain safely immune to its dangers. It is almost as though history were a dream, full of colour and drama, from which we know we will wake up, nicely tucked up in our warm modern beds.

History has yet more to offer. Many look to it for clarity in a world of confused certainties. How nice, after a day grappling with the complex judgements of daily life, to be able to sit back and relish the 'greatness' of Lincoln or Churchill or the 'evil' of Attila the Hun, Ivan the Terrible, Stalin or Hitler. The past offers clarity in another way too. 'Real life', as you and I experience it, consists of a mass of interconnected experiences, most of them trivial and without clear-cut lines of demarcation between them. But anyone wishing to communicate something of the past must define and edit his or her material. Thus, there are studies of political, social or cultural history, biographies, books about the Tudors or Stuarts, volumes on a particularly decade or century – all of which inevitably omit more than they include. In much the same way, there are places marked off as 'historic sites' – implying that other places aren't. Much history is presented as 'national', even when concerned with periods before the nation state took shape. The fact that the past is packaged in such ways suggests that it had shape, pattern

and point, far more than our lives would seem to do while
we are living them, and that its conflicts and problems were
neatly resolved, usually by colourful and decisive personalities.
Unlike the messy real lives that we have to live, history appears
to have been composed of discrete lumps that can be safely
labelled and categorized; unlike those at the time, we know
how things worked out later. History, in other words, allows
the comfort of 'closure'.

It offers one other thing, too – currently perhaps the most
important. A generation or two back, most people in the West
tended to be happy identifying themselves by reference to
various more or less immutable institutional criteria. You had
a name and address, a nationality, an educational and income
level, a job and probably a family and a religion. But in recent
years, the authority of many social and political institutions
has come to be questioned. The family is no longer the tightly
defined, generally accepted unit of society it once was. Similarly,
there has been a sharp erosion of respect for political elites,
the judiciary, the church, the academy, the medical profession
and the police. When people come to have doubts about the
integrity of such formerly defining institutions, their own self-
definition comes under scrutiny, a tendency further stimulated
by the growing ease with which people could move from one
job, partner, home or part of the world to another. If I am no
longer sure I see myself primarily in terms of my nationality,
domicile, work or political, church or family affiliation – who
am I? The question of identity lies at the heart of Natalie Davis'
Martin Guerre.

Many have come to seek new forms of identity: in ethnic
origin, for example, or sexual orientation or theological
commitment. New identities can be fragile and take time to
substantiate. They do not grow on trees, to be plucked with
every passing desire. But they can be enriched if nourished by
ancient roots so that many people found themselves turning
to the past for guidance, reassurance and validation. This

was probably in part what lay behind the growing popularity of historical re-enactment and the boom in family and local history. You could detect it in countless small bookshops, too, where, alongside works on the Pyramids, doomed duchesses and the triumphs and tragedies of World War II, space came to be devoted to old maps, do-it-yourself genealogy guides, 'then-and-now' photographic albums, new histories of Wales and Scotland or of Irish or Arabic nationalism, and biographies of hitherto underappreciated women or members of ethnic minorities. Down the flagpost of popular history came the banners of such former heroes as Richard the Lionheart, Columbus, Raleigh, Drake or Clive, to be replaced by newly iconic figures as varied as Saladin, William Wallace, Olaudah Equiano, Mary Seacole or Roger Casement. Historians of art gave new prominence to the homosexuality of Michelangelo and Leonardo da Vinci, music historians to the black creators of jazz or the work of hitherto obscure composers like the medieval nun Hildegard of Bingen or the 'Black Mozart' of eighteenth-century France, Joseph Boulogne, the Chevalier de Saint-Georges. The lesson was clear: for anyone seeking intellectual ballast for new forms of identity, an excellent place to look was – the past.

In sum, history can provide many messages to those who turn to it for succour. It can provide opportunities for escape, blame, resentment, consolation, vindication, nostalgia. For some it can be a gateway into unparalleled aesthetic fulfilment, or an opportunity to enjoy the frisson of safely viewed horror. It can feed an appetite for 'experience', reinforce pride in heritage and tradition and proffer a degree of reassurance and reaffirmation regarding the closure of the past and the nature of our own identity in the present and future. It can also fuel serious – sometimes explosive – social and political aspirations.

These are heavy burdens to bear. They are not born by the real past, of course, but by a marketable commodity created in our own time that we call 'History'. It is important to make this distinction. The 'past' is always there. It is what happened. And even if nobody ever wrote about it – or even knew about it – the past would still be there. What happened in the past did happen. But what happened in 'history' is another matter altogether. History is not what happened; it is what has subsequently been said or written or exhibited or broadcast about what happened. And every age, it has often and rightly been pointed out, has to re-create its own history, its own version of the unchanging past. This book is not about the past. It is about some of the highly talented people in our own time who have tried to transmit to those in the present something of what happened in the past. They are the conduits between past and present, the alchemists who conjure up lost eras. And since, as we have seen, people look to the past for all kinds of potent messages, those who conduct them there are, surely, Very Important People.

*   *   *

I sometimes think that historians are like the high priests of modern society. History, after all, has acquired many of the qualities of a religion. It provides ancient justifications for present-day actions and beliefs and recounts colourful tales of larger-than-life characters whose doings and misdoings provide examples and warnings to those living long afterwards. It adds legitimacy and pedigree to nations and would-be nations and to the new, less institutional forms of identity many seek. And it bestows dignity upon time-honoured practices and places which become sanctified as 'heritage'; history, like religion, has what amount to its sacred relics. And as in any religion, adherents delve into the past as prologue to the future. Some indulge in what virtually amounts to ancestor worship. In this sense, it is perhaps not altogether fanciful to regard historians, like priests, as mediating between our present anxieties and the ancestor gods looking down on us from an elevated past. Priests are important figures in all the religions they serve. As priests in the new quasi-religion of history, in which the Past is used and abused in the service of the Present and Future, historians play an absolutely crucial role.

There are of course good and bad priests, good and bad historians. The historians I have written about in this volume are among the best, though I can think of several who might be faintly surprised, and amused, to hear me refer to them as anything so elevated as high priests. Honest, workaday scribes, I suspect they'd respond, with a twinkle. And, it is true, no historian in this anthology would claim to have created (as perhaps Ranke, Marx, Braudel or Toynbee aspired to do) an all-embracing, systemic interpretation of the past capable, at least in principle, of embracing the whole of human history. Ambitions nowadays are more limited. The growing demands of academic life haven't helped, with their built-in insecurities and the pressure to publish. One by-product, to use a metaphor much beloved by David Cannadine, is that too many historians adopt the perspective of the truffle-hunter and too few that of the parachutist. More and more historians these days, it seems, know more and more about less and less.

It is true that we have no grand system-builders in this volume. But we have included some pretty intrepid parachutists. They have been helped in their ambition, I would suggest, by a number of recent developments, each of which has offered the imaginative and enquiring historian the opportunity of a more panoramic view of the past. The first is the opening up of new material from a huge and growing range of sources. For example, since the fall of Communism, historians such as Ian Kershaw, Geoffrey Hosking, Orlando Figes and Norman Davies have been able to benefit from the new availability of archive sources in Russia and Eastern Europe that would have been the envy of older colleagues.

But it is not just the amount of material that has expanded. Not so long ago, the respectable historian relied almost entirely on written documentation, those sacrosanct 'primary sources' kept in great libraries and other formal collections. Today's top historians are much more adventurous and many have learned to incorporate sources and methodologies from other disciplines into their work. In *Theatres of Memory*, Raphael Samuel wrote of 'an expanding historical culture, in which the work of inquiry and retrieval is being progressively extended into all kinds of spheres that would have been thought unworthy of notice in the past'. He himself used to give as an example the analysis of biota above gravesites that gave indications of diet. Several of the historians in this volume (for example, Peter Burke, Natalie Davis, Lyndal Roper) have clearly benefited from the insights of cultural anthropology and ethnography, while Christopher Dyer acknowledges his debt to archaeology and local history. Oral history is represented here, too; Laurence Rees' television programmes and books have relied extensively on the lengthy interviews he has conducted with people who were active participants in the wars he has documented. Niall Ferguson, capable of the most rigorous, statistically based economic history, also reveals (as do Schama, Brewer and Davis) the signs of the novelist *manqué*, while Antonia Fraser has clearly walked through the palaces and battlegrounds she describes so evocatively. John Keegan's battlefields are strewn not only with bodies but also with a rich harvest of literary references, while Lisa Jardine has enriched her historical writings with more than a laywoman's understanding of science and art. Natalie Davis has gone further and drawn on film, a self-evidently fictionalized recreation of the past, and on what she frankly acknowledges is her own historical imagination.

Most of the historians in this volume are as much concerned with context as content (Asa Briggs placed 'contextuality' at the heart of the educational revolution he spearheaded at Sussex). When Peter Burke writes about the Renaissance or

Louis XIV, he asks what these meant to ordinary people at the time and subsequently. He is also one of several historians who strengthens his analysis by comparative reference to other cultures. Thus, Eric Foner enriches his account of the emancipation of the American slaves and the Reconstruction era with illuminating parallels from European and Caribbean history. Whether Jeremy Black writes about domestic politics, diplomatic history or international warfare, he is always at pains to emphasize the links between them.

Finally, of course, historians, like everyone else, have begun to get used to the unprecedented opportunities – and hazards – offered by the revolution in information technology. It is still early days, and none of us can be sure what kinds of sources and methods might be available in years to come. But for a decade now, most historians have been routinely using computers to facilitate forms of work in a way that would have been unimaginable to previous generations of scholars. Nor is this just a question of Googling some historical figure to check birth or death dates, printing off a learned article, or working out complex statistical correlations. John Morrill's Royal Historical Society bibliography on the History of Britain and Ireland, containing nearly a quarter of a million cross-indexed, digitized items, would have been unthinkable before the arrival of the microchip.

So the historians represented in this anthology (or most of them) are men and women inspired by a wide and catholic view of the past and of the sources and methodologies by which it can be captured. They are also good writers. I can honestly say that there is not a single historian here whose work it was not a pleasure to read. That is no empty compliment, as seasoned readers of academic history will attest. Even when tackling the (to me) more unfamiliar or abstruse topics – John Keegan on ancient or medieval warfare, or Fernández-Armesto on the Maya Renaissance – the sheer élan of their scholarship and literary ability carried me through. There is of course no single way of writing history, and these historians don't by any means all write the same way. Where Hobsbawm or Roy Foster tend to be coolly analytical, even a little patrician in their approach, Jardine and Black prefer straightforward narrative interspersed with lengthy quotations from the sources, while our TV dons – notably Starkey, Schama and Ferguson – have the rare facility of marrying painstaking historical scholarship with seductively accessible prose. Many have written about historical subjects with strong contemporary resonances. Some, indeed, have probably played a part in setting the contemporary agenda. Antonia Fraser's biographies of Mary Stuart and Cromwell appeared just as feminism, and then concerns about the monarchy, were approaching a first high tide. Important works by Linda Colley and Natalie Davis have given a strong impetus to current concerns about individual and national identity and the importance of cross-cultural understanding, while Richard Evans has provided reassuring intellectual ballast against some of the more tendentious relativism that shook the historical establishment a few years ago. The environmental history assayed by Schama and the bold globalism of Fernández-Armesto, too, have helped open up areas others have gone on to explore.

*   *   *

Good priests help their flock to learn from the past in the hope that they might make better use of the present and future, and we might construe a good historian as doing much the same. But, quite apart from whether the historian should be concerned with drawing lessons, there is one mighty difference between the two. The priest is at liberty to embroider the past and use it as myth, parable or allegory, whereas whatever inferences the historian might derive from the past must normally be based on demonstrable, verifiable fact. This is both a limitation and a liberation. It is a limitation because it restricts the historian's room for inspirational manoeuvre.

No serious historian nowadays would feel free to embroider the story of Charlemagne, Henry VIII or George Washington in order to fashion a morally uplifting myth. These days, scholars routinely subject what they discover about the past to rigorous intellectual scrutiny. But it is precisely this professional discipline that provides the good historian with a degree of intellectual leverage unavailable to the priest. The priest, usually preaching to the converted, will hold views unlikely to sway those inclined to be sceptical. The conclusions of the good historian are harder to resist. As I worked my way through the *oeuvre* of the 28 historians represented in this volume, I did not (as you will see) always find myself accepting the analysis and conclusions of each and every book I read. But at the same time I found myself, again and again, pressed by a powerful and persuasive mind to reconsider some of my own prejudices, predispositions and arguments.

History is not a religion, of course. Its relics are not worshipped and historians are not priests. But a lot of people these days take history extremely seriously, and, as I have suggested, its widespread use and abuse can have momentous consequences. Those who purvey the past to the present therefore perform a highly sensitive function and bear a profound responsibility. Not quite priests, perhaps. But Very Important People nonetheless.

*   *   *

I have been immensely enriched by my reading of the historians I have written about here. I hope they feel I have done justice, if only brief journalistic justice, to the breadth, depth and sheer humanity of their scholarship. I would also like to record here one further debt of thanks. It is to Peter Furtado, editor of *History Today*, who encouraged me to undertake this series of essays in the first place and proved an ideal editor, and a good friend, throughout.

Daniel Snowman, June 2006

David Cannadine

BIOGRAPHY

David Cannadine is the Queen Elizabeth the Queen Mother
Professor of British History at the Institute of Historical
Research, University of London. He is a graduate of Clare
College, Cambridge, St John's College, Oxford, and Princeton
University. Between 1975 and 1988 he held a succession of
posts at Cambridge University: first as a Research Fellow
at St John's College, and later as a Fellow and University
Lecturer of Christ's College. In 1988 he became Professor
of History at Columbia University, New York, and in 1992
he was appointed Moore Collegiate Professor of History at
Columbia University. Between 1998 and 2003, and at the time
this article was written, Professor Cannadine was Director of
the Institute of Historical Research and Professor of History at
the University of London. He took up his present position as
Queen Elizabeth the Queen Mother Professor of British History
at the Institute of Historical Research in September 2003. In
2003–06 he has held visiting fellowships at the Council of the
Humanities, Princeton University, the Humanities Research
Centre, Australian National University, and the National
Humanities Center in North Carolina.

Since 2005 Professor Cannadine has been Chairman of
the Trustees of the National Portrait Gallery. He is also a
Trustee of the Kennedy Memorial Trust, the British Empire
and Commonwealth Museum, and the Rothschild Archive,
a Commissioner for English Heritage, a Member of the East

of England Regional Committee for the National Trust, and
a member of the Advisory Committee of the Royal Mint. He
is Vice-Chair of the Editorial Board of Past and Present, a
member of the Editorial Board of the History of Parliament,
and a judge for the Wolfson Prize for History. He has been a
member of the Advisory Council of the National Archives, a
member of the Archives Task Force, and a Historical Advisor
to the Cabinet War Rooms/Churchill Museum. He is also a
regular broadcaster on television and radio in the UK.

PRINCIPAL PUBLISHED BOOKS

Lords and Landlords: The Aristocracy and the Towns, 1774–1967
(1980)

Patricians, Power and Politics in Nineteenth Century Towns (ed.)
(1982)

Exploring the Urban Past: Essays in Urban History by H.J. Dyos
(ed. with David Reeder) (1982)

Rituals of Royalty: Power and Ceremonial in Traditional Societies
(ed. with Simon Price) (1987)

The Pleasures of the Past (1989)

'Blood, Toil, Tears and Sweat': Winston Churchill's Famous Speeches
(ed.) (1989)

*The First Modern Society: Essays in English History in Honour
of Lawrence Stone* (ed. with A.L. Beier and James Rosenheim)
(1989)

The Decline and Fall of the British Aristocracy (1990) (winner of
the Lionel Trilling Prize)

G.M. Trevelyan: A Life in History (1992)

Aspects of Aristocracy: Grandeur and Decline in Modern Britain
(1994)

History and Biography: Essays in Honour of Derek Beales (ed. with
T.W.C. Blanning) (1996)

Class in Britain (1998)

History in Our Time (1998)

Making History Now (1999)

Ornamentalism: How the British Saw Their Empire (2001)

In Churchill's Shadow: Confronting the Past in Modern Britain (2002)

What is History Now? (ed.) (2002)

History and the Media (ed.) (2004)

Churchill in the Twenty-First Century (ed. with Roland Quinault) (2004)

Admiral Lord Nelson: Context and Legacy (ed.) (2005)

Andrew Mellon: the Official Life (2006)

Trafalgar in History: A Battle and its Afterlife (ed.) (2006)

PROFILE, October 1998

The new Director of the Institute of Historical Research marches through his domains with obvious relish. 'The best job in Britain any historian could ever want or have', David Cannadine recalls Asa Briggs once telling him, as he finds his way, through the interwar marble grandeur of London University's Senate House, through one of the best history libraries in the country, to his lofty but as yet somewhat bare office. Near the door is a pile of boxes. 'Oh, that's Andrew Mellon', Cannadine says with a characteristic raising of his eyes to the heavens. 'I do not intend in my time as Director to stop writing history', he announced at a reception to mark his arrival at the IHR; 'I would not know how to do that, and have no intention of finding out.'

Good news for the rest of us. For Cannadine is one of that small band of historians whose writings, while highly regarded by his academic peers, have also found a wide, popular audience. His work on the decline of the British aristocracy became something of a cause célèbre among both admirers and critics, while his review essays have long been required reading on both sides of the Atlantic. It may be said of Cannadine, as he himself wrote of G.M. Trevelyan, that his aim has been 'to reconcile the evidential rigour of the professional historian with the broad appeal and educative function of the literary historian'.

Cannadine was born in 1950 and brought up in Birmingham, a grammar school lad who went on to become the first member of his family to go to university. Was history a schoolboy interest? Cannadine recalls that he was pretty good at a number of subjects, among them maths, geography and divinity ('Who knows – I might have become a bishop!'), but acknowledges the influence of an inspiring history teacher named Graham Butler. After his A Levels, Cannadine read History at Cambridge, did his graduate work at Oxford (a D.Phil. under Peter Mathias) with a year at Princeton (where the most important influence was Lawrence Stone). Still in his mid-twenties, he returned to Cambridge where, after a two-year sojourn at St John's, he was appointed a Lecturer in History and Fellow of Christ's.

At Christ's College, the presiding genius, and Cannadine's principal patron, was J.H. Plumb, Britain's premier historian of the eighteenth century. A man of immense energy and enthusiasm, Plumb was a riveting performer in the lecture room and a prolific writer, pouring out a stream of zestful, restless prose on a wide variety of topics. Like his own master, Trevelyan, Jack Plumb felt that a good historian should communicate not just to his professional peers but also to a wide public – a message he has passed on to his own protégés, a list that includes John Brewer, Roy Porter, Simon Schama, Linda Colley, Niall Ferguson, David Reynolds, Geoffrey Parker – and David Cannadine.

A year or two after Cannadine joined Christ's, Linda Colley arrived as the first woman Fellow of the college. Academic lore has it that Plumb acted as a marriage broker between Cannadine and Colley, a splendid story that Cannadine only half deflates, acknowledging that 'When Jack told me that Linda was going to arrive, he said to me: "You never know, you might end up marrying her!"'

A few years later, Colley (by now Mrs Cannadine) was appointed to a post at Yale and, after a period of strenuous transatlantic commuting, her husband followed her to the States with a chair at Columbia. For a decade, history's most celebrated couple merely had to travel between New York and New Haven to see each other, while summers were spent back in the UK at their retreat in Norfolk. These were productive years for both, Cannadine's published opus including his book on the decline and fall of the British aristocracy, his assessment of Trevelyan and a volume of Churchill's speeches which he edited and introduced, as well as publication of an anthology of his review essays and a further book about 'aspects of aristocracy'.

How did a boy from lower-middle-class Birmingham become preoccupied with the modern history of the British aristocracy and monarchy, with class and ritual, and with figures of such aristocratic lineage as Trevelyan and Churchill? Cannadine's first book, on aristocracy and the towns, arose from his D.Phil. thesis. It was in essence a study of the Calthorpe family of Birmingham, and more broadly the changes in Birmingham society in the nineteenth and early twentieth centuries – a way, perhaps, of helping Cannadine understand his own background. This research led to Cannadine's *magnum opus* on the decline and fall of the British aristocracy, a book vaster in its range and sweep, and one, moreover, that takes its tale forwards almost to our own times.

In the prologue to the book, Cannadine outlines three principles that guided him – or, rather, three things he says he was keen to eschew. First, he is writing in dissent from what he calls the 'present craze for national heritage', the tendency to sentimentalize the aristocracy and their country houses. This kindly man can become quite fierce against what in one of his essays he dismisses as the 'Ruritanian theme park' approach to British history, a 'contrived fantasy of hype and heritage ... [and] ... a deluded pageant of self-indulgent historical backwardness'.

Cannadine's aim is to treat the aristocracy seriously rather than sentimentally, to 'rescue the British upper classes from the endless (and mindless) veneration of posterity'.

If Cannadine's lance was bound to ruffle some upper-class plumage, his second and third principles reveal him tilting at academic colleagues. The book 'is written in protest against the current fashion in British history writing that stresses continuity at the expense of change'. Was Cannadine wishing to reinstate the emphasis on conflict and discontinuity so popular in the historiography of the radical 1960s? Maybe his *Decline and Fall of the British Aristocracy* was a kind of homage, or complement, to E.P. Thompson's *The Making of the English Working Class*.

The statement of intent was certainly taken by some as a provocation. As was Cannadine's third principle – that he was not writing 'tunnel' history, the kind that can lead an investigator to know more and more about less and less ('a weakness to which the study of the recent British past is particularly prone'). On the contrary, he lays claim to 'panoramic ambitions', and asserts that he has sought 'to poke my head above the many specialist molehills'.

So, realistic rather than sentimental history, an emphasis on change (in particular, decline) – and, for all the detail, a constant awareness of what would nowadays be called the 'big picture'. Cannadine enjoys quoting the distinction between those historians who are 'parachutists' and those who are 'truffle hunters'. While his own writing is packed with evocative detail and apposite quotation, he is unquestionably of the parachutist persuasion. He talks with pride about the way his book on the decline of the aristocracy was a large-scale, epic work covering a broad sweep of history. Most books on modern British history, he says, trying not to sound sniffy, have tended to be specifically political or social or economic monographs on particular people, ministries, institutions or events.

And he should know, for it seems there is nothing by his peers he has not read. Over the years, indeed, Cannadine has built up a reputation as a formidable reviewer, an eloquent essayist in the grand style capable of introducing, explaining, assessing, comparing and consigning the works of others with magisterial ease and authority. A master of paradox, metaphor and alliterative wordplay, Cannadine will coax and cajole, tease and taunt, laud and lament. Like Plumb, Cannadine positively bursts with exuberant wit even (especially?) when at his most withering. Prince Albert, he opines, discovered 'the impotence of being earnest', while to Kitty Kelley's claim that her book on the Windsors takes an 'unblinking look' at its subject, Cannadine remarks dryly that that 'might, of course, mean that her eyes are permanently open or permanently closed'. But, as befits one in the succession of Macaulay, Trevelyan and Plumb, he also calls upon his literary dexterity in defence of those he admires. In an entertaining review of Peter Gay's *The Bourgeois Experience*, much enlivened by stimulating verbal foreplay, Cannadine argues that in writing on sex 'it is probably better to be Whiggish than priggish'; and of the peripatetic, industrious Asa Briggs he says that 'in one guise he is a supersonic G.M. Trevelyan' and in another 'the thinking man's Mountbatten'.

This autumn sees a further collection of his essays ('my last') and a study of the idea of class in British history. Both contain the usual Cannadine wit and erudition and display his infectious enjoyment of the achievements, foibles and failures of grandees of the recent past. *History in Our Time* includes trenchant reviews of books on the royals and of lives of people like Beaverbrook, Boothby, Buchan, Churchill, Macmillan and Mosley. We also encounter the acute historiographical antennae with which Cannadine senses shifts in the writing of history itself. One of his reviews (of *The Cambridge Social History of Britain*, edited by a predecessor as IHR Director, F.M.L. Thompson), begins with a masterly survey of changing approaches to social history from Trevelyan and Plumb, through the avowedly class-based, Marxist interpretations of Edward Thompson and Eric Hobsbawm and the subsequent 'experience rather than analysis' school of social history, to what Cannadine regards as the postmodernist uncertainties and little hegemonies that characterize much of today's writing. Though disavowing the simplistic Marxism of some earlier writing, he argues that social history is nothing if it does not take account of that British obsession – class. What is needed, he says, is 'a comprehensive study of social structure and social attitudes over the last three centuries for Britain as a whole'. A daunting task. 'Who, if anyone, is willing to try?'

The answer, of course, is Cannadine himself, in his other new book, *Class in Britain*. In some ways, the rise and fall of class is a kissing cousin of the decline and fall of the aristocracy, chronicling aspects of social status and hierarchy over time against a background of increasing social equality. But this book is not about class as an objective fact or structure in British history, but about shifting perceptions – class, that is, seen subjectively. He outlines three basic ways in which the British have seen their own society: a seamless hierarchy with everyone having, and knowing, his or her place; a three-way split between upper, middle and lower; and a more adversarial dichotomy between 'us' and 'them'. With this schema as background, Cannadine traces perceptions of class from the eighteenth century to the present.

More than any of his other works, this is a book about interpretations of the past. In its pages, Cannadine assesses, and often takes issue with, the conclusions of many of his most illustrious predecessors – not just the historians, but the novelists, politicians and polemicists whose images of British society have been influential. This is, perhaps, Cannadine staking out his territory – an anti-Marxist big enough to be interested in class, a working-class boy capable of understanding social hierarchy, a man of letters able to develop a theoretical framework and sustain it through three centuries of history, a crystalline intelligence arguing that other people's interpretations over-simplify, above all a man who relishes past grandeur yet (like Gibbon) is at his most eloquent chronicling its decline.

Is there something elegiac about his subject matter and his ways of dealing with it? If so, this is perhaps appropriate to a *fin-de-siècle* historian, a product of the once-proud Welfare State and a man raised in the fading shadow of an eroding empire. Cannadine does not regret the passing of the old order; indeed, he is capable, when appropriate, of having a lot of fun at its expense. But he is profoundly taken with Trevelyan's view of history, that its poetry 'lies in the quasi-miraculous fact that once, on this earth, on this familiar spot of ground, walked other men and women, as actual as we are today, thinking their own thoughts, swayed by their own passions, but now all gone, one generation vanishing into another, gone as utterly as we ourselves shall shortly be gone, like ghosts at cockcrow'.

Is Cannadine now a different kind of British historian for having spent a decade in the USA? He feels able to regard British institutions and attitudes with a detachment that can only come from living abroad for a while. Thus, the book on class concludes that, if anyone is serious about wanting to make British society more egalitarian (which he doubts), they could learn from America – for example, by abolishing the sense of hierarchy associated with hereditary peerage and titles of honour (not to mention the monarchy), and undertaking root-and-branch educational reform.

He is in the early stages of research for his first American subject: a biography of the financier, art collector and political figure Andrew Mellon. Mellon, a Pittsburgh millionaire and businessman as taciturn as his political master, Calvin Coolidge, was a banker who financed many major business enterprises, was Secretary to the Treasury in the 1920s, US ambassador to London and principal benefactor of the National Gallery

in Washington DC. Mellon's life, says Cannadine, touches
everything; he is the largest figure of his generation still
awaiting a serious biography. Meanwhile, Cannadine also
looks forward to getting down to his survey of Britain in the
nineteenth century for the new Penguin History series (of which
he is editor) and notes that, when the nineteenth century came
to an end, issues like devolution, Irish Home Rule, and House
of Lords reform were high on the agenda – as they are today.
New Labour might be seen as picking up where Gladstonian
Liberalism left off.

As he approaches 50, how far will this excellent communicator
allow himself to become a more public figure? Cannadine
sighs, and admits that he enjoys his occasional forays into the
media, especially if (like Trevelyan and Plumb) he can bring
some awareness of historical perspective to a wider audience.
He clearly has no desire to become a universal pundit with
a ready opinion on everything he is asked, and is scornful of
those who do. But he is happy to answer questions if he feels
he has something to offer. Perhaps the government should seek
his views about reform of the House of Lords.

I asked Cannadine whether he feels that we live in an
ahistorical culture, an era of fashion-led perspectives in which
history is the name we give everything that happened before
last week. The optimist in him clutches for evidence to the
contrary; he cites the popularity of history that he and Linda
met among undergraduates at Columbia and Yale, plus the
success of books by people like Simon Schama, Roy Foster,
Paul Kennedy and Orlando Figes (not to mention Linda's
Britons).

But he does worry that the view of the world projected by
today's media lacks temporal perspective and is excessively
sensationalized, trivialized, personalized – and not only by the
media. 'The present Labour government projects an image of
not being concerned with the past,' he says acerbically, 'except
insofar as it wants to get rid of it.' And he adds: 'Even if you

want to get rid of the past you probably ought to know a little bit more about it.' We live in a world, Cannadine senses, that is increasingly 'amnesiac'. Historians, he concludes, citing Trevelyan once more, have to be public communicators. 'The job of the historian is to help give people a sense of existence in time – without which we are really not fully human.'

EPILOGUE

David Cannadine writes:

When Daniel Snowman wrote his very generous and perceptive essay about me and my work, I had barely been in post as Director of the Institute of Historical Research for six months, and I was still getting my knees under the table. During my time as Director, I sought to bring a valuable but venerable organization into the early twenty-first century, by reforming and restructuring it, by increasing its public profile, and by raising £10 million, which enabled us to restore part of our building, and to expand our activities in many ways. I received a great deal of help in these endeavours, from the many friends of the IHR, not just in Britain but around the world; and I am deeply grateful to them, and to many generous benefactors. I ceased being Director in the autumn of 2003, though I continue to lead the IHR's Appeal, and I am now the Queen Elizabeth the Queen Mother Professor of History, which means I must be one of a very few professors who has delivered two inaugural lectures within the space of five years.

While helping to revive the IHR, I also believed that the Director should be more broadly engaged in the public and cultural life of London and the nation. Accordingly, I have lectured widely in universities across the country (and also in north America), I undertook a certain amount of radio and television work, and I became involved with a variety of organizations, including the National Portrait Gallery, English Heritage, the National Archives, the British Empire and Commonwealth Museum, the Kennedy Memorial Trust, and the Royal Mint, where there was scope and opportunity for contributing a historical perspective. Like fundraising, these were (to me) new ways of being an historian and (like fundraising again) I greatly enjoyed it. And I write these lines, having just returned from New York, where I appeared on a panel to discuss 'Why History Matters', with two old friends who also appear in this volume: Eric Foner and Simon Schama.

But I have also been concerned, throughout my time at the IHR, to keep working and to keep writing. Hence two books, *Ornamentalism: How the British Saw Their Empire*, and *In Churchill's Shadow*; hence three edited books, arising from IHR conferences, *What is History Now?*, *History and the Media*, and *Admiral Lord Nelson: Context and Legacy*; hence several contributions to books, including a study of Roy Jenkins as a writer, and articles on Noel Annan and G.M. Trevelyan for the new Oxford *Dictionary of National Biography*; and hence a continuing stream of articles, including the British Academy obituary of Sir John Plumb. I have also been hard at work digging into the boxes of material on Andrew Mellon, and the biography went to the publisher at the end of 2005. Then there is the 'Penguin History of Nineteenth-Century Britain' series to get on with, and after that, the Trevelyan Lectures which I shall deliver in Cambridge in the spring of 2007 on the subject of 'Common Humanity?' Whoever said that being a historian was boring?

Eric Hobsbawm

BIOGRAPHY

Eric Hobsbawm had his elementary education in Vienna, his secondary education in four schools in Vienna, Berlin and London, where he attended Marylebone Grammar School, winning a scholarship to King's College, Cambridge. He acquired a BA degree in History at Cambridge University and, after six years in the British Army (1940–46), a Cambridge PhD in 1951. He began to teach at Birkbeck College, University of London, as a lecturer in 1947, educating himself as a historian by teaching, discussions in the Historians Group of the Communist Party, exchanges with French colleagues and Mediterranean travels. He remained at Birkbeck as a Lecturer, Reader and Professor of Economic and Social History until retirement in 1982, with spells of visiting teaching at Stanford University, MIT (1967), UNAM in Mexico (1971), the Ecole des Hautes Etudes en Sciences Sociales, Paris (1970s) and the College de France (1982). From 1984 to 1997 he taught at the Graduate Faculty, New School of Social Research in New York. He has given occasional lectures in a variety of institutions on four continents. He is President of the Past and Present Society, the Society for the Study of Labour History and, since 2002 of Birkbeck, University of London.

He is a Fellow of the British Academy, American Academy of Arts and Sciences, Hungarian Academy of Sciences, the Japan Academy and the Academy of Sciences of Turin. He has a number of honorary degrees. His writings have been translated into a considerable number of languages.

He is married to Marlene Schwarz, has two children and five grandchildren, and lives in London.

PRINCIPAL PUBLISHED BOOKS

Primitive Rebels (1959)
The Jazz Scene (1959)
The Age of Revolution 1789–1848 (1962)
Labouring Men (1964)
Industry and Empire (1969)
Captain Swing (with George Rudé) (1969)
Bandits (1969)
Revolutionaries (1973)
The Age of Capital 1848–1875 (1974)
The Invention of Tradition (ed. with Terence Ranger) (1983)
Worlds of Labour: Further Studies in the History of Labour (1984)
The Age of Empire 1875–1914 (1987)
Echoes of the Marseillaise: Two Centuries Look Back on the French Revolution (1990)
Nations and Nationalism since 1780: Programme, Myth, Reality (1990)
The Age of Extremes: The Short Twentieth Century 1914–1991 (1994)
On History (1997)
Uncommon People: Resistance, Rebellion and Jazz (1998)
Interesting Times: A Twentieth Century Life (2002)

PROFILE, January 1999

'He might have been a Russian,
A French or Turk or Prussian,
Or perhaps Italian!

But in spite of all temptations
To belong to other nations,
He is an Englishman.'

These lines of W.S. Gilbert come to mind when you talk to
somebody at once so pre-eminently cosmopolitan yet also so
unmistakably English as Eric Hobsbawm. Born in 1917 in
Alexandria to Jewish parents – an English-born father and a
Viennese mother – who were married in Zurich, Hobsbawm
was taken to Vienna at the age of two and to Berlin at fourteen
and brought to live in London a couple of years later. His first
research as a young historian was on French North Africa,
while, alongside his early work on English economic history,
he was also to apply his energies to detailed historical studies of
Italy, Latin America and jazz. Best known, perhaps, for his four-
volume history of the world from 1789 to 1991, Hobsbawm
is also a prolific essayist, one of the founding fathers of the
journal *Past and Present* and a Fellow of both the British and
the American Academy of Arts and Sciences.

But he 'might have been a social anthropologist', he recalls,
or even have specialised in literature and modern languages.
So how and when did Hobsbawm come to history? The
answer takes him back to the crucial years he spent in Berlin,
in 1931–33. His parents had both died, and an uncle living
there (also an immigrant from England) took Eric and his sister
under his wing. Berlin during that period, Hobsbawm recalls,
'was the most dynamic place on earth'. It was quite clear to an
intelligent adolescent whose mind and senses were just opening
up to all that life had to offer that he happened to be there at
a pivotal moment in history. In the cultural cauldron of Berlin
immediately pre-Hitler, Hobsbawm's intellectual and political
consciousness positively seethed as he struggled to understand
the bewildering changes going on around him.

The ideological options available were limited. Again,
Hobsbawm 'might have been' a German Nationalist, or else
a Zionist. But in practice both were quite unthinkable to an
assimilated young cosmopolitan Jewish intellectual with a
British passport. Already edging towards the Left from his
childhood in Vienna (where he had learned that 'a tenant was a

Socialist and a landlord a Christian Social'), Hobsbawm found himself attracted to Communism. A schoolteacher told him he was spouting nonsense and suggested he go to the library and read something: *The Communist Manifesto*, perhaps, and some Engels. 'Which I did. And it was a knockout!' And it was through Marx that Hobsbawm came to history.

These were stimulating days for Hobsbawm. Were they also dangerous? 'I was protected from the worst kinds of anti-Semitism', he recalls, 'because my classmates thought of me as "the Englishman" rather than "the Jew". So the only thing I was blamed for was the Treaty of Versailles!' In any case, Hobsbawm was about to move once again. His uncle had been working for an American film company, and the galloping Depression, allied perhaps to the new anti-foreigner laws, put his employment in jeopardy. In 1933 the family moved to London.

It would be surprising if Hobsbawm had not been a little demoralized as, recently orphaned and having to speak and work in English, he found himself registering at his third high school, in his third country, in a mere three years. In the event, he found London insufferably dull after Berlin, full of people who eschewed all discussion of ideologies and thought that problems would go away if you did not talk about them. But he was sustained by what he had brought with him – especially his Marxism – and did well at school. Three years elapsed and Hobsbawm, now approaching twenty, won a scholarship to King's College, Cambridge, where he took his degree in 1939 and was offered a research studentship to study agrarian problems in French North Africa. Three months later, England was at war.

Many of Britain's talented Middle Europeans had an exotic war, using their linguistic skills to help with various kinds of intelligence work, for example. And Hobsbawm? 'I was called up, but did nothing interesting.' Didn't they even make use of his perfect German? He shrugs. 'You must remember

I had a record. At Cambridge I'd acquired a reputation as an active Communist, and the people in my college who set up the intelligence centre at Bletchley weren't going to give a job to someone like me!'

But army life was not completely wasted, for it was here that Hobsbawm found his interests gravitating towards English economic history. And it was in the army that he first encountered the British working class, an experience that introduced him to one of the fundamental issues that was to concern him in years to come. As a committed Marxist, he knew what the working classes ought to want and think; they should presumably wish to unite, overthrow the bourgeoisie and share the means of production with everybody contributing according to his abilities and benefiting according to his needs. But seen close up, the working classes often seemed to have different, more mundane and often unexpectedly right-wing interests and aspirations. Nor was this true only in Britain. In southern Italy, for example, a few years later, Hobsbawm encountered a local union organizer, a Communist, who told him, incredulously, how the Calabrian peasants he was trying to mobilize kept electing Jehovah's Witnesses as branch secretaries – against, as it were, their own interests.

In Britain, at least, 'the people' elected a Labour government, and Hobsbawm, demobilized in early 1946, embarked upon some research on the early history of the Fabian Society. A year later, he obtained a job lecturing at Birkbeck College, London (where – in spite of all temptations – he was to remain for virtually his entire academic career until a late efflorescence at New York's New School). But it was another dozen years before he began publishing the stream of books that were to make him famous. Why so long – and what had he been doing in the interim?

'The crucial thing for people with my Marxist background and interests was the Cold War. It isolated us. But at the same time it also created a sense of cohesion between us, riveting us together against the outside world.' Hobsbawm has in mind friends and colleagues such as Christopher Hill, George Rudé and Edward Thompson, brilliant and pioneering scholars all, but a somewhat marginalized Marxist cabal back in the years when they first used to meet together. It was from this group that *Past and Present* was born, a serious journal of academic research (somewhat along the lines of the French *Annales*) embodying what its founders saw as a more radical approach to history. Over the years, particularly over Hungary in 1956, this group became riven by the notorious fractiousness of the Left. But as *Past and Present* (like *History Today*, its close contemporary) approaches its half-century, Hobsbawm looks back with some pride at what he helped create.

Then, well into his forties, already a noted essayist and pamphleteer, he at last began to produce important books: *Primitive Rebels* (1959), *The Age of Revolution* (1962), *Labouring Men* (1964). Like an athlete who finds his stride, Hobsbawm scarcely faltered for the next 30 years, pouring out books and essays on a wide array of subjects as though compensating for a slow start. Whether writing about the Industrial or the French Revolution, bandits or the bourgeoisie, Count Basie or Count Bismarck, Wellington or Ellington, Vienna, Venice or Venezuela, Hobsbawm's erudition was dazzling and his breadth of allusion encyclopaedic. It is a rare historian who can draw upon so wide a variety of sources – in at least five languages – while yet remaining in total intellectual control of his material. With Hobsbawm, you never feel that Pelion is piled upon Ossa for effect; nor (at least for this reader) that a structural straitjacket is imposed upon the facts. Rather, the detail and the analysis appear to run together.

Hobsbawm's *magnum opus* is a four-volume history of the world over the two centuries since the French Revolution: *The Age of Revolution* (1789–1848), *The Age of Capital* (1848–75), *The Age of Empire* (1875–1914) and *The Age of Extremes: The Short Twentieth Century* (1914–91). The last, essentially a chronicle of the tumultuous world of Hobsbawm's own lifetime, has proved a bestseller on five continents (but, for reasons the author is mystified by, was only published in French – and not by a French publisher – after several years of ideological debate). Is there something faintly Germanic about the idea of writing a magisterial four-volume history of the modern world (not to mention all those lapidary titles)? 'It certainly wasn't planned that way', Hobsbawm responds with a weary shake of the head. 'That's not my style. They started as separate projects, but I think I realized somewhere between volumes two and three that it might eventually amount to a series.'

Whatever the process of creation, the result is a tour de force of great range and virtuosity. To Hobsbawm, the defining events in European (and therefore world) history include the French and Industrial Revolutions, the revolutions of 1848 and what he calls the Thirty-one Years' War (1914–45). In the earlier volumes, there is more economic history, in the last two more about culture and the arts. Class and class consciousness (and conflict) are a powerful and recurrent presence, while the traditional 'Great Men' of history, the Napoleons and Bismarcks, the Lincolns, Gandhis and Stalins, are held firmly in place by an author not greatly enamoured of biography or the insights of psychology. As in much of Hobsbawm's writing, a predilection for patrician phrase-making can sometimes tend to obscure rather than reveal the texture of life as experienced by those he describes. But his sense of the sweep and structure of the drama as a whole is unrivalled.

Some readers find Hobsbawm's Marxism bothersome, preferring to assign the philosophical insights of Marx to the historical dustbin alongside Soviet-style Communism. But to Hobsbawm, Marx 'remains the essential base of any adequate study of history, because – so far – he alone has attempted to formulate a methodological approach to history as a whole'. Does Hobsbawm's Marxism skew his history? No more so, probably, than the work of anyone guided by an overall vision

– and you surely can't write about several hundred years of
world history without one. There are pages in his writings
where one senses the old Communist having to confront
material that the march of events has forced him to reassess.
But if Hobsbawm's Marxism leads him to give short shrift to
the occasionally awkward ideological corner (for example, the
Soviet invasion of Hungary in 1956), he also claims, in a phrase
adapted from his old comrade Edward Thompson, to be as
interested in saving the king or the nobleman as the stockinger
or peasant from the condescension of the historian.

The final volume in the quartet, *The Age of Extremes*,
begins in what Hobsbawm calls the 'twilight zone' of his own
childhood. How did he approach the writing of contemporary
history? Is one better equipped to understand a period of which
one has personal memories? Hobsbawm recognizes the value
of individual experience as data, but is aware of the distorting
mirror it can provide. 'In the 1930s, for example, we on the
Left were campaigning against Fascism and I remember being
convinced we were mobilizing the people against war. But
with the benefit of historical perspective, I can see we were
a total failure, merely rallying people already sympathetic to
our cause.'

Personal experience, he suggests, can impede historical vision
in another way, too: not just what you have lived through – but
where. 'Imagine, for example, that you were an Argentine or
Brazilian trying to write the history of modern times. You'd live
in a continent that had experienced no serious international
war this century, in which both world wars impinged largely
as distant news items – but where global economic fluctuations
had immediate and dramatic consequences. That's the kind of
perspective from which a Latin American historian has to try
and emancipate himself.'

Then why, given Hobsbawm's awesome erudition, did he still
place Europe at the centre of his quartet? 'Because of the nature
of the questions I address. If you're dealing with the history

of modern capitalism and the world economy, your analysis has got to be Eurocentric right up until the late nineteenth century and the appearance of the USA as a world player.' And 'Occidentocentric', he adds, 'until the late twentieth'.

Other questions require other perspectives. In a lecture to mark the Columbus Quincentenary in which he was probably expected to consider the effect of the Old World on the New, Hobsbawm reversed things and addressed the impact of America on the rest of the world, arguing, startlingly, that 'the major contribution of the Americas ... has been to distribute across the globe a cornucopia of wild and cultivated ... plants, without which the modern world as we know it would not be conceivable.' The potato, chocolate, tobacco, cocaine – these and other plants, unknown to Europeans before Columbus, changed the wider world far more profoundly than all the gold or silver mined by the Conquistadors. This, argues Hobsbawm, with a truly global sweep, was the real significance of 1492.

Once primarily an economic historian, Hobsbawm has found himself increasingly drawn towards broader cultural issues that he probably once thought not quite his province. Thus, in his 1998 Lecture in memory of Walter Neurath, founder of the art books publisher Thames & Hudson, Hobsbawm considered the struggle of the visual arts in the twentieth century to create a credible avant-garde, a struggle that had been spectacularly lost, he argued (somewhat provocatively, considering the audience and the occasion), by the art of painting. But the twentieth century, he concluded, is best expressed via its own media.

Now comfortably into his eighties, Hobsbawm claims to have no major new project in the works. But there is no subject in history or historiography that does not continue to arouse his interest – particularly, perhaps, the future of the subject itself. He is concerned, he says, that most British and (especially) American historians confine themselves to English-language sources. Elsewhere, historians are forced (as Hobsbawm himself was) to learn other languages, and this helps give their work a freshness and perspective that no monolingual scholar can achieve. And he worries about the incursions of postmodernism into the writing of history, the moral and even factual relativism of some historical writing in which any use or misuse of evidence, any hypothesis about the past, is treated as of equal value to any other. Whether or not the Nazi gas chambers existed, for instance, can be established by evidence, he says. And he adds acerbically that because their existence has been established, those who deny their existence are simply not historians.

The job of the historian is far too important to be left to charlatans, says Hobsbawm with passion – more important, perhaps, than ever before at a time when most youngsters grow up in a sort of 'permanent present'. The old campaigner pauses. The business of the historian, he says, 'is to remember what others forget'.

Peter Burke

BIOGRAPHY

Peter Burke (born 1937) was educated at St Ignatius' College, Stamford Hill, London, and St John's College, Oxford. He interrupted work on his D.Phil. at St Antony's College, Oxford, to become one of the first junior lecturers to be appointed (in the School of European Studies) at the University of Sussex, where he remained for 17 years (1962–79) as Assistant Lecturer, Lecturer in European History and Reader in Intellectual History. He moved to Cambridge in 1979 to become Lecturer in Early Modern European History and Fellow of Emmanuel College, becoming Reader in Cultural History in 1988 and Professor in 1996. He is married to the Brazilian historian Maria Lúcia García Pallares-Burke.

He has been a visiting member of the Institute for Advanced Study, Princeton; the Humanities Research Centre, Australian National University, Canberra; the Ecole des Hautes Etudes, Paris; the Wissenschaftskolleg, Berlin; the Instituto para Estudos Avançados, University of São Paulo; the Getty Research Institute, Los Angeles, and the Netherlands Institute of Advanced Study, as well as holding visiting professorships in Nijmegen, Groningen, Heidelberg, Brussels and Princeton. He gave the Wiles Lectures at the University of Belfast in 2002.

He is a Fellow of the British Academy; Member of the Academia Europa and recipient of its Erasmus medal; PhD (honoris causa), University of Lund. He has lectured in most

European countries, as well as China, India, Japan, the USA, Brazil, Argentina, Canada, Australia and New Zealand.

He has published 23 books (as well as about 200 articles or chapters in collections). His work has so far been translated into 31 languages and will soon appear in three more.

PRINCIPAL PUBLISHED BOOKS

The Renaissance Sense of the Past (1969)

Culture and Society in Renaissance Italy (1972)

Venice and Amsterdam: A Study of Seventeenth-Century Elites (1974)

Popular Culture in Early Modern Europe (1978)

Sociology and History (1980)

Montaigne (1981)

Vico (1985)

Historical Anthropology of Early Modern Italy: Essays on Perception and Communication (1987)

The Renaissance (1987)

Küchenlatein (1989)

The French Historical Revolution: The Annales School, 1929–89 (1990)

The Fabrication of Louis XIV (1992)

History and Social Theory (1992)

Mundo com Teatro: Estudos de Antropologica Histórica (1992)

The Art of Conversation (1993)

The Fortunes of the Courtier: The European Reception of Castiglione's Cortegiano (1995)

Varieties of Cultural History (1997)

The European Renaissance: Centres and Peripheries (1998)

A Social History of Knowledge from Gutenberg to Diderot (2000)

Eyewitnessing (2001)

A Social History of the Media, from Gutenberg to the Internet (with Asa Briggs) (2002)

What is Cultural History? (2004)

Languages and Communities in Early Modern Europe (2004)

PROFILE, April,1999

After the death of Frank Sinatra, when the singer's FBI files were opened, a New York hack was asked if he thought it true that Sinatra's friends had included Mafiosi. Well, he drawled, these guys ain't exactly the Professor of Cultural History at Oxford or Cambridge. I didn't ask Peter Burke about Sinatra, but wouldn't have been surprised if he had views, perhaps relating the language and silences of Sinatra lyrics to similar patterns in Leopardi or Lampedusa, or linking the appeal of 'My Way' to that of parallel products in Java and Japan, Bulgaria and Brazil.

The clue to Peter Burke, Professor of Cultural History at Cambridge and Fellow of Emmanuel College, is his indefatigable delight in seeking links. If intelligence is the capacity to see connections, comparisons and contrasts, especially between objects and artefacts in most ways utterly disparate, then Burke is one of the more intelligent people you are ever likely to meet. His passion is to build bridges – between languages, cultures, periods, places, methodologies, disciplines – and then stride across them, open-mindedly, to see what lies beyond. I recall him at the University of Sussex where we were fellow lecturers in the mid-1960s. Lean and angular, dressed in his trademark black corduroy jacket, his bright eyes just that more alert than anyone else's, Peter would thrill his young charges with astonishing feats of intellectual derring-do. The young women all wanted to feed him. If the Sussex mission in those pioneering days was to 'redraw the map of learning', Burke was one of its most intrepid cartographers, a Renaissance prince of the mind who acknowledged no boundaries, a young Erasmus with the mien of Cassius and the sartorial mystique of Hamlet.

Ulick Peter Burke was born in England in 1937 to an Irish Catholic family and educated in a Jesuit school in north London (where a fellow pupil was John Bossy). A scholarship took him

to St John's College, Oxford, but only after National Service
which included an 18-month stint in Singapore as pay clerk
in a local regiment largely composed of Malays and Chinese
– an invaluable if unanticipated introduction to cultural
anthropology, Burke acknowledged later. At St John's, one
of his tutors was the young Keith Thomas, while the stars
of Early Modern History at Oxford included Christopher
Hill and Lawrence Stone. Poetry and the visual arts attracted
Burke's attention (he did the Renaissance special subject and
learned to read Vasari and Machiavelli in Italian), while he
was also witness to some of the fierce polemics that swirled
around the Wittgensteinian and largely linguistic philosophy
espoused at Oxford at the time.

After graduating, Burke stayed in Oxford, obtaining
a scholarship to St Antony's where he embarked upon a
doctorate under the loose tutelage of Trevor-Roper, recently
appointed Regius Professor. Initially, the topic was to be on the
seventeenth-century Jesuits; then it broadened, unbelievably, to
cover new trends in historical writing in Europe, 1500–1700
('only Trevor-Roper would have let me get away with this!').
Before this vast and probably unmanageable thesis could be
completed, Burke received a providential call from the new
University of Sussex, Balliol-by-the-Sea, and was appointed as
one of the first batch of lecturers. Soon, he was inventing new
courses, learning new languages ('the first six are the hardest!'),
embarking on unlikely journeys, reaching out towards the latest
trends in historiography, philosophy, sociology, anthropology
and literary criticism.

Gradually, all this accumulated learning began to bear fruit.
Yet Burke's books have never been just any old apples or pears.
There has always been a point, often a somewhat provocative
one, to whatever he has written. His first major book, on
culture and society at the time of the Italian Renaissance, for
example, which was published in 1972, shocked traditionalists
by making statistical use of the biographies of 600 Renaissance

artists. Cliometrics were all very well, some critics felt, if applied to arguments about economic take-off or railways; but surely not to Renaissance art. Burke's answer was disarming: if historians can make quasi-quantitative statements such as that 'more' leading artists at a particular period came from Venice than Florence, say, or that 'most' had this or that kind of parentage or education – why not try to be a little more precise? As computers have become more sophisticated and collective biography (or 'prosopography') has become a common historiographical tool, Burke's early use of both can now be seen as pioneering.

Burke's Renaissance book was also highly original in that it attempted to find links between 'culture' and 'society', to identify some of the messages of Renaissance art – not just those consciously intended by the artists and their patrons but also those perceived by recipients. This is a theme that runs through much of Burke's published work: who, then and later, actually saw the art, read the books, heard the music or poetry – and what messages did they receive? Machiavelli, Vasari, Castiglione or Montaigne may have launched their respective literary argosies. But what was the nature of the cargo their readers thought they had unpacked? Who, indeed, were the readers?

Books and articles poured from Burke's prolific pen, many of them straddling topics and methodologies normally kept respectably separate. Venice and Amsterdam (1974) was a comparative study of seventeenth-century elites for which Burke combed the archives in both cities (the Dutch language was no great problem, he recalls, 'but I found the handwriting difficult at first'). A systematic study of 563 individual local leaders became a launchpad from which Burke went on to survey the broader 'cultural' history of the two cities. For his next book, his attention widened still further to encompass a study of *Popular Culture* (two terms that were still widely considered mutually exclusive) in *Early Modern Europe* (1978).

As Burke himself flew ever-more ambitious missions, gradually becoming known as a personable but pugnacious polemicist from Budapest to Berlin, Cambridge to Canberra, Paris to Princeton, San Francisco to São Paulo and Tokyo to Tel Aviv – and as his personal life came to revolve around a young Brazilian educationalist and historian called Maria Lúcia – he moved from Sussex to Cambridge, becoming a Fellow of Emmanuel in the late 1970s. A personal chair followed a dozen or so years, and several remarkable books, later.

Looking back, Burke sometimes feels that each of his major books was in part an attempt to compensate for something lacking in what had preceded it, to widen the field. In the late 1980s, for example, he turned his attention to the culture of high politics – not in Italy or Holland this time, but in France. The result was *The Fabrication of Louis XIV* (1992), a remarkable study of the way the many images of the Sun King were created, mediated, transmitted and perceived. As always, it is the quest for connections that motivates Burke – those elusive links between culture and society, between elites and the wider public, between cultural messages as originally transmitted and their subsequent social or psychological reception. His sense of timing was immaculate. Just as Burke was beginning to unwrap the wiles of the great iconographers of yesteryear, the Saatchi brothers were learning to unleash ever more sophisticated images of political leadership upon the British electorate. Moreover, much of the final writing of *The Fabrication* was done during a period of study leave in Berlin in 1989 – precisely where and when one of the most heavily buttressed political myths of modern times was being toppled.

From the outset, Burke's writings have been peppered with references to people like Marx and Veblen, Weber and Durkheim, social and cultural theorists of an earlier vintage whose work had broadened traditional disciplines rather as Max Gluckman, Erving Goffman, Norbert Elias or Clifford

Geertz were doing more recently. Even the historians Burke cites most approvingly tend to be those with the widest conceptual and temporal boundaries such as Bloch and Braudel. As befits an admirer of Braudel and the *Annales* school, Burke has also been keen to examine how the cultural processes he investigates have worked out over time and space. It is not just the contemporary reception of Renaissance works of art or of Castiglione's *Courtier* or Rigaud's portrait of Louis XIV that interests him. The book on Castiglione, for example, leads to the *honnête homme* of eighteenth-century France and on via Beau Brummell and Lord Chesterfield to Wilde and Yeats, while the Louis XIV book ends with some provocative parallels with (among others) Mussolini and Lyndon Johnson. Burke's most recent book, *The European Renaissance: Centres and Peripheries*, ranges across a wide variety of geographical and methodological waterfronts – and ends, characteristically, with a chapter on 'The Renaissance after the Renaissance'.

The cumulative corpus of Peter Burke's writing to date reveals an astonishing intellectual trajectory, a 30-year progress towards a history of the creation and reception of 'high' and 'popular' cultural and social artefacts and attitudes over the past six or seven centuries from Stockholm to Sicily, Lisbon to the Levant. And beyond. The references to Asia, Africa and the Americas in his recent book on the European Renaissance are, Burke assures his readers, 'part of a conscious strategy' – an attempt, as ever, to explore the wider peripheries of his subject matter in order to help set the core in ever clearer relief.

It is no coincidence that the rising path of Burke's pan-Europeanism has coincided with the development in the postwar world of a growing sense of European cultural unity. Burke has always considered himself a committed European who stands somewhere on the moderate left wing of British politics; just the kind of person to write illuminatingly about the historical development of popular cultures. But his pro-Europeanism has never been limited or insular. On the contrary,

he has constantly maintained an interest in the wider outposts of European cultural influence, an intellectual orientation that the presence of Maria Lúcia has doubtlessly reinforced and encouraged.

Where does Peter Burke go from here? He already has an enviable international reputation; his writings have been translated into nearly thirty languages, and in several countries of Western Europe he has been successfully marketed as a popular essayist to a general readership. Will he ever feel impelled to write the kind of 'Big Book' by which some historians attempt to sum up their life's work and stake their claim to immortality? Probably not. The next project, Burke tells me, is a more modest affair: a book on what, for want of a better title, he calls 'the social history of knowledge'. As I gasp, he reassures me that it is limited in its aims; 'it's basically, but not exclusively, European and Early Modern'. The book will be about the production and organization of knowledge, who received it, where, in what forms – and the uses to which knowledge was put. The 'sociology of knowledge' if you like. As with much of his previous writing, these themes will first be fired and tempered in a series of academic lectures and seminars before being finally committed to print. And, as ever, Burke's interests are not, of course, merely antiquarian. For he is embarking upon a study of the nature and uses of knowledge precisely at a period when we ourselves are living through, arguably, the largest and most bewildering 'knowledge revolution' of all.

Peter Burke has long been a forceful and consistent advocate of the 'New History', arguing by precept and example for a broadening of temporal, geographical, social and methodological perspectives. When I first got to know him in the early 1960s shortly after his brief postgraduate immersion in the historiography of Early Modern Europe, the idea of 'cultural history' – the study of popular attitudes and values (or what the *Annales* historians called *mentalités*) – was widely frowned upon in a profession still much concerned with the history of official structures. Burke was not intimidated by this. But he was intellectually somewhat isolated. Today, as Professor of Cultural History at Cambridge, Peter Burke can take legitimate pride in having seen his approach vindicated – welcomed, indeed, within the very portals of a once highly sceptical establishment. And he has done it his way.

EPILOGUE

Peter Burke writes:

Since 1999, I have published the social history of knowledge on which I was working at the time of the interview, following it up with an introduction to the use of images as historical evidence and a social history of the media written together with Asa Briggs, who appointed me to my first job at Sussex. In 2004 I retired from the History Faculty at Cambridge (retaining my Fellowship of Emmanuel College) and published a short introduction to cultural history and the revised version of my Wiles Lectures of 2002, summing up the work I have been doing since the early 1980s on the social history of language. I am currently working in the cultural history of translation and, together with my wife, on a study of the Brazilian historian-sociologist Gilberto Freyre.

Theodore Zeldin

BIOGRAPHY

Theodore Zeldin was born in 1933, and graduated from London University in Philosophy, Latin and History, and from Oxford in Modern History. He then embarked on a doctorate at the newly founded St Antony's College, Oxford; of which he was a Fellow from 1957 to 2001; he helped to build it up as the university's postgraduate centre for international studies, simultaneously holding four offices – Senior Tutor, Dean, Tutor for Admissions and Dean of Degrees – for 13 years. At the same time he was a University Lecturer, tutored undergraduates as a Lecturer of Christ Church, and wrote the books listed below.

Oxford requires a physical presence for only 24 weeks a year, so he lived also in London and Paris. At first he spent most of his time in libraries, but his publications led to invitations to participate in a wide range of state, regional, municipal, business, financial, political, artistic and charitable events: he was, for example, a television commentator on French Presidential and Regional elections; President of the Commission appointed by the Regional Council of the Nord-Pas-de-Calais to prepare a plan for the twenty-first century; he spent a year as shadow to the Minister of Culture Jack Lang; and was the presenter of the Prime Minister's website. He was a frequent contributor to the British and French press, a broadcaster – for example, on contemporary issues on BBC's Radio Three, and then a member of its Brains Trust – and for a couple of years wrote a regular column for *Impact Médecin*, the French doctors' weekly. He has, by invitation, published articles in journals as diverse as the *British Medical Journal* and the *Australian Financial Review*.

He was Director of the EC Future of Work project to develop a new vision of work; a member of the Steering Committee of the Centre for European Studies, Strasbourg; Honorary President of the Centre du Paysage, established by the French government to rethink the European landscape; member of the EC Commission to establish the European Voluntary Service; a member of the Council of Europe committee to develop a European cultural policy; Vice-President of Culture Europe; President of the Scientific Committee of Paris University's Course on Cultural Management; Honorary President of the Maison de la Mobilité; a Fellow of the World Economic Forum, Davos; President of the International Festival of Geography, Trustee of Amar International Charity for Refugees; Trustee of Wytham Hall Medical Charity for the Homeless; Patron of Hearsay Charity for the Deaf; Patron of the New Academy for Writing; a member of the Management Committee of the Society of Authors, and co-founder of the Oxford Food Symposium for the study of gastronomy.

He has been elected a Fellow of the British Academy and of the Royal Society of Literature, a Member of the European Academy, an Associate Fellow of Templeton College, Oxford, and of the Said Business School, and awarded an honorary degree by the Ecole des Hautes Etudes Commerciales, Paris. He has lectured in 16 countries, been a Visiting Professor at Harvard and the University of Southern California, and a Research Fellow at the Centre National de la Recherche Scientifique Paris. He has been made a Commander of the Order of the British Empire and a Commander of the Order of Arts and Letters of France.

Since 2001 he has been President of the Oxford Muse Foundation. His books have been translated into 24 languages.

PRINCIPAL PUBLISHED BOOKS

Political System of Napoleon III (1958)

Journal d'Emile Ollivier (ed.) (2 vols, 1960)

Emile Ollivier and the Liberal Empire of Napoleon III (1963)

Conflicts in French Society (ed.) (1970)

A History of French Passions, originally published as *France 1848–1945* in the Oxford History of Modern Europe, vol. 1. *Ambition Love and Politics* (1973) and vol. 2, *Intellect, Taste and Corruption* (1977)

The French (1983)

Happiness (1988)

An Intimate History of Humanity (1994)

Conversation (1998)

Guide to an Unknown City (ed.) (2004)

Guide to an Unknown University (ed.) (2006)

PROFILE, July 1999

Once upon a time, Theodore Zeldin wrote books about nineteenth- and twentieth-century France. Nowadays he prefers to reflect upon the nature and future of intimacy, happiness, conversation and patterns of work. Is he still a historian?

'I'm a historian in the sense that I'm constantly thinking about how things came to be the way they are and what lessons we can draw from that. The ultimate aim is to discover what one should do with one's life – where we should go from here.' The historian as futurologist. So where is Zeldin going from here?

'At the moment I am looking at the nature of work. I visit the workplace and meet young people who tell me that they are dissatisfied with the traditional world of work.' Zeldin defines work very broadly to mean what most people do, one way or another, for most of their waking hours. Many people tell him they feel they are wasting their lives in their work, enslaved to it in some cases. 'Clearly one cannot just continue according to the patterns of the past. One has got to reinvent work. And I am interested in having a vision of what is possible.' The historian as visionary.

Zeldin's ambition is literally boundless. He is one of those intellectuals – or philosophers (he finds the word 'historian' too limiting) – whose ambit embraces the entire human experience: all times, all peoples, all places, all knowledge. Typically, a Zeldin chapter in one of his more recent books starts with the microscope; a more or less verbatim report of an encounter with someone. Then he substitutes the telescope, linking that individual conversation to the wider human experience. His best-known book, *An Intimate History of Humanity*, published in 1994, is constantly broadening from a chat with, say, a schoolteacher or a policewoman in provincial France (they are all women) to gobbets of knowledge carved from ancient Babylon or Portuguese Africa, Ptolemaic astronomy or seventeenth-century Japan, the Don Juan myth, Helen Keller or modern genetics. The texts of some recent BBC radio talks on 'Conversation' were published last year (in a kind of 'Little Book of Calm' format) and filled out with some of Zeldin's own whimsical abstract illustrations and a list of suggested topics of conversation. Chapter headings do not describe or summarize; rather, they offer enticing revelations such as 'How respect has become more desirable than power' or 'Why the conversation of love is moving in a new direction'. He says of his current 'work on work' that the aim is to attempt to help set humanity on a more productive course – 'to enable people to do things that they haven't been able to do before'. The historian as self-improvement guru perhaps?

Zeldin is used to the jibe and has a ready answer. 'All the greatest books have been self-help books', he says without a hint of affectation. 'What is the Bible but a self-help book? What is *Das Kapital* but a self-help book, telling you how to stop being exploited? A book from which you get nothing is a failure.'

Now in his mid-sixties, Zeldin has become something of a peripatetic global celebrity and is consulted by bankers, industrialists, architects, civil service departments, charities, the French Millennium authorities, Iranian ayatollahs and Latin American generals. Courted by establishments, installed as one of the BBC's new Brains Trusters, Zeldin remains self-consciously subversive.

From his base at St Antony's, Oxford, Zeldin fulminates in his civilized way against universities and their restrictive curricula. Relieved of the burdens of teaching or supervising ('That's not what interests me now'), Zeldin is developing ideas for what he calls a 'Super-university' of the future that would expose its students to the practical worlds of agriculture, survival, the process of manufacturing things, the creation of art and beauty, voluntary service – to equip them to live better, more fulfilled lives. With his high brow, sculpted face and leonine mane, Zeldin is the very model of a modern polymath. Einstein without the moustache; Russell with a sexier voice – and just a hint of a cross-national accent.

Where did this global guru come from? The facts as Zeldin recounts them are clear enough, though they leave a lot unexplained. Zeldin's parents were assimilated Russian Jews, both obviously extremely bright and able to transcend the restrictive anti-Semitism of late Tsarist times. His father became a highly respected mathematician and engineer and his mother (amazingly for that time and place) a qualified dentist. While broadly sympathetic towards socialism, they were disturbed at the directions taken by the Revolution and Civil War, left Russia, and settled for a while in British Palestine, where Theodore was born in 1933. Were his parents Zionists? Not at all. Zeldin *père* chose Palestine because of the accident of a British acquaintance (with whom he spoke German) who helped get him work there.

During the war, the family moved to Egypt. The Francophone community in Alexandria, I wondered? Was that where Zeldin's interest in French history and the French language were kindled? Again, the answer is no. They lived among English-speakers, it seems, and Theodore, already a precociously gifted pupil (and excellent athlete), was sent to an English school at Heliopolis where his teachers were mostly refugees from the British public school system, and where he started learning French as a foreign language. One of Zeldin's abiding regrets is that he never really mastered any of the various other languages on offer – Russian, Hebrew, Arabic – during his youthful peregrinations.

Once the war was over, the Zeldins moved to England where their bookish son went to Aylesbury Grammar School. By the age of 15, with his Higher School Certificate exams (the equivalent of A Levels) already under his belt, Zeldin looked for a university that did not exclude people on account of their age. Thus, the boy entered Birkbeck College, London, studying Latin, Philosophy and History alongside fellow students, many of whom were well into their forties and fifties. Wasn't this a deeply disorienting experience for a young adolescent? 'Not at all,' says Zeldin, 'I was totally untroubled by it. I was so busy reading all day and all night that I never really thought about anything else!' At Birkbeck, he was taught philosophy by Dr C.E.M. Joad, famous as one of the BBC's original Brains Trust panellists.

Zeldin duly got his degree from Birkbeck, and then went up to Oxford to study for another undergraduate degree, this time in Modern History, and he stayed on at Oxford (Christ Church) for a doctorate. His thesis on the politics of Napoleon III (later published) was supervised by A.J.P Taylor, whose *Struggle for Mastery in Europe* in the Oxford History of Modern Europe series was later joined by Zeldin's own monumental study of France, 1848–1945.

I wonder what the general editors of the Oxford History series, Alan Bullock and William Deakin, expected when they commissioned young Zeldin to write for them on France. Probably a broadly political history similar to the volumes contributed by Taylor, Raymond Carr (on Spain, 1808–1939) and Hugh Seton-Watson (The Russian Empire, 1801–1917). Perhaps they anticipated an interpretation of nineteenth- and early twentieth-century French history as an unfolding dialectic between revolution and reaction – a series of democratic experiments interspersed with flirtations with the latest 'man on a white horse'. Or maybe they thought Zeldin would enter another traditional historiographical debate and consider how far stolid bourgeois virtues provided a continuity behind France's apparent political discontinuities. One way or another, they presumably thought they would get a book looking at the nation state called France and the vicissitudes it had experienced between the mid-nineteenth and mid-twentieth centuries.

What they finally got – and it took Zeldin nigh on 20 years to complete – was a multivolume 2,000-page work primarily devoted to the history of the passions of ordinary French men and women: their ambitions and frustrations, their intellectual and imaginative life, their tastes and prejudices, their loves, hates and anxieties. Along the way, as Zeldin garners his material from every imaginary source, the suspicion arises that he is not talking about a single place called France at all. The very idea of France as a definable, stable nation state – an agreed focus for all who lived within its boundaries – fades away like Alice's Cheshire Cat before his dazzlingly diverse data. Instead, Zeldin turns most of his attention to the French people – millions of them, all with their different personal, social and local problems and fulfilments. In a section on sport we read of the man who introduced soccer to the Catholic

University of Lille, and learn that the poet Paul Valéry was a keen cyclist; in a chapter on marriage and morals Zeldin quotes the local regulations for prostitutes in Vichy and St Etienne.

Statistics of newspaper readers or teachers' salaries enrich his texts, while writers from Flaubert to Proust, Daudet to Montherlant, are liberally quoted. The French nation and its leaders and legislation are there, and Zeldin writes forcefully about the appeal of Bonapartism, for example. But he is not one to pronounce the prominence of national politics and politicians; rather, their obsequies – or at least the death throes of the traditional image of La France. 'This book has been not quite a post mortem examination of French nationalism', he writes at the end of a *magnum opus* which largely bypasses the central political concept it was presumably intended to investigate, 'but a summing-up of its achievements as it reaches the age for retirement, or as it prepares to merge itself in a new European nationalism.' Has Zeldin disregarded the historical categories his readers might have expected him to adopt? What if he has? 'There is no reason why historians should accept the frameworks that have been bequeathed to them.'

In a strict sense, these great volumes were the last history books Zeldin wrote. By the 1980s, he was turning his attention more and more towards the individual people he encountered and using them as paradigms of human experience. The past as such was no longer of primary interest to him. In *The French* (1983), he tells us that 'every reflective person is a historian' and gives his chapters headings such as 'Why it is hard to meet an Average French Person' or 'How to understand what they are trying to say'. The text is packed with quotes from newspaper small ads, opinion poll results, medical minutiae – and the sayings and doings of the countless 'ordinary' people Zeldin has met. Gaby, a welder in the dockyards of St Nazaire, is full of utopian plans to reform industry and society, but is at war with his wife and son. Didier, a 20-year-old book-keeping clerk in Arceuil, is worried that if he lost his job he'd have difficulty finding another. A schoolteacher from Le Havre, married to an industrialist, likes being beaten when she makes love because it liberates her from the guilt that a religious education instilled into her. Always, the particular is related to the general, the present reinforced by reference to the past. An endearing aspect of this particular book is the way Zeldin has highlighted the work of many of France's leading cartoonists. Throughout, he emphasizes the pluralistic rather than the unitary nature of French society. And he ends with deliberate bathos, a quote from a French comedian, Pierre Dac. To the eternal triple question 'Who are we, where do we come from and where are we going?', Dac answers: 'I am me; I come from down the road, and I am now going home.'

And who, or where, was Zeldin by this stage in his career – no longer really a 'historian' in the conventional sense nor yet the Wise Man of today? The answer, at least briefly, was that he became a novelist. In *Happiness* (1988), he takes his protagonists – a woman called Sumdy (that is, 'Somebody'), along with her dog and her cockroach – on a journey to paradise and back. What do people ultimately want? Zeldin asks in this book. They say they want 'happiness' – but do they? Suppose you were taken to heaven and granted perfect happiness. What then? Sumdy and her retinue encounter the denizens of paradise, among them familiar characters from the past like the Archduke Franz Ferdinand, Henry Ford and other illuminati. At first blush, there is a touching naivety to the book as Sumdy engages in earnest dialogue with the dead of our own and earlier civilizations. She is a utopian traveller somewhat in the tradition of Gulliver or Candide (though without quite the grotesqueries they encountered). But towards the end of the book, as Sumdy prepares to return to the world of the living, she mounts a kind of Tower of Babel from where the view is supposedly clearer than anywhere else. Here, finally, she realizes that perfect happiness is akin to boredom and that the real goals of life include things like the courage to embark upon new adventures.

These mid-career volumes represented an astonishing intellectual journey, and one is bound to ask again: where, in the deeper sense, had Zeldin come from? Was Alan Taylor an intellectual influence, or Zeldin's undergraduate tutor Hugh Trevor-Roper? What about Braudel who was, after all, also thinking beyond nation-state history? Zeldin professes himself bewildered when asked to name his intellectual influences. He's a scavenger, he says, an autodidact. He read all the works of Shaw and Wells as a boy, he recalls, and jumps up to show me a 1,000-page document-based history of ecclesiastical politics during the Second Empire that he devoured as a student. But he says he cannot think of any particular historian, or school of historians, who have especially influenced him, and he is proud that, in his own writings, he never engages in polemics with any of his predecessors. Zeldin is evidently one of nature's 'originals'. But even originals have originals. When I push him, he is prepared to claim some identity, at least of ambition, with the Encyclopédistes of the eighteenth century – universalists (like Bacon, Humboldt, even Comte) who took the whole of human knowledge and, from this base, tried to think how to improve the lot of mankind.

'I'm an optimist, like Leibniz, in the sense that I like to look for solutions to problems – such as those associated with the nature of work.' Is he also a Pangloss? No, he replies: he is far from complacent. His present project, on work, is impossibly ambitious, he concedes. But that doesn't discourage him. It's always useful to have a goal ahead of you, Zeldin says, even if you know you will never completely achieve it. 'I am trying to deal with universal problems that all people who have tried to think universally have grappled with', Zeldin concludes. 'So if you want my lineage, I suppose I'm concerned with the problems that all moralists have thought about.'

Clearly, Zeldin loves thinking. Particularly, he says, about women, 'the revolutionaries of our time'. He seems to obtain 'sybaritic delight' from the sheer process of having thoughts – especially about the future: 'What people could do in the future seemed to be more worth noticing than what they had done in the past', as he put it in Happiness.

It is the desire to help people shape the future to their own interests that is Zeldin's preoccupation now. And absolutely pivotal for this task, he acknowledges, was his early training as a historian. 'The past', says Zeldin 'is what provides us with the building blocks. Our job today is to create new buildings out of them.'

EPILOGUE

Theodore Zeldin writes:

In 2001 the Oxford Muse, a Charitable Foundation, was established to develop Theodore Zeldin's ideas on new ways of improving personal, professional and cultural relations.

For him, personal relations depend on discovering what other people think and so on getting them to put aside the masks they normally wear. He has carried further the 'portrait' method he refined in his historical works to create a growing collection of written self-portraits, based on conversations with every social category, from scientists, authors, fashion designers and the homeless, to the UK's leading chief executive officers. A selection is to be found in *Guide to an Unknown City* which contains self-portraits of the inhabitants of Oxford, from all its different communities; rich and poor, and *Guide to an Unknown University*, which allowed professors, students, alumni, administrators and maintenance staff to reveal what they do not normally tell one another. Zeldin's prefaces draw out surprising implications, not least for the future of universities.

As a preparation for this laying aside of masks, he has been holding Muse Conversation Dinners, with a Menu of Conversation that focuses the mind on the most important and difficult topics in the art of living. The world leaders meeting in Davos, senior civil servants and managers, police chiefs, and people of many nationalities, social groups and religions have participated. They have been astonished by how willing people are to be honest about themselves at these dinners, and by how prejudices dissolve as a result.

Professional relations depend on organizations taking more notice of the aspirations of their members, to which they are often deaf. So Zeldin is investigating how the professions which no longer give the satisfactions they once did can be reinvented. His conversations with the leaders of industry show that many are not satisfied with the constraints that force them to focus on short-term profit-making, but though they are prisoners of the system, they feel they will have to change because of the pressure from young recruits who demand that work should reflect social and moral ideals. To facilitate that process, Zeldin has developed a new kind of generalist postgraduate syllabus which he has called the MCA – one stage beyond the MA and the MBA – for specialists who wish to widen their horizons and expand their sensibilities.

Zeldin is exploring the future of cultural relations with the help of the Muse website, which has attracted interest from over 50 countries. Muse Conversations, for example, have been held in Rwanda, where people say they need them urgently, for the prevention of new atrocities. Portraits are being contributed from every continent. A new role for hotels as cultural centres is being investigated. The voices in Zeldin's Muse are those of all civilizations, past as well as present.

Asa Briggs

Asa Briggs was born in 1921 in Keighley, Yorkshire. With degrees (taken simultaneously) from Cambridge and London Universities, Briggs went on to work in the Intelligence Corps, was a Fellow of Worcester College, Oxford, 1945–55, and Professor of Modern History at Leeds, 1955–1961. He went on to become one of the founding fathers of the University of Sussex where he was Professor of History, Dean of the School of Social Studies and, from 1967 to 1976 Vice-Chancellor. From 1976 to 1991, Briggs was Provost of Worcester College, Oxford, and from 1978–1994, Chancellor of the Open University. In 1976 Briggs was made a Life Peer. He has been President of the British Social History Society and of the Victorian Society. Briggs has produced a great many books and articles, mostly on aspects of nineteenth- and twentieth-century social and cultural history.

PRINCIPAL PUBLISHED BOOKS

Victorian People (1954)
The Age of Improvement (1959)
Victorian Cities (1963)
The History of Broadcasting in the United Kingdom (5 vols, 1961–79)
The Power of Steam (1982)
Victorian Things (1988)
A Social History of England (1983; rev. edn 1994)

The Channel Islands: Occupations and Liberation (1995)

Fins de Siècle: How Centuries End, 1400–2000 (with Daniel Snowman) (1996)

Chartism (1998)

Michael Young: Social Entrepreneur (2001)

A Social History of the Media: From Gutenberg to the Internet (with Peter Burke) (2002)

PROFILE, October 1999

Thought, work and progress: the key words of mid-Victorian England according to Asa Briggs. And they might stand as the personal motto of Lord Briggs of Lewes, a man whose monumental productivity as scholar, author and doer of good public works would have won him the plaudits of a Prince Albert or a Gladstone. But if the burghers of Leeds or Lewes ever decide to erect a statue of Asa Briggs, I hope they don't make it look too earnest, for he is the most engaging of men, utterly without pretension. 'I suppose I am a bit of a Victorian', he acknowledges, but with an almost schoolboyish grin which instantly offsets any suggestion of stuffiness.

The author of *The Age of Improvement* was born in Keighley in 1921 and rose through sheer ability and an unquenchable thirst for hard work to become Professor of History at Leeds, co-founder and Vice-Chancellor of the University of Sussex, Provost of Worcester College, Oxford, Chancellor of the Open University, Chairman or President of a score of learned and historical societies and author of countless articles and books great and small. You can read Briggs on Victorian cities, people and things, on steam and transportation, public health and education, science and technology, music and literature, food and drink, sport and public entertainment, print and publishing, Chartism and the Channel Islands and, in five mighty tomes, on the history of British broadcasting. Chronologically he ranges from prehistory (in the opening chapter of his *A Social History of England*) to the present and future (in *Fins de Siècle*), while his core writings about Victorian England are peppered with comparative material from or about Sydney and Melbourne, New York and Chicago, Dublin, Lyons, Tokyo and Berlin.

Samuel Smiles, apostle of self-help, would have approved. Grandfather Briggs, an engineer (like Asa's father), heard Smiles lecture and told his grandson about it years later. 'My grandfather got me interested in history', Briggs recalls. 'He took me to every abbey and castle and small town in Yorkshire when I was a boy.' It was through his grandfather, too, that Asa developed a lifelong interest in science and technology. His mother's family farmed land in nearby Oxenhope where the cashier in the mill was a Mr Butterfield – whose son Herbert was also to become one of England's best-known historians.

A scholarship to Keighley Grammar School led Briggs, under the influence of a forceful and encouraging headmaster, to Sidney Sussex College, Cambridge. Here he famously obtained not only a Double First in History but also – concurrently (and in secret from his college) – a First in Economics as an external student at the LSE, which was evacuated to Cambridge during the war. Thus, Briggs was able to feast at the table of Postan and Saltmarsh, Oakeshott and Ernest Barker, Hayek, Laski and Eileen Power. He revelled in the richesse, devouring lectures, consuming books and pouring out weekly essays for both sets of masters on such diverse subjects as medieval and constitutional history, political philosophy and economic theory.

His versatility was soon to be stretched yet further. After a brief stint teaching at his old school, Briggs was called up into the Royal Corps of Signals where he learned Morse Code and was trained in fast interception. Then he received a call: he was to go on a cryptographic course – and thence to Bletchley where he spent three years as part of the top-secret team that broke the Enigma code.

While still at Bletchley, Briggs was wooed by both Oxford and Cambridge, finally accepting a Fellowship at Worcester

College, Oxford, where he obtained a Readership and stayed for ten years. He was wooed by Churchill, too, who had asked Bill Deakin to recruit bright young historians (Alan Bullock was another) to help check the text of his forthcoming *History of the English-Speaking Peoples*. Apparently the curmudgeonly old aristocrat was graciously receptive to the strictures of the Keighley scholarship boy, even when Briggs accused him of having been – of all things – too Marxist in his interpretation of the American Constitution. But the most substantial products of Briggs' Oxford years were his history of Birmingham (a work of 'total history', not to mention urban and social history, well before such things became commonplace) and a bustling volume of essays on mid-Victorian 'persons and themes' which he entitled *Victorian People*.

In October 1955, Asa Briggs, recently married and still only 34, became Professor of Modern History at Leeds University. Here, this natural bridge-builder brought the history of social and scientific thought into the syllabus, introduced an experimental series of History 'general' subjects and discovered a taste for spotting and hiring new talent. He also developed a profound distaste for academic territoriality and departmentalism. At Leeds, Briggs was already 'redrawing the map of learning', something he was soon invited to do on a far wider scale.

The University of Sussex was to Asa Briggs what the Great Exhibition had been to Prince Albert or the BBC to Reith: a visionary undertaking for the betterment of the nation. Sussex was the first of seven 'New Universities' planned for the 1960s, all placed near coasts and cathedrals in deliberate contrast to the urban 'redbrick' of Leeds, Manchester and the rest. Briggs was there from the start, appointed to take overall charge of academic affairs.

Briggs at Sussex was a torrent, a dynamo, an engine. Buildings were designed and assigned, deans and dons appointed (I was lucky enough to be one of them), new concepts coined.

Students would major in the 'core subject' of their choice (somewhat in the American style) while also studying a series of 'contextual' subjects in the 'Schools of Study' to which they were assigned. Quality control was guaranteed by an Oxbridge-style tutorial system. Buzzwords in this academic terra nova were 'interdisciplinary' and 'cross-cultural'. There were taboo words, too; what 'sex' was to the Victorians, 'departments' were to Sussex.

Throughout this surge of social engineering, Briggs remained an active historian. He had already embarked upon what must have seemed the commission of (and doubtless for!) a lifetime: a multivolume history of British broadcasting. The first instalment appeared in 1961: 400 packed pages chronicling the birth of the British Broadcasting Company and its transformation into a Corporation. Briggs had research help throughout the broadcasting project. If the outcome sometimes reflects the official sources on which it is largely based, it is worth remembering that there was little 'media' or 'cultural' history when Briggs began, and it is perhaps unfair to criticize a pioneer for not having adopted an approach that his own work helped stimulate. One of the by-products of Briggs' work, incidentally, was that he was able to persuade the BBC to set up a properly catalogued written archive at Caversham.

He also found time during the early years at Sussex to write *Victorian Cities*, a richly allusive set of essays on the pattern of *Victorian People* which brought together years of accumulated research and personal experience of Birmingham and Leeds, Manchester, Melbourne and Middlesbrough, and that great 'world' city, London.

Briggs became Vice-Chancellor in 1967 and soon found himself having to pilot Sussex through the choppy waters of student protest. But not even the most disaffected student could accuse the VC – self-evidently a conscientious academic who wrote books, gave lectures and talked to students – of being a grey administrator. As a result, Sussex was a pretty happy ship, experiencing nothing like the disruption that afflicted (for example) the University of Essex or the LSE. Briggs remained at the helm for a decade, finally leaving Sussex in 1976. That year he was given a life peerage. Before accepting, he made it clear to the Prime Minister, James Callaghan, that he would not accept a Party Whip in the Lords, and would not have time to attend very often. Apart from everything else, he had a new job.

As Provost of Worcester College, Oxford, Lord Briggs was, in a sense, going home. This was where he had done his earliest historical research and penned his first books. To many great men of action, the headship of an Oxbridge college is a final reward for a life of service, grassland for a warhorse no longer required for serious battle. Retired Cabinet ministers, ambassadors and even professors have learned to enjoy the unrelenting round of drinks and homage that come with the territory, and who can complain if their presence brings the college added lustre? Briggs is not averse to such pastimes and good company, but he went to Worcester for more than that. For 15 years (until 1991, when he was 70) he moved and shook with the mightiest of them. But he also tried, as he had at Sussex, to break down the barriers between teachers and taught, artists and scientists, town and gown. One of Briggs' proudest achievements as Provost was to make the house (previously the abode of the formidable Oliver Franks) more accessible to undergraduates.

Meanwhile, the great broadcasting juggernaut pushed its way through to the war years and beyond, while in 1983 Briggs published the most important longitudinal study of English social history since Trevelyan, a book bursting with typically Briggsian detail about coins and medals, ballads and baubles, cities and seasides – plus much of the politics which Trevelyan had proclaimed inappropriate to social history. A couple of years later Briggs' collected essays began to appear in volume form.

My own favourite among Briggs' books, and I suspect it may be his, is *Victorian Things*, a companion piece to its predecessors on *People* and *Cities*, which appeared in 1988. The Victorians filled their lives and packed their homes with objects: hats and bonnets, stamps and matches, pots and pans, tongs and coal scuttles, photos, phones and phonographs. *Victorian Things* makes no claim to be comprehensive, nor does Briggs squeeze arcane symbolism from his multifarious bits and bobs as a French semiologist might have done. But, in its undemonstrative way, the book breaks new ground as Briggs gives pride of place to the objects themselves. Things, more than documents, are the new emissaries from the past.

Here, as so often, it is Briggs' insatiable curiosity about the past that drives his history. If he tends to give less prominence than some historians to analysis and explanation it is because he objects to 'premature generalization' and the sterile academic debates this can lead to. Rather, he attempts to communicate the direct experience of the past to his readers via the detail, backed up by an army of apposite quotations. Briggs typically dazzles with detail – especially, perhaps, in the Victorian trilogy where an overall picture emerges of a sensible, bourgeois world populated by energetic people genuinely dedicated to the idea of ameliorating their lot and that of their progeny. An age of improvement, indeed.

At 78, Asa Briggs, looking and sounding like a man ten years younger, remains as industrious as ever. Projects and presidencies come and go. The Workers' Educational Association and the Open University, the University Grants Committee, the Labour and Social History Societies, the Commonwealth of Learning, the Booker Committee and Glyndebourne Trust, the Bronte Society, Ephemera Society, Victorian Society and the editorial board of journals and magazines (including *History Today*) – Briggs has sat on them all and chaired most. With homes in Lewes and Scotland, an office in London and a hideaway in Portugal, he still rushes

to and from trains and planes. Deadlines loom. New projects
are accepted while previous ones lie unfinished. Recent books
include collaborations with Patricia Clavin on a volume on
European History since 1789, Roy Porter on Bethlem and
myself on *Fins de Siècle*, plus a short history of Chartism (for
a series of pocket histories of which he is general editor). Next
off the assembly line are a book about Michael Young and
a history of the Royal College of Physicians, while awaiting
completion are a history of Longman, a book with Peter Burke
on the history of communications and a project about forms of
work during World War II. As for the BBC, Briggs was furious
when the Corporation closed its broadcasting history unit and
is determined to do a volume, entirely under his own steam,
to include the John Birt years.

What has driven the engine so ferociously for so long? Why
does Briggs still work so hard, travel so extensively? Has he
written too much? Briggs knows all the jibes about 'Lord Briggs
of Heathrow' and laughs them off without quite denying their
truth. 'I love writing,' he says, 'and am never completely happy
unless I have a book on the go.' There is a moral dimension,
too. 'I always feel there are certain questions that I ought to
look at', says Briggs, evidently inspired by the sense of service
that also motivated the Victorians. His critics say that no one
man can master the range of topics Briggs writes about, and
point to phrases, quotations and examples that recur in Briggs'
writings. Some of his writings are indeed partly reworkings of
earlier material. Also, the style and subject matter are highly
discreet in a rather old-fashioned way; if you want to find
out about Disraeli's sex life or Rowntree's drinking, don't go
looking in Briggs. This is doubtless because Briggs abhors the
modern obsession with prurience. But some readers also sense
a busy writer skating along the public surface of a topic and
missing some of the more suggestive crevasses beneath.

As this chronicler, beneficiary and product of Victorian
idealism looks back over our own times he perceives what

he believes to be the rise and decline of many of our great institutions of public improvement – the BBC, the Arts Council and the National Health Service, for example. It is deeply ironic that this apostle of all that was best in Victorian values should have seen them evoked, erroneously in his view, by a prime minister, Margaret Thatcher, who aspired to tear down so much that genuine Victorian values had helped to erect.

There is a further reason why we are losing touch with the qualities bequeathed by our Victorian ancestors, of course, and that is the sheer passage of time. The Victorians, so well remembered (and in some cases encountered) when Briggs was a lad, have long since passed away, and the Victorian era itself will shortly become 'the century before last'. The revival of interest in the Victorian era, which Briggs (with John Betjeman) did so much to pioneer and spearhead, is ebbing away as younger scholars gravitate towards more recent periods.

Perhaps each generation is attracted to the era just outside its own collective memory. That is healthy enough, and Briggs holds no special brief for the primacy of Victorian studies. But he worries that our political leaders encourage very little sense of history (and fulminates about the lack of history in the Dome – an exhibition presumably mounted to mark a calendrical watershed). To Asa Briggs, nobody can expect to plan the future who does not also understand the forces which have created the present. But this preternatural optimist is not given to cursing the darkness. Briggs' instincts, rather, are to light a candle by which to get on with the next job. Whichever of the many on his plate that might be ...

Eric Foner

Eric Foner was born in New York in 1943. He was educated at Columbia and Oxford Universities and did his PhD at Columbia under the supervision of Richard Hofstadter. Foner is currently DeWitt Clinton Professor of History at Columbia, a post he has held since 1988, and he has served as President of all three major professional organizations in the USA: the Organization of American Historians, the American Historical Association, and the Society of American Historians.

He has also been the Co-Curator, with Olivia Mahoney, of two prize-winning exhibitions on American history: 'A House Divided: America in the Age of Lincoln', which opened at the Chicago Historical Society in 1990, and 'America's Reconstruction: People and Politics After the Civil War', which opened at the Virginia Historical Society in 1995 and travelled to several other locations. He revised the presentation of American history at the Hall of Presidents at Disney World, and 'Meet Mr. Lincoln' at Disneyland, and has served as Consultant to several National Parks Service historical sites and historical museums.

He is a winner of the Great Teacher Award from the Society of Columbia Graduates (1991), and the Presidential Award for Outstanding Teaching from Columbia University (2006). He was named Scholar of the Year by the New York Council for the Humanities in 1995. In 2006, he received the Kidger Award for Excellence in Teaching and Scholarship from the New England History Teachers Association. He is an elected

Fellow of the American Academy of Arts and Sciences and the British Academy, and holds an honorary doctorate from Iona College. He has taught at Cambridge University as Pitt Professor of American History and Institutions, Oxford University as Harmsworth Professor of American History, and Moscow State University as Fulbright Professor. He serves on the editorial boards of *Past and Present* and *The Nation*, and has written for the *New York Times*, the *Washington Post*, the *Los Angeles Times*, the *London Review of Books*, and many other publications.

Foner's published work has tended to concentrate on the intersections of intellectual, political and social history and the history of American race relations. His books have been translated into Chinese, Korean, Italian and Portugese.

PRINCIPAL PUBLISHED BOOKS

Free Soil, Free Labor, Free Men: The Ideology of the Republican Party Before the Civil War (1970; reissued with new preface 1995)

Tom Paine and Revolutionary America (1976)

Nothing But Freedom: Emancipation and Its Legacy (1983)

Reconstruction: America's Unfinished Revolution, 1863–1877 (1988)

The Reader's Companion to American History (with John A. Garraty) (1991)

The Story of American Freedom (1998)

Who Owns History? Rethinking the Past in a Changing World (2002)

Give Me Liberty! An American History (2004)

Voices of Freedom (2004)

Forever Free: The Story of Emancipation and Reconstruction (2005)

PROFILE, January 2000

Eric Foner was Harmsworth Professor of American History at Oxford a few years ago, when he was invited to take tea with

Isaiah Berlin and told his little daughter that he was going to meet a famous philosopher. 'What's a philosopher?' she asked. 'Someone who tries to answer difficult questions,' Eric began to explain, 'like – what is freedom? – that kind of thing.' 'Well, I've got one for him', she chimed in. 'Ask him: if you choose your own master are you free?'

Asking pertinent questions runs in the Foner family. So, it seems, does an interest in the concept of liberty. The first thing that strikes you about Eric Foner's books is their titles. His first (1970) was *Free Soil, Free Labor, Free Men*, while his most recent is *The Story of American Freedom*. In between, there were books about such icons of liberty as Tom Paine and Nat Turner, works about the emancipation of slaves (entitled *Nothing But Freedom*) and the Reconstruction era that followed, and a Who's Who of black officeholders during Reconstruction that Foner called *Freedom's Lawmakers*. Evidently a man with a rondo theme.

The second thing – obvious as soon as you start reading Foner – is that, while he may have spent his professional life buzzing industriously around the most dazzling themes of American history, he has not allowed himself to get burned by them. When all around him other historians have lost their heads to popular rhetoric and mawkish sentimentality, Foner has conspicuously kept his – no small feat in the 'Land of the Free', that 'Sweet Land of Liberty' with its Liberty Bell and Statue of Liberty where people have demanded 'Freedom Now', defended the 'Free World' and universally retort that it's 'a free country'. Foner relishes 'freedom' as much as the next man and, like the pragmatic American that he is, is not inclined to define it. Definition, after all, means assigning limits, which is precisely what Foner does not want to do. On the contrary, his particular contribution has been to illustrate the chameleon-like quality of freedom and to suggest the diverse, elusive, mercurial nature of the concept. What 'freedom' has meant, to whom, when and where – these themes run through the entire skein of American history, and they inform and inspire much of Eric Foner's work.

He was lucky in his lineage. His father Jack Foner and his uncle Philip were both New York historians with Old Left leanings, early proponents of black and labour history, while two other uncles were union leaders. Jack and Philip were made to suffer for their radicalism, being blacklisted for many years. Eric (born in 1943) was a child during the McCarthy era, and by the time he was an undergraduate at Columbia in the early 1960s, Foner family values were once more in the ascendant. In particular, the emerging civil rights movements taught the young man that history casts a long shadow, linking the past with the present. Also – as his father and uncle had always maintained – that history, properly told, must embrace those out of power as well as those who exercise it.

At Columbia, Foner was given warm encouragement by the stars of the history faculty. James Shenton awakened and inspired his interest in nineteenth-century black history; Richard Hofstadter was especially kind (possibly because of residual guilt at having accepted a job many years earlier from which Jack Foner had been ousted), and helped Eric get to Oriel College, Oxford. Here he took a second BA – including the Special Subject on Slavery and Secession under that year's visiting Harmsworth Professor, the great Allan Nevins, who had once taught Jack and Philip.

Back at Columbia, at the hub of the late-1960s 'counter-culture', Foner wrote a PhD thesis on the libertarian ideology of the Republican party in the years immediately preceding the American Civil War. Eric McKitrick, who supervised the dissertation, paid Foner what, to this day, he thinks was intended as a compliment: 'Eric,' said McKitrick 'this is a lot better than I expected!' It must have been well-intended because McKitrick encouraged Foner to adapt the thesis for publication as a book.

Free Soil, Free Labor, Free Men contains many Foner hallmarks. It opens with a *tour d'horizon* of the existing literature, respectful of predecessors yet suggesting the dated or partial schools of thought into which their work fell. Thus, earlier Civil War historiography (rather like conflicting interpretations of World War II) tended to fall into one of two camps. There were those who thought war inevitable, and those who saw it as the outcome of a series of blunders by incompetent politicians. Both tended to concentrate on politics and economics and to minimise the significance of moral or ideological issues, as if to imply that people's beliefs were really a mask for material interests.

Foner's approach is both narrower than these and broader. Focusing unashamedly on ideology, he proceeds to treat his topic as the hub of a wheel whose spokes reach deep into many aspects of ante-bellum America. Thus, *Free Soil* considers Republican attitudes towards not only the economy and politics of North and South but also the pros and cons of gradual, as opposed to radical, constitutional reform, the dignity of labour and what we would call social and geographical mobility.

In *Free Soil*, as in all his work, Foner eschews any single-thread approach to the complex warp and weft of history. His method, rather, is to hold up a particular concept, personality, party or event and then turn it around and examine its multifarious facets from various perspectives, like a diamond in light. How, he will ask of his subject matter, did things look to these or those people, from this or that position, time or place? Foner's next book, *Tom Paine and Revolutionary America*, took him back to the eighteenth century, across to England and France and into the new (to him) field of biography. If *Free Soil* was a book about ideas with links into social history, *Tom Paine* was a book of social and personal history rooted in ideas. Both, and much that followed, examine the links between what goes on in the mind and what actually happens in the streets. You may not be able to prove a relationship between ideas and action; but to write about the one and ignore the other is, to Foner, palpably bad history. It is not how we experience life.

He is refreshingly open about the links between what we believe and what we do. Raised on New York liberalism, Foner has devoted much of his professional life to the study of American slavery and its aftermath. Far too good a historian to let his liberal instincts bias his approach, he has nevertheless carried a torch for the radicalism of his father and his uncle in his choice of subject matter. Nor has this done Foner any harm professionally. Present-day America may be deeply antipathetic towards the tax-and-spend liberalism of the Old Left, with its romanticization of the 'working man' and belief in civil rights for the 'Negro'. But the new political correctness of our own times, while latently obscurantist, has undoubtedly helped generate renewed interest in the black past just at a time when Foner has reinstated the centrality of the black experience in American history.

He was to do this most forcefully in *Reconstruction: America's Unfinished Revolution, 1863–1877*. Here, too, Foner acknowledges a debt to another senior historian at Columbia, Richard Morris, who kickstarted Foner into undertaking the book for a series that Morris and Henry Steele Commager were editing for Harper and Row. As with the Civil War itself, the Reconstruction era that followed it divided historians. The standard view, still common when Foner was a student, portrayed a saddened and subdued South that would have been prepared to accept its defeat under the conciliatory politics of Lincoln ('with malice towards none'). But Lincoln's assassination, followed by the inept presidency of Andrew Johnson, permitted the vindictive radical Republicans of the North and their opportunistic agents to ride roughshod over Southern sensibilities, thus exacerbating racial hatreds and ensuring that rancour towards the North remained intact for a further century. It is the story portrayed towards the end of

Gone With the Wind, one of simple moral polarities in which all the principal actors, heroes and villains alike, are white.

The most notable voice to question this interpretation belonged to the W.E.B. Du Bois in his *Black Reconstruction*, published in 1935. Du Bois died in 1963, living long enough to see himself transformed in the popular mind from dangerous radical to quasi-sainthood. But in the 1930s, his was a lone voice as historians tended to paint a generalized portrait of Negro slavery or purvey potted biographies of admirable, patient figures like Booker T. Washington or George Washington Carver. Jack and Philip Foner knew and admired Du Bois and taught his kind of history; when Philip wrote about a great figure from the past, he chose the ex-slave and black activist Frederick Douglass. Thus, Eric Foner grew up understanding – as few of his contemporaries did – the crucial, proactive importance of black experience in nineteenth-century America.

By the time Foner was asked to write about *Reconstruction*, a large new literature had emerged about slavery and its aftermath, in part an intellectual response to the civil rights movement. Foner thus found himself researching one of the most prominent and controversial of historical subjects. In *Reconstruction*, as in his earlier writings, he assesses the existing literature, goes on to create a work of synthesis and gives proper attention to the relationship between ideas and action. But he does far more than that. Reconstruction is a major work of original scholarship, using sources unknown to previous historians (for example, a large cache of papers from the archive of the South Carolina governor's office). In addition – and in defiance of the tradition of American 'exceptionalism' – Foner calls upon his knowledge of British and European history to draw occasional parallels with and lessons from the emancipation of slavery in the Caribbean or Latin America (a comparative approach used in his book *Nothing But Freedom*). *Reconstruction* is also the first of Foner's major works to contain pictures, carefully chosen to counterpoint rather than merely illustrate the text. No wonder a book originally intended to fill a gap in a publisher's series took ten years to complete! In *Reconstruction*, Eric Foner finally placed the black community centre stage, not in the passive role of slaves but as active participants after emancipation in a series of complex social and political processes. The book was thus a major act of historical reassessment – one, moreover, that accorded precisely with the temper of the times.

Reconstruction won its author a clutch of plaudits and national renown and thrust him firmly into that select company of historians with impeccable academic credentials also capable of reaching out to a wide audience. Foner is one of nature's communicators, a man whose vigorous prose style is matched by an engaging and voluble presence. Firmly ensconced at the top of his tree (as DeWitt Clinton Professor of History at his old Alma Mater, Columbia), Foner talks fast and thinks faster. He evidently writes quickly, too ('I learned that at Oriel when I had to do an essay or two a week on subjects, like the medieval wool trade, that I knew nothing about!'). To Eric Foner, the past is a living present which he has a compulsion to share. Talk to him about Tom Paine and you will quickly be reminded that Paine helped create much of the currency of modern political discourse ('rights', 'revolution', 'republic', 'common sense'); racial tensions, similarly, still arise because of the discrepancy between the political emancipation but economic inequality meted out to America's ex-slaves.

Does Foner gravitate towards topics in the past that illuminate the present? Not consciously. Nor is he one of those American 'Whig historians' who, like the frontiersmen of old, try to conquer the obstinately variegated landscape they encounter in order to present it as a smooth story of ever-increasing success. Foner's most recent book, *The Story of American Freedom*, may look like one of those celebratory volumes that used to pass for history. The perfect Commencement Day gift, you might think, from sentimental old Mom and Pop to young

Joe or Lindy as they graduate into the big wide world. But if Joe and Lindy are alert, they may sense an irony, or double meaning, behind Foner's title, for the book is as much about the unfolding mythology of freedom as about its reality.

With *The Story of American Freedom*, Eric Foner returns to his rondo theme, expanding it indeed into a great symphonic coda – a narrative history of the United States using the constantly shifting concept of freedom as its guiding principle. Grand narrative history was more common a generation or two ago when people could write comfortably about 'the American mind' (or 'character' or 'love of liberty'). Today's academic historians are more likely to be of the 'Yes, but …' school of thought, acutely conscious of conflict and nuance, the victim and the exceptional, and more likely therefore to specialize, for example, in women's history, black history, the history of the family or urban history. While these subdivisions have yielded valuable insights unavailable to earlier historians, Foner feels, they have also tended to bring about the fragmentation of the discipline and set up invisible walls between its once-collegiate practitioners.

It is thus no small thing for a high-profile American historian to undertake a work of creative synthesis. It was also courageous for someone with intellectual roots in the mid-nineteenth century to write a book containing over 200 pages on the twentieth. What Foner has produced is not a simple, linear story, but one in which the nature and meaning of its central concept, freedom, is constantly up for grabs. Jefferson, Lincoln, FDR and Reagan all wave the banner of liberty, but so do the followers of such non-establishment figures as Frederick Douglass, Margaret Sanger, Eugene V. Debs and today's anti-government militia groups. Both sides in the Civil War claimed to espouse the cause of liberty; so did both Lyndon Johnson's liberal Democrats and the right-wing Goldwater Republicans in the 1964 presidential election a century later. Throughout

Freedom, as in all his work, Foner seeks links between ideas and actions and, by implication, between past and present.

Freedom ends with a whinge and a prayer. 'Americans', writes Foner, 'have sometimes believed they enjoy the greatest freedom of all – freedom from history.' That is of course foolish thinking. But he does not advocate a retreat into historical determinism. 'We can decide for ourselves what freedom is', Foner asserts, noting wryly that freedom as economic security, for example, or as social justice for the disadvantaged are currently in eclipse. And he concludes with the sanguine hope that what Lincoln called 'the better angels of our nature' will reclaim their place in the unfinished story of American freedom. Jack and Philip Foner would surely have agreed. And I suspect that Isaiah Berlin would have approved, too.

EPILOGUE

Eric Foner writes:

Daniel Snowman's profile of me appeared in early 2000. At the time, I was busily engaged in writing a survey textbook of American history, aimed at introductory undergraduate classes. Its theme, like many of my previous works, was freedom, and it was published in 2004 with the title, *Give Me Liberty! An American History*.

While I was at work, of course, the terrorist attack of 11 September 2001 took place, which unexpectedly elevated freedom to an even more central place in American political discourse than it had previously occupied. President Bush quickly announced that the reason for the attack was 'they hate our freedom'. In 2002, the government issued the National Security Strategy, a document that announced the doctrine of pre-emptive war. It began with a discussion not of weaponry or of geopolitics, but of freedom. The United States, it declared, had achieved the 'single sustainable model' of social organization, and our current understanding of freedom was 'right and true for every person in every society'. Soon, the country would be thrust into Operation Iraqi Freedom, as the invasion of Iraq was christened. As at many other times in our past, the United States had assumed a self-proclaimed role as the embodiment of freedom for the entire world. The possibility that other peoples may have given thought to the question of freedom, and arrived at their own conclusions, did not arise. At the same time, a crusade described as a titanic worldwide struggle between freedom and its opposite went hand in hand with restrictions on freedom at home. This, too, had historical precedents.

No one today can predict the outcome of the Iraq war, or the resolution of the tension between liberty and security at home. But recent events highlight even more powerfully than in the past the importance of developing a historical – as opposed to mythical – understanding of the idea of freedom and its evolution, and of making discussions of freedom a dialogue with the entire world, not a complacent monologue with ourselves.

John Keegan

BIOGRAPHY

John Keegan was born in 1934. He is married to the biographer Susanne Keegan and they have four children. He was educated at King's College (Taunton), Wimbledon College and Balliol College, Oxford, of which he is an Honorary Fellow. From 1960 until 1986 he taught military history at the Royal Military Academy, Sandhurst. Since 1986 he has been Defence Editor of the *Daily Telegraph*.

John Keegan is the author of 20 books, including *A History of Warfare* (1993), which won the Duff Cooper Prize, and *The First World War* (1998), which was awarded the Westminster Medal. In 1998 he gave the BBC Reith Lectures, which were published as *War and Our World*.

He has been Lees Knowles Lecturer in Military History at Cambridge, 1986–87, a Fellow of Princeton in 1984 and Delmas Distinguished Professor of History at Vassar in 1997. He was a Trustee of the National Heritage Memorial Fund and Heritage Lottery Fund from 1994 to 2000 and is now a Commissioner of the Commonwealth War Graves Commission. He is a Fellow of the Royal Historical Society and of the Royal Society of Literature. He was awarded the OBE in the 1991 Gulf War Honours List and was knighted in 1999 for services to military history.

PRINCIPAL PUBLISHED BOOKS

The Face of Battle (1976)
Who's Who in Military History (with Andrew Wheatcroft) (1977)
World Armies (1981)
Six Armies in Normandy (1982)
Soldiers (with Richard Holmes) (1983)
Zones of Conflict (with Andrew Wheatcroft) (1984)
The Mask of Command (1987)
The Price of Admiralty (1988)
The Second World War (1989)
Times Atlas of the Second World War (1989)
Churchill's Generals (1991)
Battle At Sea (1993)
A History of Warfare (1993)
Warpaths (1995)
The Battle for History (1995)
War and Our World (1998)
The First World War (1998)
The Penguin Book of War (1999)
Winston Churchill (2002)
Intelligence in War (2003)
The Iraq War (2004)
The American Civil War (2006)

PROFILE, May 2000

In and all around his desk piles of books jostle for space with
as yet unanswered letters of congratulation. John Keegan was
knighted in the Millennium honours and is still not quite used
to the idea. We were sitting in Keegan's office in the large
manor house in rural Wiltshire that he and his wife Susanne
(author of books on Alma Mahler and Kokoschka) acquired
15 years ago.

Maybe it was the West Country air. Or the fact that,
shortly after the house move, Keegan quit his job lecturing

at Sandhurst and joined the *Daily Telegraph*. Whatever the cause, the effects were a cascade of major works: *The Mask of Command* (a study of generalship), substantial military histories of both world wars, an elegant peregrination around the battlefields of North America, the colossally ambitious *History of Warfare* and the BBC's 1998 Reith Lectures, *War and Our World*. All these (not to mention an anthology of 'great military writing') constitute an astonishing efflorescence of talent that, by Keegan's own admission, remained many years in the bud.

Born in 1934, Keegan is of Irish Catholic extraction on both sides. His father was a schools inspector in Clapham whose district was evacuated during the war to the Dorset–Somerset border, where Keegan still remembers seeing US troops mobilizing for D-Day. Struck down by tuberculosis as an adolescent, Keegan spent his mid-teens in hospital beds just when other boys were learning the rituals of emerging masculinity. A pair of kindly teachers in the hospital school, followed by two years at Wimbledon College, a Jesuit school, helped equip the boy to get into Oxford in 1953.

At Balliol, Keegan, walking painfully with a stick, was surrounded by robust, self-assured young men, most of them just out of National Service. They were a bright lot and included a future Lord Chief Justice (Bingham), two Northern Ireland Secretaries (Peter Brooke and Patrick Mayhew), the writer Ved Mehta and the historians Keith Thomas and Maurice Keen. Keegan read history at Balliol, learning about the Middle Ages from Richard Southern and the seventeenth century from Christopher Hill, and chose as his special subject 'Military History and the Theory of War'. After a six-month trip through the USA with Maurice Keen (later a brother-in-law), Keegan worked for a couple of years at the American Embassy in London. He was nearly 26 when, in 1960, his first 'proper' job materialized; he was to keep it for the next 26 years.

In many ways Keegan found the Royal Military Academy, Sandhurst, to be like an Oxford college, with beautiful grounds and buildings and the camaraderie of intelligent and motivated young men. But there was a fundamental difference. At Oxford, the intellectual ethos had encouraged the dialectic of debate, dispute and disagreement and the active entertaining of alternative hypotheses; at Sandhurst, Keegan lectured on military history to officer cadets who were training to become part of a chain of command in which you learned to accept, not argue with, the instructions of superiors. As Keegan acknowledged in the opening pages of his first important book, *The Face of Battle*, published in 1976: 'the atmosphere and surroundings of Sandhurst are not conducive to a realistic treatment of war'. So how did this Balliol-trained historian adjust to what he called the 'stern, professional, monocular outlook' of the student-officer? The answer is that Keegan loved Sandhurst and Sandhurst evidently loved him. The company was congenial, the library well stocked, the institution endowed with a sense of purpose. 'The British army,' Keegan maintains, 'is a remarkably liberal and open-minded organisation in which there is great freedom of discussion – so long as you don't undermine or condemn its central values.' Like a Jesuit college perhaps.

In *The Face of Battle*, Keegan addresses what he calls 'the central question': what it is like being in a battle – something none of his young charges at Sandhurst could have known and which he himself, because of his disability, would never experience. Concentrating on three very different confrontations – Agincourt, Waterloo and the Somme – Keegan begins with an elegant historiographical essay on the nature of military history. He reflects on why military history tends be written by victors, or at least from territories that have not hosted great wars, and whether this has to be the case, and he pays homage to predecessors from Thucydides to Ranke to Michael Howard.

In this most humane of battle books, Keegan calls upon a wide range of data: priests who wrote eye-witness accounts of Agincourt, William Siborne who sent a questionnaire (possibly the first in history) to surviving British officers who fought at Waterloo, official reports, letters, memoirs, anecdotes and poetic recreations. Not for Keegan a simple tactics-and-triumph approach. The battles he describes unleash the deepest fears and most violent passions, and Keegan reflects on what leads men to expose themselves to the possibility of severe pain and death. In the final chapter he attempts the bold task of comparing the three battles as to severity, length, danger to participants, technical difficulty, and so on, and draw broad conclusions. Keegan – writing at the height of the Cold War – concludes that, whatever the soldiers and politicians might say, 'the suspicion grows that battle has already abolished itself'.

This was not Keegan's first book; there had been half a dozen pot-boilers in the 1960s for 'Ballantine's Illustrated History of the Violent Century' (where fellow toilers included Paul Kennedy, Roger Manvell, Noble Frankland, Nicolai Tolstoy and Christopher Hibbert). But *The Face of Battle* was the work that catapulted him to fame. And once adopted as the US Book of the Month Club choice, it brought John and Susanne a welcome burst of unaccustomed wealth as they raised their four children.

Over the next decade, Keegan worked on a number of writing projects. He conceived the idea of a military equivalent of *Jane's Fighting Ships*, an encyclopaedia of the world's armies which, naturally, he would have to update each year. It lasted for two editions. He wrote a book about Normandy and the bulk of John Gau's TV series *Soldiers* (with his Sandhurst colleague Richard Holmes).

By now, the love affair with Sandhurst was cooling. Keegan had been there for a quarter of a century, was himself over 50 and felt he still had a lot more 'proper' books in him. Few people keen to write learned tomes leave an academic environment for a newspaper. But Keegan had already acquired a taste for journalism, notably when he wrote on the Falklands War for *The Spectator* (under an assumed name), and he joined the *Daily Telegraph* in 1986 as Defence Correspondent (later restyled Defence 'Editor', which meant more think-pieces and less travelling).

He celebrated his change of life with the publication of *The Mask of Command* (1987), a counterpart to *The Face of Battle*. Each studied a variety of military confrontations from different times and places and drew general conclusions. But while the earlier book had examined the experience of battle for ordinary participants, *The Mask of Command* reversed the telescope and looked at military leaders: Alexander, Wellington (the only point of overlap between the two books), Grant and Hitler. As before, Keegan starts and ends with speculative chapters, this time reflecting on the heroic – or 'anti-heroic' – nature of generalship. Throughout, he is concerned to identify the nature of the mask that all leaders, especially perhaps military leaders, are required to wear if they are to be effective.

What comes across is the energy, tenacity, stamina – and ruthlessness – of military leaders. Alexander 'moved with ferocious rapidity' to quell plots against him; Wellington at Waterloo slept nine hours in ninety. The general must show himself to his followers and create a bond of kinship between himself and them – perhaps (like Alexander) by seeming godlike and invincible, or else (like Grant 'galloping from place to place … to rally shaken regiments, encourage subordinates and send reinforcements to the front') by seeming to be one of them. The military leader who loses the confidence of his followers, as Hitler did even before the military tide had begun to turn against him, is lost.

The parallels with politics are close and it is striking that all the commanders Keegan considers – like Caesar, Napoleon and Eisenhower – exercised political as well as military power. Keegan is much concerned throughout his writing with the relationship between the two. War, he starkly asserts at the outset of his *History of Warfare* (1993), 'is not the continuation of politics by other means'. He hastens to explain that what Clausewitz actually wrote (that war is the continuation of 'political intercourse with the intermixing of other means') was subtler and threw useful light on warfare in an age of nation states. But he feels that the Clausewitzian analysis had little relevance to pre- and non-state conflict. The Prussian sage was useful, but primarily about his own time and place.

A History of Warfare stretches the parameters of military history (and one senses it probably stretched its author) to the limits. It certainly takes the subject way beyond Clausewitz. Chronologically Keegan covers 4,000 years of history and geographically the entire world. In the course of a dazzling survey, we visit places as far apart as Easter Island, Ancient China, imperial Rome and the Aztecs of Mexico and encounter Attila, Genghis Khan, Muslim Mamelukes and Japanese samurai, in addition to the great landmarks of European and American military history that more commonly delineate Keegan's chosen territory. The book is structured around the great technological developments in military history from stones to swords, forts to horses and guns to bombs, but Keegan also considers social and economic influences upon warfare, psychological and anthropological drives and factors such as climate and terrain. The plot is complex but the conclusion simple: politics must continue, but war cannot.

Many historical surveys fatten out as they approach modern times. *A History of Warfare* tapers off once it enters the nineteenth century. Keegan had after all already written about Wellington and Grant, the Somme, the armies of Normandy and Hitler. For those who wanted more, he had recently completed a military history of World War II (*The Second World War*, 1989) and was soon to publish one on World War I (*The First World War*, 1998). Between times he had also managed to produce an excursus on the military sites of

North America (*Warpaths*, 1995) that cleverly married theme and chronology. Keegan has a big following in the USA and was invited to advise President Clinton on what he should say at the D-Day fiftieth anniversary celebrations. (His advice, which Clinton took, was not to forget the contribution of the Canadians.)

As he looks back over his furious productivity these past 15 years, Keegan remains passionately convinced of the importance of military history. Yet he manages to retain a healthy distance from its idiosyncrasies. He laughs in hearty agreement when, with apologies to Joseph Heller, I suggest that in order to want to become a soldier you must be a bit mad – but that anybody who is mad isn't allowed to be one. Is there something hidden away deep inside his own constitution that would love to have been a soldier, perhaps one of the great generals he admires? 'No, never, never, never,' he repeats with staccato emphasis. 'I'm quite unsuited to being a soldier.' Why? 'Oh, I'm the wrong temperament. I'm very rebellious by nature', he asserts and, spotting my scepticism, adds: 'I know I don't appear to be but I am. I fly off the handle very quickly. I'm super-critical.' One can see why he and Sandhurst finally parted company.

Keegan fell to musing on further paradoxes, catches and misconceptions of military life. Armchair strategists love to talk of 'decisive' battles; but few battles are truly decisive in the sense of solving the problem that stimulated them. Easy victories may cause temporary exultation among the victors (for example, Israel in 1967), but the results rarely stick. Nor do conflicts where the vanquished do not believe they were fairly defeated (the French in 1870, the Germans in 1918). The 'ideal' war, or battle, is a struggle such as Waterloo between two more or less equal sides in which one eventually suffers collapse and both accept the result and agree to move on. Such conflicts may be conclusive, Keegan says, but they are rare. People also talk glibly about military strategy; yet Keegan has found that,

time and again, extrinsic events rather than strategic intent
determine the outcome of a military campaign. In his book on
World War I, Keegan shows how the Schlieffen Plan, a formula
for 'quick victory in a short war', directed Germany towards
an unachievable strategy, thus helping plunge Europe into a
four-year conflict no one wanted. Indeed, since World War II
was in many ways an outcome of World War I, he suggests that
the Plan was arguably 'the most important official document
of the last hundred years, for what it caused to ensue on the
field of battle, the hopes it inspired, the hopes it dashed, were
to have consequences that persist to this day'.

Keegan is no peacenik, and he claims that the Gulf War, for
example, was a classic 'Just War' as defined by Grotius. But he
has no love of war or illusions about its nature. Every day of his
life, he says, he wrestles with the further paradox that, among
those who have chosen to confront and if necessary commit
the most appallingly inhumane actions, he has encountered
some of the most charming, civilized and high-minded people
one could ever hope to meet. Nobody, says Keegan, is more
disgusted by the horror of war than the generals who, in
the last resort, are called upon to fight it. It was a point he
reiterated at the culmination of his 1998 Reith Lectures, *War
and Our World*.

Recorded in a variety of locations before invited audiences,
Keegan's lectures received extraordinary réclame. 'Give War
A Chance!' said the *Sunday Times* headline over an article
commending the series; the *Guardian*'s Anne Karpf, expecting
to scoff, was held rapt. Keegan used the BBC's prestigious
platform to present his distillation of a lifetime's learning.
He placed war in the context of history's other apocalyptic
scourges, painted a poignant portrait of the delivery and receipt
of bereavement messages from the front, asked whether a state
is defined by its capacity to make war (and was rude again
to Clausewitz) and pointed to the 'non-state' wars that have
increasingly characterized the post-Cold War era.

How does Keegan see the future of warfare? He senses that major wars have become impossible and that the great military powers seem increasingly prepared to try to contain the smaller-scale local conflicts that currently afflict the world. He cites the way the Russians, the traditional protectors of Serbia, behaved with restraint and maturity in their dealings with NATO over the crisis in Kosovo. We are not there yet, of course. A world besmirched by the bloodshed of Grozny and Dili, Eritrea and Angola, can hardly be regarded as free of warfare. Keegan argues for greater restrictions on the production and international distribution of cheap armaments, and urges that the peace-keeping and peace-making activities of the United Nations be strengthened. But when pressed, he admits to being guardedly optimistic about the future. And that, from our newest historical knight, is source for comfort.

EPILOGUE

John Keegan writes:

Such comfort as I felt at the international response to the Balkan conflict of the 1990s has been severely modified by the subsequent rise of large-scale Muslim terrorism, and the persistence of associated regional conflicts. The end of the Cold War and the quietening of interstate confrontation that resulted gave hope of grounds for genuine optimism. Few observers identified the rise of militant Islam as a movement to replace militant Communism. Yet, since the 1980s there has undoubtedly been a vigorous Islamicization of many areas of the world, particularly in regions not thought by the West to be centres of Muslim fundamentalism, such as Indonesia and nearby territories in the Philippines and Thailand. Militant Islam is alarming because religious fanatics place little or no value in the safeguarding of human life if the human beings concerned are not Muslims, at least Muslims of the right stamp. The appearance of mass murderers claiming justification in the name of Allah or his Prophet has revived the threat of warfare in a highly destructive form, not one limited or arrested by diplomacy or deterrence. Unlike Communism, moreover, Islamic militancy is not likely to be terminated by the action of internal contradictions. Indeed Islamic fundamentalism thrives on contradiction, including the ultimate illogicality of resort to suicide as a means of military action. The only recourse the non-Muslim world has to such a threat is constant vigilance and the willingness to forestall attack by pre-emptive military action, which promises a revival of international militarism. War is revealing its persistent capacity to mutate by analogy with disease. The disease is still with us and we have not found an antidote.

Geoffrey Hosking

BIOGRAPHY

Geoffrey Hosking taught Russian/Soviet politics and history at the University of Essex from 1966 to 1984, though with two years off, teaching at the University of Wisconsin, Madison in 1971–72 and at the University of Cologne in 1980–81. Since 1984 he has been Professor of Russian History at the School of Slavonic and East European Studies, University of London (since 1999 part of University College London). He has made numerous journeys to Russia, both for research and to work in the NGO sector.

PRINCIPAL PUBLISHED BOOKS

The Russian Constitutional Experiment: Government and Duma, 1907–1914 (1973)

Beyond Socialist Realism: Soviet Fiction since Ivan Denisovich (1980)

History of the Soviet Union (1985) (winner of the Los Angeles Times History Book Prize)

The Awakening of the Soviet Union (1990)

The Road to Post-Communism: Independent Political Movements in the USSR, 1985–1991 (with Jonathan Aves and Peter Duncan) (1992)

Russia: People and Empire, 1552–1917 (1997)

Russia and the Russians: A History from Rus to Russian Federation (2001)

Rulers and Victims: The Russians in the Soviet Union (2006)

PROFILE, July 2000

When I first met Geoffrey Hosking in the 1970s, he was a Lecturer in History at the University of Essex but his current enthusiasm was Russian literature. Tolstoy and Dostoyevsky? No, he said: recent and present-day Russian literature. Dissident literature, then – all that samizdat stuff? Again, no. He was interested in novelists published in the USSR of Khrushchev and Brezhnev, some of whom, he said, were really rather good. Here, evidently, was a man who sidestepped the stereotypes.

He always had. At Cambridge, Hosking read Modern Languages but his PhD was in Russian History (with a thesis on the Duma of 1907–14). In mid-doctorate, he took a year off to go to St Antony's, Oxford, for a crash course on Western European history, which he didn't feel he knew enough about. Then, with all those years of languages and variegated history under his belt (and a still-to-be completed PhD), he was offered a lectureship in yet another subject: Government. The new University of Essex did not yet have a History or Russian Studies Department, so Hosking, now in his mid-twenties, found himself having to teach (and therefore learn about) Hobbes, Locke and Rousseau, comparative political cultures, input–output theory and the structures and functions of the state. With so many topics floating seductively past his purview (not to mention a year lecturing on Revolutions to huge assemblages of students in Madison, Wisconsin), a less disciplined person might easily have become lost to serious scholarship. But if others pursued the path to dilettantism, Hosking used his intellectual versatility to help fuel his guiding light, the flame of Russian history.

Russia was still very much the riddle wrapped in an enigma it had been to Churchill. Few Westerners knew much about the country or its history. Those who did tended to be either left-leaning ideologues inclined to justify the Communist experiment or exiles and Cold Warriors avowedly opposed to it. Both groups were transfixed by the geopolitics of a dangerously bipolar world.

Hosking was neither Cold Warrior nor fellow traveller. But he wasn't a dry-as-dust academic either. He felt, and feels, that you can only really understand the present if you know what produced it. Back in the bipolar world in which Hosking learned his craft, the USSR was a vast, looming presence. Western academies were full of Kremlinologists, analysts of Soviet leaders and their policies; but the deeper internal history of the country and of its people was scarcely known except in barest outline. Here, surely, was a vital key to understanding the contemporary world. It was a door Hosking was determined to unlock.

The country and its people. These are what Hosking has particularly tried to know. His writings are sprinkled with references to a town here, a village there, a quotation from the letters column of a regional or local newspaper, a joke the workers or peasants would tell each other, a telling anecdote from his own experience. But Hosking is not a collage artist. On the contrary, his finely tuned mind loves nothing more than to alight upon an organizing principle, perhaps a Big Hypothesis, that helps explain a mass of otherwise inchoate facts. In a recent article, for example, he interpreted the whole course of Russian history as variations on the theme of Patronage and Clientelism. There were early hints of such an approach in his book about those post-Stalin novelists, *Beyond Socialist Realism*. Here, he suggested that the publication of Pasternak's *Dr Zhivago* (in the West) and of Solzhenitsyn's *Ivan Denisovich* heralded the appearance of a new fiction, less burdened than before by the ideological yoke of Socialist Realism and capable of revealing authentic insights into the nature of life at village and township level.

The book was, in some ways, a residue of Hosking's undergraduate training in languages and literature, underpinned perhaps by his years as a politics lecturer. But Essex by now had a History Department and Hosking was one of its founder members. His thesis on the Duma had been published, but it was high time he produced a 'big' history book.

Hosking took a long time writing his *History of the Soviet Union*. It was a book he knew he had to get right. In 1984 he had left Essex to succeed Hugh Seton-Watson as Professor of Russian History at London University's School of Slavonic and East European Studies (SSEES). A year later, his *History*, which takes off where the thesis on the Duma ended, finally appeared. It has been widely used as a standard text on the subject ever since.

This was and remains a source of mild surprise for, as Hosking is the first to admit, it was in some ways an unusual book. For a start, it concentrated on domestic history, scarcely touching on the USSR's relationship with its neighbours. While recounting the main political and economic outlines of his story – the 1917 Revolution, Stalin's Terror, Khrushchev's secret speech, and so on – he said little about the Battle of Stalingrad or the Cuba crisis. Leaders loomed large, but so did the led. In addition to weaving the big picture, Hosking enriched his tapestry with a rich skein of illuminating local detail. Thus, when describing the wholesale transplantation of the kulaks, he was able to call upon his wide knowledge of literary sources to help convey the brutality of the process. Having himself travelled in various parts of the USSR, Hosking also devoted substantial space to the non-Russian nationalities. And, almost uniquely among historians of the Soviet state at that time, he dug deep to mine an ore that most pointedly ignored: religion – a view of Russia that was to be triumphantly vindicated a few years later when a widespread resurgence of religious observance accompanied the demise of the Soviet Union.

By the time Hosking delivered his inaugural lecture at the SSEES in 1987, the USSR, having recently survived a series of weak and inefficient presidents, had an intelligent, energetic man of vision at the helm. Mikhail Gorbachev, Hosking argued, had to lead a modern, well-educated, largely urbanized society governed via an old-fashioned, totalitarian yet ineffective political system. Hosking saw him trying to bring the two into phase by introducing greater openness in public discourse and restructuring the forms of government. In the West, Gorbachev gained respect for these policies of 'glasnost' and 'perestroika'. To many Russians, however, the reforms meant you weren't allowed to drink and that you lost the back-of-the-shop arrangement whereby, for a few roubles, you could obtain the little luxuries of life. Political restructuring did not deliver 'sausage'. Furthermore, the introduction of 'glasnost' ensured that these gripes were widely aired. Freedom of speech was used not to praise the government that had instigated it but to abuse it for imposing economic stringencies. In some of the non-Russian areas, such as the Baltic states and Ukraine, people began to demand a degree of autonomy. Gorbachev's liberal reforms had loosened the ties that bound his nation together. The USSR was evidently embarking upon a series of seismic changes that were daily placing its previous history in a shifting perspective.

It was against this background that Hosking was invited to present the BBC's 1988 Reith Lectures. His brief was to try to explain the dramatic changes occurring in the Soviet Union by presenting them in historical context. He found it an exacting commission. It was not easy to compose scripts that would take the prescribed 28 minutes and 40 seconds to read – especially as they had to be recorded six weeks before transmission at a period when events in the USSR were moving with great rapidity. When Hosking began work on the first talk he wondered whether, by the last, he would be predicting the fall of the Soviet Union. The lectures were an elegant tour de force, tough arguments nicely salted and peppered with deft literary references and revealing personal anecdotes. The series began with a quote from the *Pravda* letters page signed by, in effect, 'Disgusted, Sverdlovsk'. All the Hosking hallmark subjects were there. One lecture was devoted to the many nationalities within the USSR and their uneasy and unstable coexistence with that over-powerful first among supposed equals, the Russians. In another, he told how, one day in Tbilisi, he had watched workmen refurbishing a magnificent church that had lain almost untended and unattended for 70 years, and he went on to talk about the Orthodox and other Christian cults, Islamic Central Asia and the Jews of Russia. Throughout, it was a fluid, pluralist Russia that he portrayed, one emerging from a long history of imposed rigidity and embarking on an uncharted path whose destination nobody could predict with certainty.

Hosking remains a great admirer of Gorbachev (and enjoyed a long meeting and conversation with him a year or so ago). Yet he senses that Gorbachev had very little understanding of the way the Soviet economic system worked and how, if you gave encouragement to the private sector, it would suck goods out of the public sector and create shortages. Nor did Gorbachev appreciate the depth of national feelings outside the heartland of Russia itself. To the very end, he remained a firm believer in the Communist Party and the unity of the USSR. A giant on the world stage, Gorbachev – like many of his predecessors – was never able to enter the minds of the people he was called upon to govern.

After the fall of the Soviet Union, Hosking decided to turn his attention to earlier times. It was a bold step. It was also characteristic. After all, he says, how better to understand our own era than to study what preceded and created it? Thus, at 50, Hosking embarked upon what was to prove his most influential work to date. Its title, *Russia: People and Empire, 1552–1917*, if not lapel-grabbing, precisely encapsulates what amounted to a major reinterpretation of Russian history, a Big Hypothesis, one that has since become widely accepted.

Hosking ignored the minority nationalities this time and concentrated on the Russians. He argued that there have been two Russias. First, there is 'Rus', a word that refers to the people and suggests modesty, homeliness, religion, locality, femininity ('Mother Russia'). Then there is the more grandiose, thrusting, imperial concept suggested by the word 'Rossiia'. It is the conflict between these – the expansive imperium and the more passive ambitions of the Russian people – that forms the central theme of Hosking's interpretation. In a closely argued book of over 500 pages, he showed how the emphasis on 'Empire', so attractive to Russia's leaders from Ivan the Terrible onwards, consistently stifled the more organic aspiration to authentic nationhood for which the 'People' always yearned.

The Hosking Hypothesis, this polarity between the demands of empire and the popular aspiration to nationhood, won its author considerable laurels. But he is building rather than resting on them. He has been awarded a five-year Leverhulme professorship which will eventually issue in a work systematically applying the people–empire dialectic to the period since 1917. The imperial concept, he says, clearly drove the founders of the USSR; the people and territory over which they ruled were not even mentioned in the name they gave the new state, though Hosking senses that Stalin did more to encourage a sense of Russian nationhood than did the old Tsarist empire.

More immediately, Hosking tells me he is correcting the proofs of a discursive volume covering the whole of Russian history, from Rurik and Rus to the Russian Federation of Putin. Here, too, the people–empire hypothesis remains as a building block. But for the first time, Hosking has also written about Russia's relations with its neighbours, of the Mongols, Varangians and Poles, the Swedish, Ottoman and Austrian empires and the twentieth-century challenges from Japan, Germany and China. All this is, so to speak, foreign territory for Hosking. Also, while much of his earlier writing is infused with his knowledge of Russian literature, the new text calls upon music, the visual arts and popular culture as adjuncts to his underlying argument about the suppressed sense of Russian 'nationhood'.

Hosking has given more thought than most to the nature and definition of nationhood, an issue that, until recently, was relatively dormant in sophisticated political circles where the smart talk was of multinational groupings. In the former Soviet Union, as the minority peoples reassert their separate identities, Hosking feels that the Russians may at last have a chance to achieve genuine national fulfilment. Certainly, this is something to which any Russian leader must be sensitive, he says. Vladimir Putin made his name preserving the integrity of the Russian 'empire'. Once he is properly secure as President, says Hosking, Putin should turn his attention to the national aspirations of the Russian 'people'.

Does Hosking really advocate a resurgence of ethnicity in Russia? Does not assertive cultural nationalism, a blight on the twentieth century, continue to fuel murderous hatreds in the Balkans, the Caucasus and elsewhere? Hosking's response is twofold. First, that a period of national fulfilment is probably a phase Russians need to experience before moving forward; and, second, that the successful achievement of national identity must always be not only ethnic but also civic. Both answers raise further questions, of course; but this wily historiographer and seasoned political scientist is well-equipped to deal with them. 'I do think Russia would be a happier country if it were to become a proper nation state', he adds conclusively.

The other day, I bumped into Hosking in the street and he told me he was on his way to the Wigmore Hall. Shostakovich? No. The magnet drawing him was the quartet by Robert Simpson. We waved, and I watched as Geoffrey went on his way, still sidestepping the stereotypes.

EPILOGUE

Geoffrey Hosking writes:

Since the publication of Daniel's article, I have been researching, writing and editing my book on the Russians in the Soviet

Union. In the end I decided to call it *Rulers and Victims*, partly because I wanted to publish a book without 'Russia' in the title (inevitably, it's in the subtitle), and partly because that paradoxical juxtaposition seemed to me to explain much about the strange role of the 'dominant' people of the USSR. I remember one Russian telling me that the subject was an impossible one, and by the time I'd finished I was inclined to agree. It's certainly extraordinarily complex: almost no generalization about the Russians in the USSR is wholly true, and few are wholly false. It's a book I feel strongly about, since apart from anything else it encapsulates my own experience of Russia while working there as a scholar over a total of about 40 years. But above all, reflecting on what Russians experienced and felt about their changing country in recent decades is vital for understanding where Russia is going today.

While working on that book, I found myself launching into a completely new initiative, provoked also by the experience of post-Soviet Russia. Watching the attempts to privatize the Russian economy and adapt it to globalization, I was struck by the way no economists seemed to realize that you cannot create a successful economy without understanding why people won't trust one another. After all, if they don't, they won't invest their money and they won't work together in ways that promote productivity. The 'Washington consensus' certainly didn't fit the modes of trust dominant in Russia. Hence the depressing chaos there in the 1990s.

I then found that for social scientists 'Trust' is currently a positively modish subject, being discussed in all the journals. But social scientists content themselves with a fairly simple 'premodern/modern' account of the evolution of trust. To me, reading about different historical societies, it seemed that there were many different forms that trust can take, for example in city states, ancient empires, feudal society, absolute monarchies, nation states, and so on. I led a study-

day on the subject at the Royal Historical Society in February
2004, have given a few public lectures, and am now trying
to explore further what it would mean for historians to write
systematically about trust.

Antonia Fraser

BIOGRAPHY

Antonia Fraser was born in 1932, the eldest of eight children of Frank and Elizabeth Pakenham. She was brought up in North Oxford (her father was a don at Christ Church) but in her youth both her parents were aspirant politicians, standing in turn as Labour candidate for Oxford. She went to the Dragon School, Oxford, in 1940–44, and after her mother joined her father as a convert in the Catholic Church she left her Anglican boarding school for St Mary's Convent, Ascot, in 1946–48. She went to Oxford University in 1950–53, reading History. She then worked as an editor for the publisher Weidenfeld & Nicolson until her first marriage in 1956 to the Conservative MP Sir Hugh Fraser; they had six children. She has been President of the English Centre of PEN and Chairman of the Society of Authors. In 1999 Antonia Fraser received the CBE and in 2000 was awarded the Norton Medlicott Medal of the Historical Association.

She is married to Harold Pinter.

Her historical books have been published worldwide in countries which include Brazil, Japan, Mexico and Turkey as well as Europe.

PRINCIPAL PUBLISHED BOOKS

Mary Queen of Scots (1969) (winner of the James Tait Black Prize for Biography)
Cromwell: Our Chief of Men (1973)

King Charles II (1979)

The Weaker Vessel (1984) (winner of the Wolfson Award for History)

The Warrior Queens (1988)

The Six Wives of Henry VIII (1992)

The Gunpowder Plot: Terror and Faith in 1605 (1996) (winner of the Crimewriters' Association Non-Fiction Gold Dagger)

Marie Antoinette: The Journey (2001) (winner of the Franco-British Society Award)

Love and Louis XIV: The Women in the Life of the Sun King (2006)

She has also written a short life of King James, entitled *King James VI and I* (1974) in the 'Kings and Queens of England' series which she edits; eight Jemima Shore detective stories, many of which have been televised; and has edited many anthologies, including *Scottish Love Poems* (1975) and *The Pleasure of Reading* (1992).

PROFILE, October 2000

When Antonia Pakenham was a girl living in wartime Oxford, where her father was a politics don, she would terrorize the 'dragon' at the public library by actually borrowing lots of books. Worse, she'd often consume a volume of popular history in a single day and return that evening for another. She still remembers giving a Mary Stuart biography the one-day treatment.

This pattern of enthusiastic industriousness has lasted a lifetime and seen Lady Antonia Fraser, now in her 69th year, through the production of seven or eight works of serious historical scholarship, a similar number of mystery novels, a fistful of anthologies, half a dozen children and a high-profile public life. 'Passionate zest for life combined with rigid self-discipline' was how George Weidenfeld characterized her.

The same might be said of her parents, Frank and Elizabeth Pakenham (the Earl and Countess of Longford), both of them highly educated, industrious and motivated. Pakenham, a protégé of F.E. Smith (and later assistant to Beveridge), sent a frisson of dangerous excitement through the household in the mid-1930s when he announced his conversion to Catholicism; Lady Antonia, the eldest of his children, followed him into the Church of Rome as an adolescent a few years later.

In 1953, having just finished a history degree at Oxford, Antonia joined Weidenfeld & Nicolson as an editorial assistant. One of the ways W&N remained solvent in those early days was by mass-marketing out-of-copyright children's classics at Marks and Spencer stores. One day Weidenfeld proposed King Arthur. 'But you can't just re-publish Malory', piped up his assistant, explaining in her earnest way that it was written in the fifteenth century and quite unreadable. 'Then, my dear Antonia, you will have to write King Arthur!'

Lances splintered and arrows thwacked, as they were to do again when Antonia took on Robin Hood. Much of the writing was undertaken in the early hours by a weary young lady on her return from an evening of culture and/or carousing. But her reserves of energy and ebullience saw her through and she delivered a good, professional job.

In 1956, Lady Antonia married the Scottish MP Hugh Fraser and by the mid-1960s was beginning to surface after a decade of child-rearing. Her mother had just published a biography of Queen Victoria and was thinking of following it with a book about Mary Stuart. 'You can't do that,' Antonia said cheekily, 'you're much too moral! I'll do Mary.' So Elizabeth Longford turned to Wellington instead. Thereafter, mother and daughter effectively divided up 400 years of British historical biography between them: Elizabeth taking the nineteenth and twentieth centuries, Antonia the sixteenth and seventeenth.

Antonia Fraser's *Mary Queen of Scots* was published (by Weidenfeld, like all her non-fiction) in 1969 and has never been out of print since. A scholarly yet evocative voyage into the life, loves and death of a colourful Catholic princess somewhat maligned by history, it introduced many of the themes and variations that recur throughout Antonia Fraser's *oeuvre*. Here, as in much of her writing, there is a sense not only of period but also of place. When you read about the murder of Riccio or of Darnley, or of Mary's own execution, you can see, feel, smell the locations. Readers of *History Today* got a foretaste in an article on the murder of Mary's lover, Riccio (April 1966); the prose still had a touch of the breathless thwacks, but the piece made a good read and, like the book, was painstakingly researched.

There is a strong moral sense, too, underpinning Fraser's writing (her strictures to her mother notwithstanding), as though she were anxious that her readers share her compassion for her tragic and/or misunderstood subjects. Like many people who take religion seriously, she is also at pains to communicate the importance of theological belief and controversy to those she describes. An entire chapter is devoted to the infamous 'Casket Letters' which appeared (mostly to later generations of historians) to prove Mary's adultery with Bothwell before the death of Darnley, and foreknowledge of his murder. The letters may be forgeries, but Fraser nevertheless subjects them to detailed textual analysis, going on to consider who might have composed them and why. She is excellent at sifting evidence, weighing possibilities, arguing likelihoods. Evidently, the creator of 'Jemima Shore, Investigator' is something of a lawyer *manquée*.

When she was writing, in the late 1960s, it might have been regarded as intellectually old-fashioned to undertake a biography of a doomed queen when much academic history was self-consciously eschewing the lives of monarchs and generals and embracing social and working-class history. But in other respects, *Mary* placed its author, somewhat improbably, on the high ground of contemporary historiography. Published a year before Germaine Greer's *The Female Eunuch*, it helped raise an early standard for the sympathetic portrayal of women in history, for example, while also providing a pointer to the growing interest in the Scottish past.

Mary Queen of Scots succeeded in reaching a mass audience and making its author a household name. Everybody knew of Lady Antonia Fraser, her beauty, her famous parents and siblings, her prominent husband and their numerous progeny. One or two academic snobs dismissed her as a 'popular biographer'; how could the love life of a doomed queen be regarded as serious history? But *Mary* went on to win its author the James Tait Black memorial prize for non-fiction (as her mother's life of Victoria had done five years earlier). If any doubts remained about the seriousness of Antonia Fraser's intentions and talents, they were surely laid to rest with her next book. True, it was another biography of a historical leader whose ambivalent reputation, perhaps, needed rescuing from the mischievous myths of history. But her subject was neither a monarch nor a woman, a Catholic nor a Scot, a Tudor nor a Stuart. Nor was there even much of a sex life to write about.

Oliver Cromwell was not lacking in the attention of historians and Antonia Fraser was entering a minefield of intellectual controversy with her biography, published in 1973. Would she portray Cromwell as a regicide and destroyer of Parliament or as a Carlylean hero? Would she argue the respective merits of Laud's High Church Anglicanism and Cromwell's Puritanism, or walk in the footsteps of Christopher Hill and regard the Civil War as essentially the outcome of economic forces? How well would she be able to explain how so implacable a warrior as Cromwell could have been so courteous a friend, how so relentless a Puritan could have loved music, and how so single-minded a Christian could have readmitted the Jews? What was the overall legacy of a man whose system survived him by a bare two years, yet whose statue stands – within the grounds of Parliament – across from Churchill's?

One theme running through all of Antonia Fraser's writing is the desire to uncover the reality behind the emblem, the human being beneath the encrustations of myth. As always, the myths are carefully considered: Cromwell asking his portraitist (but was it Cooper or Leyly?) to include 'these roughness, pimples, warts and everything as you see me', or visiting the corpse of Charles I alone in the depth of night and muttering the words 'Cruel Necessity'. Fraser considers the evidence, makes informed speculation and argues convincingly that the very retelling of sometimes inadequately substantiated stories such as these can throw its own light on the historical personage concerned.

The thrust of her writing is to get as close as possible to the elusive personalities, places and events at its core. This is a historian, clearly, who tramps across battlefields before writing about them. One of the surprises of Marston Moor (to Fraser and, presumably, to Cromwell) was that 'in the level, verdant flatness of the Vale of York there should be some high points of sufficient rise to constitute … strategic advantage'. The road between Preston and Skipton is 'an exceptionally deep, narrow lane, sunk down by natural formation and consequently waterlogged from the wet summer', so that in the early stages of the Battle of Preston the cavalry were somewhat incapacitated, giving way to desperate hand-to-hand fighting. From the lofty steeple of St Mary's in Drogheda (still there today), defenders of the town 'could indulge in some murderous firing'. In some of the finest passages in the book, Fraser describes Cromwell's Irish campaigns and, while acknowledging his responsibility for the butchery of civilian populations, assesses the still controversial episode with impressive fair-mindedness. She was especially gratified when the book garnered excellent reviews in Ireland.

To write one acclaimed historical biography may be regarded as good fortune; to produce a second bespeaks serious talent. After *Cromwell*, Antonia Fraser's intellectual credentials were beyond dispute. Paradoxically, the writer some had once labelled 'merely' a biographer of royalty had now earned the right to turn her attention to the monarchs of Britain. First to appear was a short volume about Mary Stuart's son, James VI (of Scotland) and I (of England) – a prelude to the hugely successful 'Lives of the Kings and Queens of England' series and first published in 1975. Meanwhile, as Fraser worked on a life of Charles II – a natural continuation, in a way, of her work on Cromwell – she also found time to produce more Jemima Shore stories as well as a number of poetry anthologies.

By now, the children were approaching or entering young adulthood and Antonia Fraser's private life went through a period of some turbulence as she approached her second marriage (to Harold Pinter). Perhaps not entirely surprisingly, her next three books all concentrated on the place of women in history. They are among her finest. The first, *The Weaker Vessel* (1984), is a tour de force describing the changing role of women in seventeenth-century England in which the mothers, sisters, wives, mistresses, cousins and courtiers who peep in from the wings in Cromwell, James and Charles II positively teem onto the stage. Four years later came a work taking off from the fiery, knives-in-the-wheels myth of Boadicea (carefully distinguished from the historical Boudicca) in which Fraser considers some of history's 'warrior queens'. And then, after a further four years, *The Six Wives of Henry VIII*.

Each is in its way an exercise in 'prosopography' in which collective biography is used to illuminate more than the sum of the parts. In *The Weaker Vessel*, Fraser documents many developments during the seventeenth century from which women benefited: not just the exigencies of war which invariably thrust women into greater prominence, but advances in health care and education, greater sexual independence, the presence of women on stage and the virtual end of trials for witchcraft. Yet she also argues that most such changes were of even greater benefit to men so that, by 1700, women were not only still the weaker vessel but relatively weaker than a century before. It is a striking conclusion, one thoroughly consonant with the spirit of the times in which the book was written.

It was perhaps a natural transition from weak vessels to fiery chariots, from handlooms to handbags. *Warrior Queens* is Antonia Fraser's best-kept secret. I have never known a book with such an exotic cast of characters: not only the constantly looming presence of Boudicca/Boadicea but also Cleopatra and Zenobia, the medievals Maud, Matilda and Tamara of Georgia, Isabella of Spain and Elizabeth I of England, latter-day Amazons from seventeenth-century Angola, eighteenth-century Russia and nineteenth-century India, and such modern handbaggers as Mmes Bandaranaike, Gandhi, Meir and Thatcher. They provide a formidable bunch, all colourfully evoked, though I am not fully convinced by the various 'Syndromes' ('Appendage', 'Chaste', 'Shame', 'Voracity') which Fraser uses as a device to try and keep her pugnacious ladies under control. Perhaps there are too many of them. Easier to write about the six wives of one man.

To Antonia Fraser, the wives of Henry VIII were not simply a collection of women rejected by an irascible tyrant but (like the warrior queens) individual human beings with their own strengths, sensibilities and susceptibilities. What stays in the mind from a reading of *The Six Wives* is the almost saintly patience and dignity of Catherine of Aragon, the volatile spirit of Anne Boleyn or the 'rare goodness' of Catherine Parr. In *The Gunpowder Plot* (1996), similarly, Fraser familiarizes us with the personalities and motives of the plotters and we virtually move with them, once the plot is uncovered, from one safe house to the next, to eventual arrest, torture and death. In both works, too, Fraser's skills as theologian and jurist are again in evidence. Especially impressive is her expert guidance through the maze of dynastic and theological thickets surrounding Henry's successive marital crises or, in the later book, the way she elucidates the ambivalent position of

Catholic Recusants in newly Protestant England, considers the legal status of information given to a priest in Confession, or examines alternative theories as to the provenance of the warning letter to Lord Monteagle which, in effect, sealed the fate of the plotters.

Antonia Fraser has an enviable knack of writing good, well-researched history books that also plug into current concerns: our anxieties about the monarchy, for example, or our growing awareness of the importance of Scottish or Irish history or of the changing social role of women. Thus, *The Gunpowder Plot*, written against a background of struggle in Northern Ireland, is an examination of terrorism. Fraser does not set out to exonerate the plotters. But she does assay a sympathetic understanding of them. Under what circumstances, she asks, might the resort to violence for political ends be regarded as justified – and (the concomitant question) how does the state deal with those who plot to destroy it? At the end of the book she quotes Nelson Mandela explaining, if not excusing, the sabotage practised under his leadership by the ANC.

If *The Gunpowder Plot* was something of a new departure for Antonia Fraser, her next project will stretch her still further: a life of Marie Antoinette. Another doomed queen? Perhaps. But the book will take Fraser across the Channel to the Continent for the first time, and from her familiar sixteenth and seventeenth centuries to the late eighteenth. It will also plunge her into the historiographical wasps' nest of French Revolutionary studies – though anyone who has negotiated the emotionally charged historical revisionism of the Reformation and English Civil Wars will doubtless emerge with head intact from the French Terror.

When I spoke to her, Antonia Fraser had checked out all the relevant locations in Austria and France, and was busy catching up with her Rousseau and poring over a plenitude of French- and German-language sources. She evidently still consumes cartloads of books. I just hope she doesn't plan to get them all out of the Oxford public library.

EPILOGUE

Antonia Fraser writes:

Antonia Fraser is now in her 75th year. Her biography of Marie Antoinette, subtitled *The Journey*, was published in the UK and US in 2001; it won the Franco-British Society Award in this country, was a bestseller on both sides of the Atlantic and has since been or is being translated into ten languages. The most recent is French. The French publishers, who ignored her work after *Marie Stuart* in 1973, presumably took courage from the prospect of Sofia Coppola's film based on Antonia Fraser's book, released in the US in October 2006. After *Marie Antoinette: The Journey* Antonia Fraser spent a year researching a book to be called *The Battle of the Boyne: Irish Tragedy 1690* before she decided that dislike (mixed with admiration) for William III and dislike (unmixed with anything) for James II was no basis for a serious book. She preferred to return to the delights of Versailles; *Love and Louis XIV: The Women in the Life of the Sun King*, her ninth full-length historical work, was published in the UK and the US in September 2006.

David Starkey

BIOGRAPHY

David Starkey is Bye Fellow of Fitzwilliam College, Cambridge. He is a winner of the W.H. Smith Prize for Biography (for *Elizabeth*) and the Norton Medlicott Medal for Service to History presented by the Historical Association. He has written and presented TV series on Henry VIII, Elizabeth I, the Six Wives of Henry VIII, Mary Tudor and Edward VI, and his books on Elizabeth I and the Queens of Henry VIII were bestsellers. He was guest Curator of the 2003 exhibition at the National Maritime Museum in London about Elizabeth I.

PRINCIPAL PUBLISHED BOOKS

This Land of England (with David Souden) (1985)

The Reign of Henry VIII (1985)

Revolution Reassessed: Revisions in the History of Tudor Government and Administration (ed. with Christopher Coleman) (1986)

The English Court from the Wars of the Roses to the Civil War (ed.) (1987)

Henry VIII: A European Court in England (ed.) (1991)

The Inventory of Henry VIII, Volume I (ed.) (1998)

Elizabeth: Apprenticeship (2000)

The Six Wives: The Queens of Henry VIII (2003)

The Monarchy of England, Volume I: New Beginnings (2004)

The Monarchy of England, Volume II: The Tudors and Stuarts (2006)

PROFILE, January 2001

'Forgive me ... .' Words that can strike terror into the hearts of witnesses on the BBC Radio Four's *Moral Maze* as Dr David Starkey stalks his next mouse in preparation for the kill. Like Henry VIII or Queen Elizabeth, Starkey can be a resolute executioner when he thinks fit. Like them, too, he strives to clothe a combative personality in the correct outward forms. Immaculately garbed and groomed, formidably and forcefully articulate, Starkey can appear armed *cap-à-pie* to those who fear him. Yet the apparel probably conceals as much of the man as it proclaims. Despite his public prickliness, Starkey can be a kind and conscientious colleague and teacher sensitive to the person beneath the posture, deeply conscious of the historical impact of human nature with all its frailties, of the all-important role of individual quirk and nuance, preference and prejudice. To Starkey, the pageantry of the past is prelude to the real drama – the intersection of power and personality.

Like Thomas Cromwell and Cardinal Wolsey, Starkey rose from the ranks. Born in Kendal, the only child of working-class Quakers, Starkey learned – especially from his mother – the value of education and self-improvement. Overcoming the childhood disability of a double club foot, he developed into a bookish lad who soon came to love history and enjoyed nothing more than to curl up with Arthur Mee's *Children's Encyclopaedia* or the Quennells' *History of Everyday Things* or to gaze at books depicting the gods of Ancient Greece. From Kendal to Cambridge may have been a long jump socially and geographically. But intellectually, says Starkey, he had been well prepared by excellent teachers at the local grammar school. When he took up his scholarship at Fitzwilliam in 1964 he already knew as much history as some of his supervisors.

Starkey remembers himself as clever, bumptious and doubtless difficult to manage, and he pays tribute to the mature understanding of his Director of Studies, the kindly

Leslie Wayper, who patiently taught his young charge how to organize material, marshal arguments and write with clarity. Starkey also discovered starrier figures in the Cambridge galaxy such as Denis Brogan, Moses Finley and Jack Plumb. It was inevitable that at some stage the young comet would come blazing into the orbit of Geoffrey Elton.

Elton had not only mastered the minutiae of Tudor history and refashioned the subject – an astonishing achievement for a refugee from Hitler's *Mitteleuropa* – but, by sheer industry and force of character, had all but obliterated those who tried to gainsay him. Admired and feared in equal measure, Elton would enthral an undergraduate audience in the morning, enjoy a genial pub lunch – and then hasten back to Clare to mow down the latest wrong-headed hack with a rebarbative review. Once David Starkey opted for the Tudor Special Subject in his third year, the immovable Elton and the irresistible Starkey soon found themselves playing a deadly game of father and son.

For his postgraduate research, Starkey staked out core Elton territory: the Tudor bureaucracy. To Elton, with his continental background and influenced perhaps by the theories of Max Weber, Tudor England was best understood – celebrated indeed – as the fountainhead of the emerging liberal bureaucracy from which Britain had benefited ever since. Elton wrote and lectured with unconcealed enthusiasm about what he saw as the administrative institutions of Tudor government (and its great innovator Thomas Cromwell) and tended to pass over with disdain such vulgarities as the religious or personal passions of the time or the shenanigans of court life. The revolution of which Elton wrote was essentially a conceptual one: the creation of an efficient and essentially benign bureaucracy. To Starkey, by contrast, the institutions of Tudor government were constantly shifting in response to the individuals and circumstances around them. Political change in general, says Starkey, tends to be erratic, episodic, unpatterned. Real history means real people interacting with each other at specific times and places. For a while, as Starkey went on to do postgraduate work under Elton, the two men with their radically different views of the way the world wags lived out a kind of heightened intellectual symbiosis, elks whose entangling antlers presumably sharpened each.

The subject of Starkey's thesis, the King's Privy Chamber, was not one of the great offices or institutions of state but the informal body of advisors around the monarch (a bit like today's Downing Street staff). What emerged was a dissertation that, far from distinguishing between court and government as Elton had done, clamped them firmly together. Courtiers were councillors under Henry VII and Henry VIII, argued Starkey.

The relationship went from sour to bitter. Starkey got his doctorate but was denied a job at Cambridge. Soon, however, he obtained a post at the London School of Economics (where he was to stay until 1998) and, as both men grew in prominence, they came to criticize each other in print with the kind of vehemence that, a generation earlier, had characterized Trevor-Roper's attacks on Tawney. There are indications of what was to come in Starkey's first solo book, *The Reign of Henry VIII* (1985), in which he writes of the 'great game of politics' over which Henry presided. It is an engaging volume, well illustrated, with chapters on the main political events and personalities of the age, all expressed with Starkey's characteristic combination of the lapidary and the colloquial. Cognoscenti doubtless noted the emphasis on the 'small group of intimates and personal attendants' who 'acted as the land-line between the King and the formal machinery of government', men who 'were supremely well-placed to rig politics and patronage to their own benefit'. And they would certainly have spotted Starkey's references to, and avowed distancing from, the work of Elton in a brief bibliographical appendix.

But the real assault came in the next two books, both of them edited and introduced by Starkey: *Revolution Reassessed: Revisions in the History of Tudor Government and*

Administration (1986, co-edited with Christopher Coleman) and *The English Court from the Wars of the Roses to the Civil War* (1987). Not the sort of titles to appeal to the general reader, perhaps. But scarlet rags to the Elton bull. Starkey's young toreros, among them star performers such as John Guy (on the Privy Council) and Kevin Sharpe (on the Court and household of Charles I), set out to question and reassess the Elton legacy. Elton, provoked, duly charged.

In particular, he charged Starkey with errors of fact. Starkey, instead of turning aside on an elegant heel, held his ground. Elton's criticisms of *The English Court*, he showed in a point by point rebuttal of his former mentor's review, were themselves misinformed. In a prominent footnote that dropped the academic courtesies, Starkey accused Elton of bullying some of the younger contributors 'for no worse crime than agreeing with me'.

Starkey looks back on his protracted battles with Elton with profound and mixed feelings. Fully aware at the time of the psychological implications of what he was doing, he found as he tore into Elton that he was reliving some aspects of his relationship with his mother, the other defining mentor whom he had outgrown. Soon afterwards, Elton's health deteriorated and there is no doubt that he was deeply wounded by the broadsides he received from Starkey and others towards the end of his life. Yet Starkey's sadness is mitigated by a sense of intellectual satisfaction. He and his colleagues had argued persuasively for a fluid, flexible interpretation of the various Tudor and early Stuart courts, showing how a subtly different pattern of government had emerged under each. Thus (for example), Henry VII, Elizabeth or Charles I retained a certain distance from their councillors, while Henry VIII and James I were more 'participatory' monarchs. Elton's somewhat static, institutional interpretation of the Tudor and Stuart administrations was no longer adequate.

Not only are personalities important, says Starkey. So are places and objects. You can't understand Henry VIII, for example, unless you know where and how he lived, whom he controlled, what he owned. As historical consultant to the Greenwich Exhibition to mark the 500th anniversary of Henry's birth (1991), Starkey clustered the display around a series of specific dates and events, many of them linked to Greenwich Palace: a particular joust or reception, the christening of Elizabeth, the marriage to Anne of Cleves. The Exhibition contained a cornucopia of authentic and evocative objects – clocks and scientific instruments, books and manuscripts, gold and silver plate, armour and weaponry, musical instruments, tapestries, maps, paintings and sculpture. In a richly illustrated catalogue, Starkey emphasized the importance of these objects – the real things, not smoke-and-light reproductions – to a true understanding of King Henry, the man who 'built and accumulated more than any other English king'. It was the work on the Exhibition that kickstarted Starkey into what was to become one of his most important contributions to scholarship: the annotating, indexing and publication of the massive *Inventory of Henry VIII*, a vast project of which Starkey was and remains overall editor.

Starkey was working on a major biography of Henry VIII that would reflect the crucial links between the private aspects of Henry's life – his marital woes, his insatiable acquisitiveness, the membership of his Privy Chamber – and the history of England and its neighbours during his reign. In the course of his researches in the Royal Archives, Starkey extended his interests to encompass the history of the monarchy as such. Indeed, for a while he was considering writing a history of the English monarchy. Neither project materialized. But the preliminary work had important consequences.

Britain at the time was much exercised with its monarchy and, in particular, with the evidently deteriorating relationship between its heir to the throne, Prince Charles, and his wife

Princess Diana. Was a royal divorce possible? Could a divorced
Prince Charles remarry? If so, who would eventually become
Queen, his first or second wife? Should Charles perhaps
renounce (or be denied) his right to the throne? These were
juicy tabloid issues. But they were also major constitutional
ones, and everybody wanted to know the precedents. Enter
David Starkey, whose knowledge of the Tudors, augmented
by a little prepping on Queen Caroline and Mrs Simpson, led
to his being taken up by the media and rebranded as one of
Britain's leading constitutional experts. Always ready with
a pithy yet highly informed answer to a complex question,
Starkey clearly enjoyed the frisson he could create with the
forcefulness and clarity of his views. As he strayed ever
further from his academic centre of gravity, some found him
opinionated and objectionable. But that only increased the
media currency of a man who wrote easily for the popular
press, had been taken up as one of the regular inquisitors
on Radio Four's *Moral Maze* (from 1992) and was soon to
have his own commercial radio talk show (on Talk Radio UK
in 1995–98). In the aftermath of the death of the Princess
of Wales in 1997, Starkey achieved international celebrity
as he explained the arcane implications with exemplary and
indefatigable lucidity to American television audiences.

Starkey continues to pursue what is, in effect, a double
career: academic specialist and media celebrity. He is not the
first to attempt this balancing act, nor the first academic to be
criticized for trying. The two careers came together in 1998,
the year in which, having finally parted company with the LSE,
he accepted a Visiting Fellowship at his old Cambridge college,
Fitzwilliam. That year, in addition to publishing the *Inventory*,
Starkey wrote and presented a three-part television series on
Henry VIII for Channel 4. Then, two years later, his four-part
series about Elizabeth for Channel 4 achieved national headlines
(and a Times editorial) for having achieved higher ratings than
the popular comedian Ali G. Both series were supposed to have

accompanying books. To date, the biography of Henry VIII still awaits completion, while *Elizabeth: Apprenticeship* shows signs of the haste in which it was written and (like the TV series) only takes the story as far as Elizabeth's accession to the throne. Will Starkey complete major works on Henry and/or Elizabeth? *Henry* is well advanced and could be published by 2002. By that time, Starkey will be at work on an ambitious Greenwich exhibition planned for 2003, the 400th anniversary of the death of Elizabeth – a project which, ironically, will delay his plans to complete her biography.

Now in his mid-fifties, Starkey radiates a sense of immense energy, ambition and intellectual power. He is negotiating to buy a house in France, with a lot of library space, to which he can repair from time to time to concentrate on his writing. Meanwhile, he enjoys his periodic bouts of teaching and (especially) working with colleagues and graduate students on shared projects. He sits on the Blue Plaque committee, helping to decide which illuminati from the past should be commemorated on the buildings they once inhabited, and is President of the recently founded Society for Court Studies. Anyone inclined to scoff from within the ivory tower would do well to read Starkey's article on 'Henry VI's Old Blue Gown' from the Society's excellent journal *The Court Historian* (April 1999) – or to await publication of the volumes of commentary on the Henry VIII inventory, a genuinely collegiate enterprise which Starkey speaks about with great enthusiasm. There is another Channel 4 series in discussion, this time about the wives of Henry VIII. Familiar territory, perhaps. But Starkey, with his outspoken views about the court and constitution, will undoubtedly illuminate the past while throwing irresistible sidelong flickers of light upon the present. He also has an ambition to write about the twentieth-century monarchy. Few serious historians nowadays write about the modern monarchy, Starkey says. Those who do tend to miss the point, either building up its supposed constitutional significance or, on the contrary, seeing it as a mere plaything of the nation's powerbrokers. To Starkey, drawing on his intellectual roots in Tudor history, the interesting thing about the monarchy in recent times is the way it has intersected with a quasi-moral debate about the nature of our national identity. 'Who are we?' people ask – and are immediately forced, willy-nilly, to address the role of the monarchy.

Is Starkey still a historian? Of course. You don't have to have an academic position or institution, he says, to qualify (and many who do, don't!). He says he is cutting back on the more 'tinselly' aspect of his work, preferring to concentrate on a smaller number of large projects. These include not only his television series and the Elizabeth exhibition, but also the publication of the commentaries on the *Inventory* and, above all, the eventual completion of his biographies of Henry VIII and Elizabeth – the works on which, I suspect, his ultimate reputation as a historian may depend. For these, he will need to give himself time, space and tranquillity. Let's hope his proposed foray to France proves furnished with cloth of gold.

EPILOGUE

David Starkey writes:

'You have a monkey mind', my mother (who was single-mindedness itself) told me sternly over half a century ago. Daniel Snowman says much the same, though at greater length and more kindly. It is true, of course. And it has been the bane of my life. But also the blessing, since I can't stand being bored.

That is why, a year after I had spoken with Daniel at the turn of 2000–01, I left the *Moral Maze*. We were debating the same topics; the same phrases echoed in my head; I had the same, stage-managed confrontations with chairman Michael Buerk. So I went.

But equally there is a time to return, and I am now presenting the rather similar *Last Word* on More 4. For this, however, Dr Rude of the *Moral Maze* has been joined by my other persona of Mr Nice. It is the classic 'good cop, bad cop' routine that panellists tell me it is hard to get the measure of.

That makes it sound as though the media half of my career has overwhelmed the historical. It hasn't. Instead, I just manage to keep the two in balance, with the one fertilizing the other. *Six Wives*, on which I had begun work in 2001, turned into another Channel 4 series, which got even larger audiences than *Elizabeth* and was likewise BAFTA nominated. It also became a big book – big enough, I hope, to escape the charge of being hastily written which Snowman levels at *Elizabeth*.

But one man's hasty is another man's (or woman's, more likely) lightness of touch. At all events, *Elizabeth* was a number one bestseller in both hardback and paperback and has sold hundreds of thousands here and abroad. This matters because history belongs, not only in the academy, but in the marketplace and on the public stage. That is also why I have become involved (along with several other of Snowman's interviewees) in the Prince of Wales Summer Schools, which are trying to rescue history teaching in schools by reintroducing narrative and content.

The quatercentennial *Elizabeth* exhibition duly took place at the National Maritime Museum, Greenwich, in 2003 and was both a popular and critical success. I shall also be guest-curating the *Antiquaries* exhibition at the Royal Academy in 2007 to mark the tercentenary of the Society of Antiquaries. Otherwise 2007 will be devoted to finishing the writing of *Henry VIII* in time for the 500th anniversary of his accession in 2009.

Nor have other projects mentioned by Snowman been forgotten. The edition of the *Inventory of Henry VIII*, after lying fallow for some years, has sprung back to life and the first volume of the *Commentary* is due for publication next year.

Similarly, the history of the Monarchy has become a 15-part TV series, broadcast over three years, 2004–06. Underlying it is a broad reinterpretation of the last five centuries of our history, which I see as driven, not by the birth-pangs of the British state (as yesterday's academic fashion had it), but by Henry VIII's assumption of the Royal Supremacy, the resulting tensions between religion and politics and their eventual resolution (at least before 9/11).

No, I haven't got bored!

Ian Kershaw

BIOGRAPHY

Ian Kershaw was born in Oldham, Lancashire, in 1943, and educated at St Bede's College, Manchester; the University of Liverpool (BA, First Class Honours in History, 1965), and Merton College, Oxford (D.Phil., 1969). In 2004 he was awarded an Honorary D.Litt., from Manchester and an Honorary D.Univ. from Stirling. He was Assistant Lecturer, then Lecturer, in Medieval History of the University of Manchester from 1968 to 1974; thereafter Lecturer (1974–79), Senior Lecturer (1979–87), and Reader Elect in Modern History (1987). He is a Fellow of the Royal Historical Society (1970–72, 1991–); was a Fellow of the Alexander von Humboldt-Stiftung in 1976–77; a Visiting Professor of Contemporary European History, Ruhr-Universität Bochum, 1983–84; Chair of Modern History, University of Nottingham, 1987–89; a Fellow of the Wissenschaftskolleg, Berlin, 1989–90, and has been Chair of Modern History, University of Sheffield, since 1989. He has been a Fellow of the British Academy since 1991. He was awarded the Cross of Merit of the Federal Republic of Germany (Bundesverdienstkreuz) for services to German history in 1994 and received a Knighthood in 2002. He has won the Wolfson Literary Prize (2000); the Bruno-Kreisky Prize (Austria) (2000); the British Academy Prize (2001); the Norton Medlicott Prize of the Historical Association (2004) and the Elizabeth Longford Prize for Historical Biography (2005). He was a Consultant on the BAFTA-winning BBC

TV series *The Nazis: A Warning from History*, and also on BBC2's *War of the Century*, and *Auschwitz: The Nazis and 'the Final Solution'*; ZDF's *Hitler: eine Bilanz*, and *Holokaust*; Spiegel-TV's *Hundert Jahre Deutschland* and *Göring – die letzte Schlacht*, and on BBC TV *Timewatch* programmes on 'Operation Sealion' (the planned invasion of Britain), 'Himmler' and 'The Making of Adolf Hitler'.

PRINCIPAL PUBLISHED BOOKS

Bolton Priory Rentals and Ministers' Accounts, 1473–1539 (ed.) (1969)

Bolton Priory: The Economy of a Northern Monastery (1973)

Der Hitler-Mythos: Volksmeinung und Propaganda im Dritten Reich (1980) (English version: *The 'Hitler Myth': Image and Reality in the Third Reich*, published in 1987)

Popular Opinion and Political Dissent in the Third Reich: Bavaria, 1933–45 (1983)

The Nazi Dictatorship: Problems and Perspectives of Interpretation (1985)

Weimar: Why did German Democracy Fail? (ed.) (1991)

Stalinism and Nazism: Dictatorships in Comparison (ed. with Moshe Lewin) (1997)

Hitler, 1889–1936: Hubris (1998)

Hitler, 1936–2000: Nemesis (2000)

The Bolton Priory Compotus 1286–1325, Together with a Priory Account Roll for 1377–78 (ed. with David M. Smith) (2001)

Making Friends with Hitler (2004)

PROFILE, July 2001

Another biography of Hitler? It was a question Ian Kershaw had to contend with throughout the 1990s as he struggled to ascend his chosen mountain top. Many others had scaled the heights before him, notably Alan Bullock and Joachim Fest, and many others had failed to reach the summit. Kershaw completed his 2,000-page, two-volume biography last year to enormous critical acclaim, and there can be little doubt that his is the flag that will flutter triumphantly for the next generation or more. But what's so special about Kershaw's *Hitler* – and why, indeed, another biography?

The nursery slopes on which Kershaw trained were not the obvious ones for an aspirant scholar of Nazism. Born to a working-class family in Oldham in 1943, Kershaw was sent to a Catholic grammar school in Manchester where he learned French and Latin and imbibed a doubtless somewhat sectarian view of the Reformation. He was not interested in such tasks as having to justify the excesses of Mary Tudor, but he loved researching the Tudor world and began to wonder what Europe was like in earlier times when Catholicism reigned supreme. An undergraduate at Liverpool University, Kershaw coincided with a cluster of talented and inspiring Medievalists, got a First and went on to do an Oxford D.Phil. on the account book of the monastery at Bolton Priory in Yorkshire. Before long he and his young wife settled down in Manchester, where Kershaw had been made a Lecturer in Medieval History.

And there things might have remained. Keen to hone his linguistic skills, and perhaps to read more about Barbarossa or the later medieval German peasantry, Kershaw took up German at evening classes offered by the Goethe Institute in Manchester. In 1972 he went off to Bavaria for a two-month intensive course. To this day he vividly recalls his encounter in a café on the outskirts of Munich with an old man who told him how wonderful Germany had been back in the 1930s. 'You English were so foolish', he told Kershaw. 'If only you had sided with us. Together, we could have defeated Bolshevism and ruled the world.' At one point, the fate of the European Jews was mentioned. 'The Jew is a louse', said the man. Kershaw was shocked and incredulous. But he reflected that, perhaps for the first time in his life, he had just obtained a tiny insight into the enigma that was already coming to preoccupy him.

Most people whom Kershaw knew, in Germany and elsewhere, tended to dismiss Hitler as an evil, possibly mad, devil figure. Yet 30 years before, millions of intelligent and cultured citizens of a modern nation state not unlike Britain had idolized Hitler and enthusiastically adopted his world view. Why?

In 1975, Kershaw was back in Munich with a grant to join Professor Martin Broszat's team researching Bavarian resistance and persecution in the Nazi period. Encouraged by Broszat, Kershaw examined how people had perceived Hitler. Why had so many followed the Führer – and why did others dissent or resist? Kershaw's first book, *The Hitler Myth* (written initially in German and published in 1980) addressed the first question, and his next, *Popular Opinion and Political Dissent in the Third Reich* (1983), the second. Meanwhile, the University of Manchester had reappointed him – as a Lecturer in Modern History. The transition was complete.

By now, Kershaw was working his way through what was already a massive bibliography, in German, French and English, and rapidly discovering that he had entered a field wracked by acrimony. Those who argued that Hitler was a uniquely demonic leader would be pounced on for letting the German people off the hook, while those who saw Nazism as a product of all that had preceded it were lambasted as 'structuralist' or 'functionalist'. Did you regard Hitler as having had a master plan? Then you were evidently taken in by *Mein Kampf*. But equally open to criticism was the view that the Führer was merely a master improviser. To Marxist historians from East Germany, the Nazis were best explained as tools of capitalism; but many who scorned such over-simple interpretations ran the risk of losing the baby as well as the bathwater and forgetting the undoubtedly nefarious role of many mighty German corporations still extant.

Kershaw reflected on such issues in a book called *The Nazi Dictatorship: Problems and Perspectives of Interpretation*, originally published in 1985. These fierce historiographical disputes, he pointed out, between (for example) the adherents of a 'structuralist' as opposed to an 'intentionalist' approach, or between those who saw the Nazis as unique and those who saw them as part of an historical continuum, were far more than mere intellectual games. For the historian of the Nazi period had a crucial part to play in the political education of postwar Germany. Indeed, the very course of modern German development depended in part on how people came to perceive the era that had immediately preceded their own, and this bestowed upon historians a social and political significance far greater than that of colleagues specializing in other times and places.

The history of Nazism, therefore, required careful handling. Kershaw began to develop a number of concepts that were later to help underpin his thinking when he came to write his big biography. In order to understand the Nazi era, he argued, the historian must take proper account of the 'historical-philosophical' and the 'political-ideological' dimensions of the subject – and, crucially, in this particular case, the moral dimension. In 1991, Kershaw published a brief study of Hitler for a Longman series called 'Profiles in Power'. Here, he called upon Max Weber's concept of 'charismatic authority' as a key to understanding Hitler's extraordinary hold. He also introduced the Greek terms 'hubris' and 'nemesis' as evocative shorthand for the epic scale of Hitler's pride and fall. As ever, Kershaw continued to reflect on the central enigma, the quasi-religious admiration Hitler was capable of arousing – and the controversies that almost any proposed explanation of the Hitler phenomenon tended to arouse.

In 1987, Kershaw had become Professor of Modern History at the University of Nottingham, moving a couple of years later to Sheffield, where he remains to this day. Before plunging into the demanding schedule of teaching and administration that came with the Sheffield appointment, he was able to spend some time researching in Berlin. He was there the night the wall came down, but had spent the evening in a café in the western suburbs with a graduate student and didn't know what had happened until he returned to his flat and received an excited call from his wife in England who had seen it all on TV!

For the historian of Nazism, the demise of Communism and the reunification of Germany brought fresh perspectives to old debates and soon began to open up new ones. The flames of historiographical controversy were not doused but refuelled. As Soviet and East German records emerged, people asked whether Soviet Communism and German Nazism – ostensibly opposite ends of the political spectrum – hadn't in some ways been comparable, two totalitarian systems in which the gulag was no less barbaric than the concentration camp. Gradually, the genocidal policies of the Nazis, arguably underplayed (though for different reasons) by earlier historians in both East and West Germany, came increasingly to occupy centre stage. By the mid-1990s, any historian thought to have given the Holocaust too little prominence was liable to be suspected of anti-Semitism; too much, and you were in danger of being dubbed part of the 'Holocaust industry' and doubtless an apologist for Israel. Political generalizations, masquerading as historical analysis, abounded. In 1996 Daniel Goldhagen caused something of a storm with his provocative book arguing that the entire German people were 'Hitler's willing executioners'. All this and more Kershaw addressed in the fourth edition of *The Nazi Dictatorship*, published in 2000. And he had to keep these issues constantly in focus during the long, lonely years while he was writing his *magnum opus*.

Ian Kershaw's *Hitler* is as magnum an opus as one might comfortably want to handle. When I asked him why he had not called upon his reserves of expertise in medieval history to flesh out the Nazi ideological lineage, the myths and monuments of earlier history, Kershaw laughed as he imagined the size of the resulting tomes. But of course what he was undertaking was a life of Hitler, not the intellectual pedigree of Nazism.

Until then, Kershaw's intellectual centre of gravity had been public perceptions of Hitler – the social psychology of Nazism as a mass movement, if you like, rather than the day-to-day activities of its leaders. His apprenticeship, furthermore, had been at the elbow of writers like Broszat and Hans Mommsen who had tended to decry biography as a substitute for serious history – especially a biography of Hitler, with the attendant dangers of over-personalizing all that happened and downplaying the responsibility of everything and everyone else. On the face of it, a big Hitler biography was an unlikely project for Kershaw to undertake.

He acknowledges this, but sees his work on Hitler as a natural culmination of all that preceded it. 'What I tried to do', he says, 'was to embed Hitler into the social and political context that I had already studied', something he feels previous biographies had not really achieved. Kershaw is full of admiration for pioneering predecessors like Bullock and Fest. But, as he re-reads Bullock's masterpiece (written nearly 50 years ago), Kershaw finds a portrait of Hitler as an unprincipled opportunist obsessed by power almost for its own sake. Inevitably, Bullock (like Fest, writing in the early 1970s) failed to give the Holocaust, for example, the centrality most historians now feel it warrants. Fest, for all his literary and imaginative flair, became somewhat sidetracked by his fruitless attempt to assess whether or not Hitler embodied a form of 'greatness'. Other writers, Kershaw feels, concentrated too closely on Hitler's personality, doubtless bringing valuable Freudian insights to bear but sometimes tending to attribute the entire Third Reich to the sexual (or asexual) idiosyncrasies of one man. None had attempted in any systematic way to relate Hitler to the wider structures of German society.

When Penguin approached Kershaw with the suggestion that he undertake a major biography, he at first demurred. But he soon got used to the idea, aware that the kind of book he could do did not exist and was needed. Apart from everything else, there were new sources to hand: the rediscovered Goebbels diaries, for example, which, like so much other material, had been hidden away until very recently in inaccessible archives in the Soviet Union or East Germany. Clearly, there were fresh perspectives to examine, new problems to tackle and perhaps new solutions to seek. 'I always imagine that historians write books on complex topics in the first instance to sort out problems for themselves', wrote Kershaw in the preface to the latest edition of *The Nazi Dictatorship*, adding disarmingly that 'it is a bonus if others then find interest in their musings'. Thus, one senses that the real reason Kershaw finally agreed to take on the big book was that he personally was burning to confront, head on, the question that had possessed him for nigh on 30 years: how had Hitler been possible?

It was only once he had started work on what was originally intended to be a single-volume biography that Kershaw slowly realised the full scale of what he had taken on. He continued to run the Modern History Department at Sheffield and, as he tried to wrest research and writing time from a busy schedule, took comfort from what he called the Magnus Magnusson principle: 'I've started so I'll finish!' Fully ten years later, Kershaw completed what is an engagingly written and dazzlingly documented account of a man whom he sees not as some sort of demonic genius but as the product of an exceptional interaction of personality and circumstances.

In some ways, Kershaw clearly reveals himself as a product of the 'structuralist' school of German historiography in which he was trained. Thus, many pages are devoted to the social, political and economic context of his story: the Vienna of Karl Lueger, for example; the failure of Weimar democracy; the political manoeuvrings that led to Hitler becoming Chancellor, or the Realpolitik preceding the invasion of the USSR or the declaration of war against the USA. But, especially in his second volume, Kershaw is also something of an 'intentionalist', showing beyond doubt the indelible impact left upon events by Hitler personally. Thus, there may be no single document signed by Hitler ordering the annihilation of the Jews (of course there wasn't, says Kershaw: Hitler consistently created an atmosphere within which his henchmen knew what he wanted done without his actually having to say so). But to Kershaw, without Hitler there would have been no Holocaust and probably no war.

Kershaw's ambition, and perhaps his great achievement, is to have bridged the hitherto conflicting insights of historians of Nazism and, as in a great drama, to have linked Hitler to his times, the times to the man. Kershaw sees a continuum, too, though not always direct cause and effect, between Hitler's ideology and his actions. The passionate desire to avenge Versailles, or the virulent anti-Semitism he acquired in Vienna, were of a piece with Hitler's desire to crush Bolshevism. The Holocaust was not a barbarous sideshow but integral to Hitler's war aims.

Page by page, detail by detail, Kershaw builds up a picture of overweening arrogance followed by catastrophic downfall – for Hitler as for those he led. The story has elements akin to those of Greek tragedy. Thus, the first half of the story, culminating in the spectacular triumph of Hitler's occupation of the Rhineland, Kershaw entitles *Hubris*; the second volume is *Nemesis*.

Kershaw was keen to produce a work that would command respect among German readers and academics. This he has achieved, and he is in constant demand as a star speaker throughout Germany. By now, indeed, his books have been translated into some 15 languages and Kershaw has spent much of the past couple of years on promotion trips at the behest of his publishers. A man of great charm and obvious integrity, Kershaw speaks with enviable and indefatigable balance and intelligence about his emotion-laden subject. Offers of lucrative posts from the USA, Germany and glamorous places closer to London are routinely turned down by this cheerfully unrepentant Northerner who still lives in Manchester and teaches at Sheffield. I asked him what he will do next. (What do you do next, once you have completed a vast, authoritative biography of one of the giant figures of modern history?) He says he needs to recharge his intellectual batteries and is giving up being Head of History at Sheffield, but has no large-scale project in mind. A period of stasis perhaps? Maybe. But not, I suspect, for long.

Roy Foster

BIOGRAPHY

R.F. (Roy) Foster holds the only endowed chair of Irish History in Britain. He was born in Waterford, Ireland, in 1949 and educated in both Ireland and the United States. A graduate of Trinity College, Dublin, where he was a Foundation Scholar in history, he subsequently became Professor of Modern British History at Birkbeck College, University of London, as well as holding visiting Fellowships at St Antony's College, Oxford; the Institute for Advanced Study, Princeton, and Princeton University. In 1991 he became the first Carroll Professor of Irish History at Oxford and was elected a Fellow of Hertford College. He was elected a Fellow of the British Academy in 1989, was elected a Fellow of the Royal Historical Society in 1986, a Fellow of the Royal Society of Literature in 1992, and has received honorary degrees from the University of Aberdeen, the Queen's University of Belfast, Trinity College Dublin, and the National University of Ireland, as well as an Honorary Fellowship at Birkbeck College. In the spring of 2002, he was the Whitney Oates Fellow at Princeton.

In 1998 he was awarded the James Tait Black prize for biography for the first volume of his Yeats biography, *W.B. Yeats, A Life, Volume I: The Apprentice Mage, 1865–1914.* In 2003 he won the Christian Gauss Award for Literary Criticism for *The Irish Story: Telling Tales and Making It Up in Ireland.* His most recent book is *Conquering England: Ireland in Victorian London* (2005), co-written with Fintan

Cullen, to coincide with their exhibition at the National Portrait Gallery. In 2004 he also delivered the Wiles Lectures at Queen's University Belfast, on 'Metamorphoses: The Strange Death of Romantic Ireland, c.1970–2000', which will form the subject of his next book. He is a well-known critic, reviewer and broadcaster.

PRINCIPAL PUBLISHED BOOKS

Charles Stewart Parnell: the Man and his Family (1976)
Lord Randolph Churchill: A Political Life (1981)
Modern Ireland 1600–1972 (1988)
Paddy and Mr Punch: Connections in Irish and English History (1993)
W.B. Yeats, A Life, Volume I; The Apprentice Mage, 1865–1914 (1997)
The Irish Story: Telling Tales and Making It Up in Ireland (2001)
W.B. Yeats, A Life, Volume II: The Arch-Poet, 1915–1938 (2003)
Conquering England: Ireland in Victorian London (with Fintan Cullen) (2005)

PROFILE, October 2001

On the face of it, there is nothing particularly controversial about the Carroll Professor of Irish History at the University of Oxford. With his mop of hair and casual-chic style, Robert Fitzroy Foster seems the very model of the modern don, a thoughtful, sophisticated historian at ease among books and bookmen, whose own erudite, elegant writings have won widespread plaudits.

Widespread, but not universal. For Roy Foster, *malgré lui* (as he might say), has also stirred up periodic pockets of protest. Furthermore, he is routinely labelled a 'revisionist'. To you and me, that might simply mean someone who checks and revises the conclusions of his predecessors, perhaps upsetting accepted nostrums in the process. It is what any good historian is bound to do. But, in the hothouse that is Irish history, 'revisionist' is used by some as a term of abuse levelled at those like Foster who don't accept the traditional totems and taboos of the Irish past. When Foster writes of the great emblematic milestones of Irish history – the Battle of the Boyne, the Wolfe Tone rebellion of 1798, the Easter Rising – he does so with the cool intellectual detachment of one who has actually re-examined the evidence. Not for him the celebratory mythologizing that still sometimes passes for Irish history. If previous interpretations are not borne out by the facts, Foster regards it as his duty to say so.

Such a stance has attracted brickbats. Foster, an Irishman of Protestant background with a chair at Oxford, has been accused of concentrating too much on 'Posh Protestants' (Parnell, Lord Randolph Churchill, Yeats, Elizabeth Bowen). Some have even seen him as having sold out to Britain – the ultimate Irish betrayal – when, for example, discussing the dilemmas faced by the British at the time of the Famine or in 1916. Such labels, Foster says, tend to come from people who haven't actually read his books: Irish-Americans drawn to a sentimentally 'Green' view of Irish history, or journalists looking for a headline. In any case, he adds philosophically, the labelling comes with the territory. Irish history (like German history) is intensely political: any stance is liable to be examined for its supposed political agenda. It's the price you pay for choosing to write about – and for – people who are hugely interested in their own history. Foster considers it a price well worth paying. 'We write for an engaged readership!' he says emphatically.

Roy Foster was born in 1949 and raised in Waterford. His parents, nominally members of the Church of Ireland, were teachers at a Quaker school where Roy was educated. After a year in America, Foster attended Trinity College, Dublin, where he studied history and political science. At Trinity, he encountered one of the seminal figures of modern Irish historiography, Theo Moody. Under Moody's inspired tutelage,

Foster became interested in the Anglo-Irish history of the Home Rule period, the late nineteenth century, and went on to write a PhD thesis on Parnell. Casting around for a job, Foster was interviewed by Eric Hobsbawm at Birkbeck College in London and was offered a Lectureship in Modern British History. The job was for a year; by the time he left, 17 years later, Professor Foster was head of the department.

Parnell was published as a book in 1976, and a biography of Randolph Churchill followed a few years later. Neither is a conventional political biography. The Parnell volume, indeed, is ostensibly not about politics at all but about family, lineage and location. As in much of Foster's writing, there is a wonderful sense of place; you can almost smell the old country estates of nineteenth-century Wicklow as you watch Parnell playing cricket as a lad or struggling later on to reconcile his growing belief in land reform with his position as landowner. By examining the social and personal milieu in which Parnell was raised, Foster establishes a strikingly original context in which to approach the central enigma of Parnell: how someone from the Protestant gentry should have come to espouse land reform and nationalist politics.

If the Parnell book approached politics obliquely, the Churchill biography places it at the centre. Every chapter, indeed, has 'politics' in its title. But this, too, is no mere conventional political biography. Rather, Foster sees Lord Randolph as the central figure in a political novel, a Trollopean figure whose spectacular rise and fall provide an entrée into a world of high political society. Churchill, like Parnell, was both a highly privileged figure yet also in some ways a marginalized one, a representative of a small but powerful enclave entering decline. Both were men of immense ability whose very talents contributed to the downfall each was to suffer. And, like so many before and since, both Parnell and Churchill found themselves caught in up in the turbulent relationship between Ireland and England, their lives enriched, moulded and debilitated in consequence. These are themes that run, like a brightly coloured skein, throughout the complex textures of Foster's *oeuvre*.

In 1981, Foster was asked to write a popular textbook on the history of 'Modern Ireland' (i.e. since about 1600). The commission (from Allen Lane) sounded like a godsend. Foster and his wife Aisling had just had their first child, and a textbook on Irish history would surely provide the young family with much-needed extra income, especially from American sales. Yet Foster soon found himself asking his patient editor for extensions to his contact. This was partly due to the sheer bulk of material to be covered. But it was more than that. 'I found', says Foster looking back, 'that to write the history of modern Ireland, you had the write "the history of the history" of modern Ireland.'

The eventual result was both less and more than originally envisaged. *Modern Ireland* is no typical textbook, parts of it proving difficult to penetrate unless you are already familiar with the basic facts. True, it contains a helpful chronological table, plus illuminating biographical footnotes about every major character and many minor ones. But you would have to know quite a lot about previous interpretations of the Famine, the Phoenix Park murders or Patrick Pearse, or for example, to understand the furore that Foster's cool reassessments were capable of arousing in the breast of old-fashioned patriots. Foster is a fine and subtle wordsmith. But he rarely uses his talents merely to describe or evoke what happened, much less to 'empathize'. What he produced in Modern Ireland, rather, was a book that encapsulated in a single volume the work – and approach – of a new generation of Irish historians: sceptical in tone, scholarly, balanced, detached and eschewing the cheap moralism of the past. The book was thus a reinterpretation of Irish history, a 'revision' of much that had popularly passed for history when Foster was a boy.

Foster is no giant-killer, however, and is generous in his praise for those historians, like Moody, who pioneered the 'revisionism' with which he himself is associated. He acknowledges that he learned much, too, from the work of historians as diverse as E.P. Thompson, Natalie Zemon Davis, Eugene Genovese and Hobsbawn: not only the importance of the social and cultural forces that lie behind political history, but also the need to write with style if you want anyone to read what you have written. Foster recognises a shift in his own centre of intellectual gravity as he has increasingly drawn upon literary sources in his writing – a trend prefigured in the work of another friend and mentor, F.S.L. Lyons. Leland Lyons died while still in the early stages of his official biography of William Butler Yeats. That mantle was to pass to Roy Foster.

Modern Ireland was published in 1988 and is still in print. In 1989, Foster was elected to the British Academy; two years later, he took up the first permanent chair of Irish history in Britain, becoming Carroll Professor of Irish History (and a fellow of Hertford College) at Oxford. Already, he was toiling away at Yeats. 'It was the subject that had been waiting for me!' he says, his enthusiasm evidently undimmed, for Yeats meant 'history, politics, literature, biography – virtually an alternative history of Ireland over exactly the period that interested me'. W.B. Yeats came from a highly connected Protestant, Anglo-Irish background, knew everyone of consequence from the 1880s to the 1930s, was a pivotal figure in the Celtic revival and wrote some of the most highly wrought and evocative poetry of the past 100 years. He repeatedly fell under the spell of unattainable women and intangible spiritual cults, but lived to become the grand old mage of Irish letters, going on to attain the Nobel Prize and a seat in his country's Senate. Foster's life of Yeats will comprise two volumes. The first (*The Apprentice Mage*), published in 1997, is dedicated to Lyons and takes the story to the outbreak of World War I; volume II is largely complete and should appear in 2003.

Many of the themes that appear in *Yeats I* are prefigured elsewhere in Foster's work. In the *Oxford Illustrated History of Ireland* (1989), which Foster edited, his own contribution was a lengthy essay on the eighteenth-century Protestant Ascendancy, its gradual decline in the nineteenth and the historical myths that came to be associated with it. The book had an impressive cast list (including fellow 'revisionist' David Fitzpatrick) and ended with an essay by Declan Kiberd touching on another favourite Foster topic: the relationship between Irish literature (both English-language and Irish) and Irish history.

The theme of men and women 'caught' between Ireland and England was the central thread in a collection of essays that Foster entitled *Paddy and Mr Punch* (1993) while his latest compilation of writings, *The Irish Story* (just published), considers the various ways in which the 'story of Ireland' has been told, or fabricated. These volumes contain many old friends: Parnell, Lord Randolph Churchill, Yeats, Synge and Elizabeth Bowen are all there, as are Foster's sensitivity to the importance of literature, language, lineage and locale. There is much on Irish historiography, too, in Foster's essays, including a sophisticated analysis – and dismissal – of the concept of revisionism ('there are no professional historians who are not revisionists', he says at one point).

As in much of Foster's writing, the essays assume considerable prior knowledge. He has a tendency to refer obliquely to the work of others, as though we had all read what he has read, and there is a patrician tone to his writing. He knows that historians are often exhorted to write for the 'general reader'. But, to Foster, the general reader is 'a bit like the stray neighbourhood cat; you feel vaguely sympathetic towards it, but you know it's someone else's responsibility to look after it, and you're damned if you're going to do it yourself'.

Yet it is well worth persevering, for Foster has a subtle and important message to impart. He resolutely and rightly refuses to simplify the complex or to impose the facile judgements of today upon the events of yesterday. The best historical writing, argues Foster, should be informed by an understanding of what people thought at the time, whether or not we happen to agree with them. His own credo, he admits engagingly, 'is that the most illuminating history is often written to show how people acted in the expectation of a future that never happened'.

Herein, perhaps, lies the key to Foster's view of Yeats. Yeats may have been a Mage. But he was no Prophet. Yeats, says Foster, 'lived out his life constantly expecting various kinds of future'; indeed, as a man attracted to astrology, he probably felt he had a better purchase on the future than the rest of us. But, of course, 'the expected future never happened'. Much of Yeats' life can thus be understood, Foster suggests, as the constant adaptations to the unexpected of a man with a 'protean ability to shift his ground, repossess the advantage, and lay claim to authority – always with an eye to how people would see things afterwards'.

In the first volume we enter the world of the Yeats and Pollexfen families that produced William Butler Yeats, his artist brother Jack and their sisters; we dwell in the Irish and London milieux in which W.B. was raised; encounter major literary figures like Wilde and Shaw; follow the vicissitudes of Yeats' personal obsessions, among them Maud Gonne and the occult; and move into the very heart of the Irish literary revival and the creation of the Abbey Theatre. In volume II, Foster will introduce Yeats' response to the Easter Rising (the subject of one of his most emblematic poems), his preoccupation with Maud Gonne's daughter, his marriage and his career in politics.

Yeats has been the subject of several previous studies, notably those by Joseph Hone and Richard Ellmann (not to mention W.B.'s own Autobiography). Foster's opus is no personal memoir, apologia or 'literary' biography, however, but a piece of rigorous historical research documenting the life of a man who among other things happened to be a major poet. Thus, Foster relates the story largely as it seemed to unfold at the time. No grand theme or thesis runs through the text, nor has

Foster any time for hagiography or demonology. Yeats was a person of impressive and variegated accomplishments whom Foster clearly admires. But he was also someone riddled with doubts and insecurities, a man who reflected aspects of the times in which he lived but was scarcely their architect. No man, Foster implies, is that.

In Yeats, as in all his work, Foster refuses to over-simplify, reduce or polarize. His plea – one that it is not easy to accept in Ireland – is for what in one of his essays he calls 'the acceptance of ambiguity'. If you want to 'possess' your history, he says, 'you may have to give some of it up' – thereby, he would argue, inheriting a past greatly more enriching. One is not a whit the less Irish, Foster insists, for accepting a broad, pluralist perspective. He quotes the writer Hubert Butler (whose essays he has edited), another of those liberal, cosmopolitan Protestant Irishmen to whom he is drawn, as saying that great cultures 'have always risen from the interaction of diverse societies'. All this amounts to a bold position for an Irish historian (in both senses) to adopt.

When Foster pours scorn on the 'stage Irishry' of the brothers McCourt for 'trading on misery', or at the sentimentalized 150th anniversary commemorations of the Famine, he knows he is inciting Nationalist critics to accuse him of taking an 'English' line. It is a danger that will doubtless surface once more if he fulfils his post-Yeats ambition to write a 'little book' on the history of Ireland from 1968 to the present. But, as Foster emphasizes, the whole drift of his work is to transcend mere politicized history, to liberate his subject from the thrall of preconceived pieties. He acknowledges that a completely impartial mind may be impossible for the historian to achieve. But, 'like virtue, it is there for us to aim at'. Is this what is meant by 'revisionism'? If so, Roy Foster is reluctantly prepared to accept the 'r' word.

Lyndal Roper

BIOGRAPHY

Lyndal Roper grew up in Melbourne, Australia, and graduated from the University of Melbourne in 1977. Immediately after, she went to Germany on a German Academic Exchange Award, where she studied at the University of Tübingen and started archival research in Augsburg, going on to write her doctorate on women in the German Reformation with the late Bob Scribner, finishing her doctorate in 1985. She held a Junior Research Fellowship at Merton College, Oxford, from 1983 to 1986, and, after a brief period working at King's College, London, took up a Lectureship at Royal Holloway, University of London, where she stayed until 2002. A year at the Institute of Advanced Study in Berlin (1991–2) and another period as a Humboldt Fellow in 1997–98 at the Max Planck Institute for History were major influences. She is married to the historian Nick Stargardt, and in 1996 their son was born. In 2002 she moved to Balliol College, Oxford, where she is Fellow and Tutor in History (Professor 2004), and, with Chris Wickham, she co-edits *Past and Present*, a major historical journal.

PRINCIPAL PUBLISHED BOOKS

The Holy Household: Women and Morals in Reformation Augsburg (1989)

Oedipus and the Devil: Witchcraft, Sexuality and Religion in Early Modern Europe (1994)

Witch Craze: Terror and Fantasy in Baroque Germany (2004)
Dreams and History: The Interpretation of Dreams from Ancient Greece to Modern Psychoanalysis ed. with Daniel Pick (2004)

PROFILE, January 2002

Religious fundamentalism, mass hysteria, mysterious poisonings, coded messages, the subjugation of women, the demonization and slaughter of outcasts and a struggle for hearts and minds between opposing ideologies – and that's just seventeenth-century Augsburg! But it would not be surprising if Lyndal Roper's subject matter also suggested messages for our own troubled times.

I sometimes think there are two Lyndal Ropers. The first writes vivid and often searing accounts of the experiences of women accused of witchcraft in southern Germany in Early Modern times. Thus Regina Bartholome was tried and incarcerated for (among other things) confessing to having had intercourse with the Devil, while Catharina Schmid, it seems, caused a young girl to be possessed and also used mysterious means to bring about the deaths of the wife and children of a neighbour. Anna Megerler, a supposed healer and sorceress, claimed to have given occult and astrological advice to the great Augsburg banker Anton Fugger. Roper Mark II, meanwhile, operates on the more elevated level of theory, examining the links between the social and the psychological, penetrating the arcana of Weber, Elias and Klein, and struggling to advance and integrate the latest insights of feminist history, psychohistory and cultural studies.

The two come together in a string of stimulating essays and a pair of pioneering books which, between them, suggest a major reassessment of the history of Early Modern Europe and, thereby, of the world to which we are heir. This connection between our forebears and ourselves is important to Roper. Although she is Professor of Early Modern History at Royal

Holloway (University of London), and obviously devoted to her craft, she protests quite unselfconsciously that 'I've never really thought of myself as primarily a historian!'

She is a historian – and much more. Lyndal Roper was born in Melbourne in 1956 (a few months before the Olympic Games came to town). Her first encounters with history were probably at the knee of her grandfather, a passionate trade unionist, who would pour out animated and angry reminiscences of Gallipoli. Lyndal's mother taught drama and literature and had a strong interest in psychodrama; her father, who had done intelligence work in Germany after World War II, went on to obtain a theology degree and for a while became a somewhat heterodox minister of religion.

By the time Lyndal entered the University of Melbourne, where she sailed through a degree in History and Philosophy, several strands of her later work were beginning to emerge: an interest in the Early Modern past and in the changing role of women and the family, and a curiosity about the states of mind that lead people to label themselves and others by reference to irrational dogma. At 'Uni' Lyndal encountered a succession of inspiring teachers. One, the historian Charles Zika, encouraged her to go to Germany for her postgraduate work.

From her base in Tübingen, Roper undertook research on the role of women in Early Modern Germany, journeying to various towns, among them Ulm and Stuttgart, seeking documentation, such as Council minutes, that, on inspection, often proved elusive, indecipherable or non-existent. For a 22-year-old Australian girl in Europe for the first time in her life, equipped with (as yet) somewhat shaky German, these were lonely and demoralizing days. But she persevered and eventually discovered in Augsburg just the kind of documentation she needed: a wonderful cache of criminal records that brimmed over with information about domestic life. Herein lay the basis of Roper's PhD about women and morals in Reformation Augsburg (supervised by Bob Scribner, another important influence). It was eventually to materialize (in 1989) as her book *The Holy Household*.

'My thanks, first of all,' Roper proclaims at the top of the Acknowledgements page in *The Holy Household*, 'to the Women's Movement, without which this book could not have been written.' And the text is, indeed, a major contribution to women's history, packed with tightly organized material about changing attitudes towards sex, sin, marriage, prostitution, sexual abstinence, the family and convent life in an age of religious transformation. Roper argues that gender relations were at the crux of the Reformation. We may have thought, somewhat simplistically, that, as Medieval Catholicism ceded ground to the Lutheran Reformation (and priests began to marry), a more liberal, egalitarian regime came to govern relations between men and women. In some ways, argues Roper, the opposite was true. The Reformation tended to reinforce the centrality of the family, and thus woman's subservient role as wife and mother – thereby outlawing and anathematizing any female role perceived as non-familial or (especially) anti-familial.

The Holy Family was well received as an important contribution to scholarship, one that used new insights from the women's movement, but with subtlety and discrimination. Roper was by now a History Lecturer at Royal Holloway, having previously had brief research and teaching posts at King's (London) and Oxford. By the time she published her next book, *Oedipus and the Devil* (1994), she had a Readership; a chair followed a few years later.

Oedipus and the Devil is in essence a collection of essays, many previously published elsewhere. Together, they amount to a substantial critique of the history and historiography of witchcraft, sexuality and religion in Early Modern Europe. As in much of Roper's writing, the brew bubbles with steamy information about some of the seamier and more bizarre aspects of life in early modern Germany. Thus she tells of

Anna Ebeler who was accused of poisoning the woman she worked for, as well as a number of local children in mysterious circumstances, and was put to death as a witch. Appolonia Mayr strangled her new-born baby because the Devil promised that, once she had done so, her lover would marry her. Readers of the *Sun* and *News of the World* need go no further.

But readers of the broadsheets should turn to Roper too. For what is really interesting is the use she makes of these and similar fragments. Originally, she had intended to undertake a straightforward work about sexuality and the Reformation. The Reformation (this was to be her argument) left a legacy of sexual repression which led to a moral crackdown; and this, in turn, led to people placing their repressed sexual fantasies onto women they labelled as witches. An easy, pat argument, which Roper went off to try to prove. The problem was that the evidence (from witch trials and the like) seemed to lead elsewhere. Instead of the plethora of repressed sexual fantasies she had expected, Roper kept stumbling over references to milk, to babies – to the accoutrements of motherhood, in fact. This was a theme that, she concedes, she had underestimated in her earlier writings (there is surprisingly little about motherhood in *The Holy Household*). In *Oedipus and the Devil* and subsequent essays by Roper, it is striking how often accusations of witchcraft were brought by mothers, soon after giving birth, against older women concerned with the care of children.

Unlike some earlier historians of witchcraft, Roper does not revel in the absurdity (to us) of witch trials or the irrationality (to us) of imputing magic powers to certain otherwise ordinary people. She reminds us of the astrological advice that Nancy Reagan sought out for her husband the President, and points out acidly that most of us happily accept the axioms of subatomic physics, for example, not in response to the evidence but on trust from those we regard as experts. No. Roper's concern, rather, is to enter the minds of those who believed in witchcraft. What did the world look like to a woman who confessed, and in a sense genuinely believed, that she had had intercourse with the Devil, or who claimed to have helped a great banker by giving him advice derived from her dealings in the occult? And (just as important), what was the mindset of a local official who was quite prepared, as part of his civic duty, to consider condemning such a woman to torture and a painful death?

Such questions lie at the heart of Lyndal Roper's work. In order to address them, she transcends her work as historian, marshalling arguments from psychoanalysis, sociology and cultural anthropology. After all, any woman accused of (or confessing to) witchcraft is someone whose personal pathology and cultural context equally warrant study – especially if that context was the turmoil that followed the Reformation. How (Roper asks) does a great cultural transformation, such as the Reformation, affect the self-perceptions of people living in its midst? What is the relationship between the 'subjective' world in which people felt themselves to be living at the time and the 'objective' world out there that subsequent historians might recognise? Where lay the organic links between the two, the realms of the psychic and the social?

Part of Roper's underlying agenda in *Oedipus* is to reinstate the body – bodily protuberances, orifices and fluids – at the centre of our understanding of the past. One might balk at the occasional shorthand ('Sixteenth-century culture can clearly be described as a phallic culture'). But Roper is surely right to emphasize the obvious fact that our bodies are the inescapable framework from within which we perceive everything around us.

She has a further mission, one equally provocative, perhaps, yet equally obvious when you think about it. Like all good historians, Roper pores over her evidence. But, for her, it is less important to pin down the 'facts' of what this or that 'witch' may have done, or been accused of doing, than to understand how people perceived a world containing witchcraft. Her 'project' (a favourite word) is to delve beyond the facts and seek a deeper truth, to 'get people out of this condescending feeling towards people in the past, the feeling that we're rational but they weren't – and the idea that human actions always arise from conscious causes'. People, ourselves included, have always been driven by partly unconscious motives, Roper avers, and one of the jobs of the historian is to try to dig into these deeper strata.

Roper sees important implications in her work for our own troubled times, too. Our basic psychological makeup may not have changed. Yet there has been a clear shift, she says, in our collective consciousness over the centuries. We don't demonize witches nowadays, nor do many women suffer from the kind of hysteria Freud identified in his patients. Today, we worry about new forms of 'mass hysteria', debate the best ways of enabling women to reconcile the competing pressures of motherhood and work – and seem far more concerned than our predecessors with fears and fantasies about the sexuality of children. Roper, acknowledging that there have been both gains and losses, wants to find out how and why such shifts occur. In addition, she is concerned to tie such psychological changes to alterations in the lived, physical experience that occurred in parallel – particularly to those of birthing and motherhood. Herself a mother of a five-year-old, Lyndal Roper is struggling to achieve a synthesis of these themes in a book tentatively entitled *The End of Fertility*.

The new book (much of which is already in draft) will examine the way society views women especially those beyond the years of fertility – in seventeenth-century Germany as, by implication, in our own time and place. As Roper says, we seem to live in an age that clings on to the appearance of female youthfulness, an era of HRT, fertility drugs and seductive images of 45-year-old Cherie Blair with her new-born baby (not to mention the 68-year-old Joan Collins parading in bra and panties). Women

are highly valued, it would appear, for as long as they can
retain the trappings of fertility. An 'old woman', in popular
parlance, is a gasbag, a fusspot, somebody who suffers from (or
clogs up) hospital queues. Was this always so? What roles have
been assigned in the past to 'old' (that is, post-menopausal)
women, and what are the nature of the fantasies projected onto
them? How far do these preoccupations correlate with wider
demographic trends and anxieties?

Roper's new book will range across southern Germany,
its themes reaching from cannibalistic witches to sex with
the Devil – who, by the way, often appears as a sexy young
man dressed in such beguiling clothes as red velvet doublet
and hose and a plumed hat. Roper says she wants readers
to know what it felt like to be a witch. What these women
confessed, she argues, can offer us a window into women's
fantasies. Furthermore, since confessions were the outcome
of an interaction between interrogator and victim, they can
illuminate collective psychology. At the same time, Roper
emphasizes, a witch's confession is always full of surprises
which offer tantalizing glimpses of individual subjectivities.

Witch-hunting was not mere women-hunting; after all, men,
too, were accused of witchcraft. But Roper finds in trial records
a deep seam of hatred towards women, particularly older
women. Early Modern society, she says, was keenly concerned
about fertility – human fertility and that of animals and crops –
which the witch was out to destroy. What more powerful image
of these fears could there be than that of an old, sterile woman,
in sexual league with the Devil, killing and roasting babies,
rendering men impotent, laming animals and destroying crops?
This demonization of older women, and the corresponding
idealization of the young, fertile wife, were particularly
common, Roper finds, during and after the recurrent plague,
warfare and dearth of the Thirty Years' War.

Thus Roper argues that motherhood and fears about fertility,
far from being a quaint by-way of sixteenth- and seventeenth-

century German social history, lay at its core. Too much recent history, she feels, has described people as though they were simply 'heads spouting discourses'. Roper aims to bring back the body – and by that she means real bodies, not writings about the body, but the physical facts of birth, lactation, ageing – and to link it to the history of psychology. Body and mind aren't separate, she says pointedly. We have to consider both, and the links between them, if we are truly to understand the life of our predecessors.

Roper is one of those historians who loves opening up new archives ('It's like an Aladdin's cave!'), discovering new material, trying new hypotheses, debating new issues. Some of the ideas in the new book have already been let off a limited leash in seminar or conference papers or as articles; she is clearly at home in the dialogue and dialectic such work involves (her writings are replete with generous acknowledgements to friends and colleagues). Roper has been a frequent contributor to, and sometime editor of, *Past and Present* and *History Workshop Journal*. A recent *P&P* article concerned child witches; the spring 2000 edition of *HWJ* was devoted to psychoanalysis and dreams and began with an editorial by Roper and Daniel Pick emphasizing the centrality of the body to the ego. Meanwhile, the new book (Roper promises) is nearing completion. But for the time being, the cauldron simmers away as this most engaging of witch-hunters strives to produce the perfect brew – one in which the two Ropers will become one.

EPILOGUE

Lyndal Roper writes:

When I gave this interview, I was in the middle of writing *Witch Craze*, and unsure what the final shape of the book would be. The book took 14 years to write, partly because I had a baby during that time; and partly because of the contrary pulls in my intellectual interests, the 'two Lyndal Ropers', as

Daniel termed it. *Witch Craze* was deeply influenced by my experience of becoming a mother. Watching my son as a baby made me even more sceptical about the claims historians make about the primacy of discourse, and also convinced me that it's impossible to write the history of women – or indeed of society – without thinking about motherhood.

The way I use psychoanalytic ideas in my work has changed quite a bit since this interview. Originally, I had been interested in the subjectivity of individuals accused of being witches, the area in which Freud himself had contributed one of the most significant studies in his account of the possessed painter Christoph Haitzmann. What fascinated me was the relationship between the interrogator and the witch. I wanted to know why it was so often older women who were accused of witchcraft. Psychoanalysis is a method that works best for individuals; and so *Witch Craze* is full of stories about individuals – the girl who was accused of poisoning her little stepbrother, stepsister and six children in the orphanage to which she had been packed off by her family; the old woman who appeared naked at night by her window, with a body 'like alabaster'. I wanted to re-create the overwhelming emotions that gripped individuals at the centre of these dramas. I came to think that the witchcraft accusations were not just about the deaths of infants and the early weeks of motherhood, but featured animals and crops; in short, fertility itself. To be a fertile wife with plenty of children was to be honoured and respected. To be an old woman frequently meant poverty, infirmity, and humiliating dependence on the young. Why were old women so hated?

The problem I faced at this point in writing *Witch Craze* was how to go beyond individual dramas and to try to understand why witch-hunting was prevalent in some places at some times, and not others. This meant thinking much more about the social and religious importance of fertility. The unconscious fantasies that lay behind the witch craze made sense in a world where fertility was precarious, death threatened, and the religious struggle between Catholicism and Protestantism nourished the conviction that Satan was at work in the world. In short, we need both psychoanalysis and history. I hope that I've managed to incorporate areas of human experience that often elude the historical record, realms such as fantasy, envy and terror, or the apparently ahistorical sphere of the bond between mother and baby, into an account of why, for a period of over two hundred years in Western Europe, acts of such appalling ferocity could take place against apparently harmless old women.

Christopher Dyer

BIOGRAPHY

Christopher Dyer's father was a builder's foreman and his mother a primary schoolteacher. He was born in 1944 near Stratford-upon-Avon, and was educated at King Edward VI school in that town (1955–62), and went on to gain a BA and PhD at Birmingham University. He wrote his doctoral thesis on the estates of the bishopric of Worcester between 680 and 1540, which was a useful training as it made him think about many of the developments in society in the whole medieval period. The research was especially stimulating as it was supervised by Rodney Hilton. As a schoolboy he began to take part in archaeological excavations, and at university was taught medieval archaeology by Philip Rahtz. He was appointed Assistant Lecturer at the University of Edinburgh in 1967 at an unusually early age, and moved back to Birmingham in 1970 where he was successively Lecturer, Senior Lecturer, Reader and Professor. He was taken briefly out of the routine of teaching and administration in 2000–01 when he gave the Ford Lectures at the University of Oxford, and was appointed to a Visiting Senior Research Fellowship at St John's College, Oxford, 2000–01. He was then emboldened to take on a new permanent post, and became Professor of Regional and Local History at the University of Leicester in 2001.

He has served as an Editor of *Midland History* from 1978 until 1988, and of the *Economic History Review* between 1990 and 1995. He was also General Editor of the Worcestershire Historical Society in 1987–2004. He has always been an active supporter of the societies and groups which promote the study of history and archaeology, and currently belongs to more than 20 of them. Having served as Secretary, Editor and other time-consuming offices in various societies, he now enjoys the less demanding role as President, successively of the Medieval Settlement Research Group; the Society for Medieval Archaeology; the Bristol and Gloucestershire Archaeological Society; and currently of the Agricultural History Society. He is also Chairman of the Dugdale Society (which publishes records relating to Warwickshire) and Chairman of the Records of Social and Economic History committee of the British Academy. He was elected Fellow of the British Academy in 1995. His work is rooted in English localities, but he addresses historical problems which are universal, and this enables him to maintain contacts with historians in continental Europe and the English-speaking world. He has supervised students from the far East, and keeps in touch with Russian historians.

PRINCIPAL PUBLISHED BOOKS

Lords and Peasants in a Changing Society: The Estates of the Bishopric of Worcester, 680–1540 (1980)

Standards of Living in the Later Middle Ages: Social Change in England c1200–1520 (1989)

Everyday Life in Medieval England (1994)

Village, Hamlet and Field: Changing Medieval Settlements in Central England (with C. Lewis and P. Mitchell-Fox) (1997)

Making a Living in the Middle Ages: The People of Britain, 850–1520 (2002)

An Age of Transition? Economy and Society in England in the Later Middle Ages (2005)

PROFILE, May 2002

One of the charming things about Christopher Dyer is that many of his articles and all his major books – including a new

400-page volume just published – have 'life' and 'living' in their titles. Thus, Dyer writes about getting a living, about standards of living and everyday life; about what people in medieval England ate, what they did with their work and leisure time, and how peasants emerged from serfdom to achieve a degree of independence. He is not a subscriber to the old-fashioned 'Merrie England' school of medievalists and is not comfortable with sweeping generalizations. On the contrary, Dyer's careful writing is exhaustively documented and impeccably balanced, constantly returning to the individual instance evinced by the evidence. Yet, within the constraints imposed by the requirements of scholarship, he might be said to document 'Life, Liberty and the Pursuit of Happiness' *avant la lettre*.

It may seem absurd to say of a medievalist that he writes about topics of which he has personal knowledge. But Dyer, who was born to a lower-middle-class family in Stratford-upon-Avon (to 'a long line of carpenters') and active in the Labour Party when a young man, has always been attracted to the study of the Midlands, of small towns, of individual economic survival at the local level. In addition to the written records familiar to all medievalists, Dyer found himself drawn to anything that would get him closer to the experience of life in Britain 1,000 years ago, such as landscape history, aerial photography and archaeology. He went on his first archaeological dig at the age of twelve; and today, 45 years later, he still gets out whenever he can, loves the camaraderie that develops around an archaeological site and is a good friend of TV's *Time Team*.

In the mid-1960s, Dyer went up to the University of Birmingham to read History. Here he soon came under the influence of Rodney Hilton and found himself at the core of an intellectual revolution. Hitherto, medieval history had tended to concentrate on those who had owned property and had left written records: royalty, lords, knights, clergy, lawyers. The poor, the peasantry, the criminal and vagabond classes and the rest were usually regarded as a large undifferentiated group more acted upon than acting, the victims rather than the protagonists of history, even by such leading and innovative medievalists as Michael Postan. Experts on later periods, too, had tended to concentrate on the visible elites who, after all, were easier to research and write about. But now a new generation of historians, motivated in part by a shared political radicalism and influenced by the *Annales* school in France, were beginning to emphasize economic and social history and, by delving into new kinds of source material, to retrieve 'the people' for the historical record. Among the pioneers were Christopher Hill on seventeenth-century Britain, Edward Thompson on the eighteenth century and Raphael Samuel on the nineteenth. In this quasi-Marxist historiographical revolution, the leading medievalist was Rodney Hilton.

At Birmingham under Hilton's tutelage, Christopher Dyer soon found his *métier*, learning to apply the new insights of economic history to the minutiae of individual (often 'ordinary') lives in specific locations. But he also learned to combine this worm's-eye view with that of the high-flying bird. Going on to do a PhD under Hilton, Dyer chose to research the Estates of the Bishops of Worcester. A straightforward enough topic, you might think – until you note the astonishingly wide terminal dates: 680–1540, a span of nearly 900 years. No wonder it took him close on a decade to complete!

After a few years lecturing at the University of Edinburgh (teaching survey courses which, he recalls, had to cover 'Alfred to Attlee'), while also trying to concentrate on his doctoral research, Dyer returned to Birmingham in 1970. Here he stayed for a further 30 years, becoming Professor of Medieval Social History in 1990 and head of the Medieval History department a couple of years later. In 2001, he exchanged the West Midlands for the East, accepting an appointment as professor at the University of Leicester's Centre for English Local History.

Yet if Dyer remains rooted close to the heartland of his youth, he is also a frequent flyer. His conference papers have been published in the United States of America, Canada and most of the countries of Western Europe, as well as in a score of British scholarly journals. You can read him in French on medieval diet, in Italian on leisure among the peasantry, in Russian on the rise of the yeoman, in Flemish and German on the decline of the village. Dyer's *Niveles de vida en la baja edad media* is available in all good Spanish bookshops.

It was with this book – *Standards of Living in the Later Middle Ages* – that Dyer announced himself as an important new historical voice. First published in 1989 by Cambridge University Press and recently revised and updated, the book is marketed as a textbook and is widely used by American MA courses (for which the Dyer household remains grateful). But it is far more than that. Behind its bland title and its formal mien, Dyer's *Standards of Living* contains a little bombshell. The first clue is in the table of contents. After a chapter on 'Aristocratic Incomes' comes one on 'The Aristocracy as Consumers'; and, more remarkably, a chapter on peasant living standards is followed by one on 'Peasants as Consumers'. Peasants as consumers? This is a topic which reveals the central thrust of a great deal of Dyer's research. 'All too often,' he complains in a telling phrase, 'agriculture is seen as a matter of cultivation and productivity, and the end products of bread, porridge, ale and fodder are forgotten.'

There is plenty of food and drink in *Standards of Living*. Thus, we read of the aristocratic predilection for white bread, which necessitated milling off a sizeable proportion of the grain; the resulting bran was fed to the animals – often in the form of specially baked horsebread. Analysis of animal bones found in excavated villages provides data suggesting the amounts of mutton, pork and game consumed. Ale was usually brewed in the lord's household, utilizing barley malt, though malted wheat or even oats are recorded. Beer, a continental

CHRISTOPHER DYER   159

invention using hops, appeared in England in the fifteenth
century. Peasants, through maintenance agreements with their
lords, sometimes had the right to cultivate small gardens, thus
providing themselves with onions, leeks, garlic and cabbages,
as well as apples and pears.

Dyer writes, too, of housing, of fuel (more available after
the Black Death because of the dearth of consumers), of
clothing (shorter and tighter after the 1340s, to the dismay,
or even consternation, of old-fashioned moralists), of the rise
and temporary decline of cities, and of the key importance of
weather and climate (a rainy summer could sometimes mean
starvation). His writing is packed with details plucked from a
plethora of local studies. But the bird's-eye view is also there.
Hence, while the incomes of the aristocracy rose in and after
the thirteenth century, 'the sources that historians can use to
investigate aristocratic incomes are', he tells us, 'the product
of worried men'. As the aristocracy tottered (and yet somehow
managed to survive), peasants learned to take increasing
control over the decisions that affected their own lives.

The result is not the traditional world of Breughelesque
peasants (or of worried aristocrats) slurping their way across
the thin ice of medieval England. Nor does Dyer paint a lurid
portrait of people morbidly obsessed with the priesthood,
superstition and death, or a romantic elegy for a 'world we
have lost'. All these might make for better entertainment, but
certainly not for better history. Christopher Dyer's vision of
medieval society, rather, is of individual men and women,
caught up in a shifting social structure, primarily concerned
with the fulfilment of practical needs and desires.

Standards of Living has become something of a classic in
its field, staking out territory that Dyer has occupied and
expanded ever since. In a collection of essays entitled *Everyday
Life in Medieval England*, we find him writing about housing
and settlements, food and drink, wages and earnings. Again,
the striking thing is Dyer's emphasis not on what people were

obliged to consume but on what they chose to eat. Similarly, he highlights the growing capacity of people in the lower orders to take initiatives. To Dyer, faithful to the socialism of his youth, it is simply false history to regard the peasants, particularly in Later Medieval times, as having been merely the passive recipients, or victims, of other people's decisions and actions.

In his quest to explain the dynamics of social change, Dyer emphatically rejects determinist interpretations of history, including the Marxist view that what happened to people was largely the product of impersonal economic forces over which they had no personal control. Nor is he much attracted to Marxist phraseology, showing how the supposed 'transition from feudalism to capitalism' in late medieval England, for example, fails to take account of the continued survival of lordship or the non-emergence of a genuine wage-based proletariat.

Historicism of any kind is anathema to Christopher Dyer, a man clearly more at home with specific instances and individual free will. Thus, the peasants' lot may have improved after the Black Death. But it is simplistic, he insists, to regard this as merely the product of a more favourable ratio of people to resources. Similarly, he argues that the Peasants' Revolt was far from an inevitable concomitant of the arrival of a money economy. Did a strong state promote economic growth in the tenth century, and did high population before the Black Death lead to land hunger in the early fourteenth? Yes, for many people in many parts of the country, Dyer acknowledges. But just as important is the way in which hundreds of thousands – indeed millions – of individual people learned to adapt to changing circumstances and struggled, with varying success, to turn them to their personal or local advantage.

This is a theme to which Dyer returns in his latest book, *Making a Living in the Middle Ages*, a work of immense ambition and erudition. For the first time, Christopher Dyer attempts to cover not only England but the whole of Britain, a vastly more complex enterprise for a medievalist. And, as if to ratchet up the challenge still further, he has chosen terminal dates nearly seven centuries apart (850–1520). Why begin so early?

Originally, Dyer had been asked to start in 1066, but he had sound reasons for insisting on an earlier date. 'The Norman Conquest had virtually no economic significance', he told me emphatically. 'It was purely a political change. The various economic and social institutions you find in Domesday Book and thereafter – the towns, villages, fields, big church estates and the basic social structure – all these can be traced back to their origins in the ninth and tenth centuries.' People tend to think of the traditional English village as having been there since earliest recorded times, he continued; but all the latest research suggests that, around 850, most people were living on scattered farmsteads or hamlets on different sites from the ones that are now inhabited. Yet two centuries later, the pattern of village habitation that prevails to this day was well established. Hence this was the process with which the book had to start. And it was much the same with the towns. 'If you were to name the top twenty towns on the eve of the Industrial Revolution, they would mostly be towns formed in the tenth century.'

The broad themes in *Making a Living* are those you would expect: rapid urbanization in the twelfth and thirteenth centuries, social crisis around the period of the Black Death followed by economic growth. But, as in so much of Dyer's writing, the spotlight falls not on the great events, places, institutions or magnates. Rather, he concentrates on the experience of individual people, especially perhaps the peasants, and on life in small towns. The two were inextricably linked. 'The story of English rural society', he says, 'is in outline the story of how peasants became farmers, something that only became feasible as peasants came to have access to markets. Most didn't live near the few big cities. So the gradual transition of countless small towns – places like Northallerton or Henley-upon-Thames – into fully-fledged marketplaces was absolutely pivotal. This is what provided the engine that drove the transition from the medieval economy to the modern.'

For 30 years, Dyer has been steadily expanding his remit, first from Worcester to England and then from England to the whole of Britain; and in addition his writing is sprinkled with periodic references to the conclusions of his French and German counterparts. Dyer likes to regard his work as part of a wider continuum, with important points of comparison with developments on the continent – until the mid-fifteenth century, at least, when England, with its low population and high sense of economic enterprise, 'takes off'.

He is also aware of parallels between medieval life and the struggle for modernization undertaken in parts of the Third World. But Dyer cautions against taking such analogies too literally. 'When I started out,' he says, 'it was almost an article of faith that thirteenth-century England was like nineteenth-century India.' But he cites recent research, derived from the newly fashionable emphasis on cultural history, that has highlighted the differences – between (for example) the family structure, gender relations and religious rituals of the two societies. Dyer, clearly, is not a man to ride off and tilt vainly at vast but impregnable intellectual windmills.

His instincts, rather, have been to till familiar soil. His next book, based on the Ford Lectures delivered in Oxford last year, will examine the well-trodden issue of the transition from the 'medieval' to the 'modern'. Furthermore Dyer continues to pursue his interest in local history, in landscape history and in archaeology. Thus, he has a pair of research fellows currently examining the borders of Buckinghamshire and Northamptonshire – a programme that requires them, with their professor in tow (in the best Rodney Hilton tradition), to spend part of the summer digging in pursuit of the origins of the English village. But don't let Christopher Dyer's (literally) down-to-earth approach mislead you. He is not a man given to great rhetorical flourishes. On the other hand, Dyer is driven by a passionate commitment – to the people and places of our shared past. An indication of his lifelong credo can be found at the end of his recently published *Making a Living in the Middle Ages*. It is a moving 'Fanfare for the Common Man'. We should never forget, he concludes,

> that the medieval world developed in the way that it did because Wulfhelm developed his goldsmith's craft in a new urban environment; Stephen de Fretwell mismanaged his affairs and went bankrupt; Robert Broun cleared new land; Nicholas Symond the spurrier demanded higher wages and Thomas Vicars managed his farm in the most profitable fashion.

These individuals, says Dyer, may have had little impact on their own. But they nevertheless are vital agents in Britain's historical story. It was the accumulated actions of real people such as these that created the transition from the medieval world of our ancestors to the modern world we ourselves now inhabit.

EPILOGUE

Christopher Dyer writes:

The book based on my Ford Lectures, *An Age of Transition?*, has now been published. I appreciated Daniel Snowman's insights into my writing, and the warmth of his response to my work. He emphasized my concern for individuals and specific examples. I regard the experience of individual people and communities as important and worth recording, and I believe that for most readers concrete examples and specific episodes make the past more interesting and immediate. But the details are never included for their own sake – there is always an underlying purpose. I am addressing the big questions in history – the origins of feudalism and capitalism, the interaction of social groups and classes, the identification of the agents behind change, the role of environment in human history, and the reasons for the differences between regions and countries. My next project is a book about a Cotswold wool merchant, John Heritage, who lived at the beginning of the sixteenth century. It will be concerned with the many people with whom he did business, and with the places where he bought wool. But the reason for the detail is to understand the dynamics of a society, economy and landscape at a crucial stage in the emergence of the modern world.

Peter Stansky

BIOGRAPHY

Peter Stansky is the Frances and Charles Field Professor of History, Emeritus at Stanford University. He was born in New York City in 1932 and educated at Yale College, King's College, Cambridge, and Harvard University. He first taught at Harvard and then came to Stanford in 1968. He is now officially retired, but will be teaching half time for several more years. He has held various fellowships, including visiting ones to All Souls College and St Catherine's College in Oxford. He is a member of the American Academy of Arts and Sciences and the Royal Historical Society. He has been on the Boards of academic journals and was President of the North American Conference on British Studies. He has edited several series, written numerous articles and reviews, and given lectures in the United States, Britain, Germany and Australia. He is particularly proud of all of his PhD students, quite a few of whom have made important contributions to the field of modern British history.

PRINCIPAL PUBLISHED BOOKS

Ambitions and Strategies: The Struggle for the Leadership of the Liberal Party in the 1890s (1964)

Journey to the Frontier: Julian Bell and John Cornford: Their Lives and the 1930s (with William Abrahams) (1966)

The Unknown Orwell (with William Abrahams) (1972)

England Since 1867: Continuity and Change (1973)

Gladstone: A Progress in Politics (1979)

Orwell: The Transformation (with William Abrahams) (1979)

William Morris (1983)

Redesigning the World (1985)

London's Burning (with William Abrahams) (1994)

On or About December 1910: Early Bloomsbury and its Intimate World (1996)

From William Morris to Sergeant Pepper (1999)

Sassoon: The Worlds of Philip and Sybil (2003)

PROFILE, July 2002

> 'It is a truth universally admitted that we all speak badly of others, even of those of whom we may in fact be quite fond.'

You have to warm to a historian who is prepared to embed such a sentiment in the midst of a learned treatise about the Bloomsbury Group. But Peter Stansky's writing, like his conversation, is full of colour, personality, flair and the Higher Gossip. Professor of History at Stanford for over 30 years, Stansky's own educational credentials include degrees from Yale, Cambridge and Harvard. At 70, he can look back on a stream of articles and books, many written in close collaboration with the late William ('Billy') Abrahams, on some of the seminal figures in British political and cultural history from the mid-nineteenth century to the mid-twentieth: Gladstone, William Morris, the 'Bloomsburyites', George Orwell, Henry Moore, Benjamin Britten.

The elite writing about the elite? Old-fashioned American Anglophilia? On the face of it, perhaps. But there are engagingly troublesome undercurrents to much of Stansky's writing. Again and again he portrays formidably endowed characters struggling to encapsulate and communicate what they believed to be the feelings of those less privileged than themselves. He writes, in addition, of people who, by crossing conventional intellectual boundaries, were obstinately hard to label. Stansky's *dramatis personae* tend to be celebrated 'insiders' much admired by contemporaries but who, deep down, nevertheless retained a sense of being 'outsiders'.

Thus, Stansky's Gladstone was a Scot of English lineage, born to a mercantile family but pushed into a patrician education, who lived as a Welsh landowner and whose final mission, doomed to failure, was to pacify Ireland. Morris, a multi-talented genius who, like Gladstone (but unlike most people), became more radical the longer he lived, crossed every boundary between art, literature and politics. Eric Blair, a son of Anglo-India and Eton, became obsessed by the evils of poverty, modified his identity and adopted the nom de plume George Orwell. E.M. Forster and Benjamin Britten canalised their homosexuality into works of art that celebrated the social outsider. Stansky's next book is about a wealthy and flamboyant pillar of interwar British society who seems to have felt excluded from the nation's highest councils because of his (albeit non-observant) Jewishness.

Peter Stansky's grandparents were Eastern European Jewish immigrants who came to New York in the late nineteenth century. His father, the first member of the family to go to college, became a lawyer, specializing in art and the art market – an interest that clearly influenced both Stansky and his sister, the art critic Marina Vaizey.

What led Peter to history? He recalls being drawn as an adolescent to a recording of the songs the International Brigade had sung in Spain just a few years before. As a Yale undergraduate in the early 1950s, he began to study history seriously, writing papers on John Cornford and Julian Bell, two of the literary *jeunesse dorée* who participated and died in the Spanish Civil War, and two who survived their Spanish forays, Stephen Spender and George Orwell. Already, Stansky was crossing conventional boundaries between 'history' and 'literature' – and, moreover, writing at the height of McCarthyism, about heroes of the political left. McCarthyism and its progenitor were soon dead. But Stansky had alighted upon what was to prove a lifetime's interest.

At King's College, Cambridge, he did a second BA, learning more about Bloomsbury from Noel Annan and E.M. Forster and of wider aspects of history from John Saltmarsh, Eric Hobsbawm and Christopher Morris (whose wife Helen had once been Julian Bell's lover). This was followed by a Harvard PhD, with a dissertation on the post-Gladstonian Liberal Party. While working on this, Stansky teamed up with the novelist, poet and editor William Abrahams. Their first joint enterprise, an article about the problems of finding a successor to Tennyson as Poet Laureate, cross-fertilized Abrahams' literary sensibility with Stansky's newly acquired expertise on late Victorian politics. The result was published, in *History Today*, in October 1961. Three years later, Stansky's thesis on the struggle for the leadership of the Liberal Party in the 1890s became his first book. But only just. It seems that Robert Rhodes James, writing his biography of Rosebery at the time, consulted the thesis with Stansky's enthusiastic agreement – and then made so much use of his research as to render the dissertation almost unpublishable.

Once the doctorate and book were safely behind him, Stansky settled down to the life of a history instructor at Harvard University. Before long, he and Billy Abrahams set to work on what was intended to be a vast work on four 'poets' of the Spanish Civil War (originally planned to include a work on Spender). *Journey to the Frontier*, about Julian Bell and John Cornford, appeared in 1966. Then, in the 1970s, by which time they were based in California with Stansky teaching at Stanford, they produced two volumes: *The Unknown Orwell* (1972) and *Orwell: The Transformation* (1979), the second culminating in Orwell's experiences in the Spanish Civil War. Orwell, unlike Bell and Cornford, was not killed in Spain. Yet he returned to England seriously injured, not only physically but also intellectually as, disillusioned with the dissimulation of the Communists, he embraced socialism while being forced to reassess its nature. The result was *Homage to Catalonia* and a succession of literary-political masterpieces. It was the experience of Spain, argue Stansky and Abrahams, that ultimately transformed Blair into Orwell.

From his base at Stanford, Stansky rapidly built a formidable reputation as a leading scholar of British intellectual and political history, training graduate students, speaking at conferences, editing anthologies, publishing a plethora of original articles and reviews and being invited to sit on countless boards, juries and steering committees. For some years, Stansky was Head of the History Department at Stanford. None of this, however, staunched the flow of books.

In 1979 came a short but strikingly original life of Gladstone in which Stansky used as his core material the texts of some of Gladstone's most important parliamentary speeches. From these, he built up a broadly chronological biography in which each chapter also concentrated on one of the great themes of Gladstone's life such as Religion, Foreign Policy, Finance and Ireland. Gladstone was by repute one of the most powerful orators of the nineteenth century, and it is breathtaking to read his rhetoric at some length. Stansky's brief but pithy biography of William Morris (1983), similarly, is peppered with quotations – not so much from speeches but from an array of poetry, letters, his novel *News from Nowhere*, and variegated political and aesthetic manifestos and writings.

The Morris biography was a by-product of work Stansky was doing for a book, splendidly entitled *Redesigning the World* (1985), on some of the institutions that sprang up around Morris dedicated to the idea that, through art and design, one might somehow improve society – the Century Guild, the Arts and Crafts Exhibition Society, the National Association for Art and Industry and the rest. Nobody straddled the disciplines as dazzlingly as Morris, a man whose late Victorian idealism led through to the Bauhaus and beyond and who, Stansky argues, has much to say to our own times. Morris was one of the first to link the values of the past to the industrial techniques of the future – and to warn against the overweening powers of the state. The way to transform society, thought Morris, was to begin in the home. Small could be beautiful, traditional and also mass-produced. Yet for all the radicalism of Gladstone and Morris, says Stansky, they remained surprisingly respectable figures. There was something incurably domesticated, too, about even the most rebellious or louche members of the Bloomsbury group, while no couple was more bourgeois than Benjamin Britten and Peter Pears.

Stansky has been repeatedly struck, in fact, by the extraordinary respectability of England's would-be revolutionaries – a tendency that continues. He recounts a revealing incident as he left London's Roundhouse a few years ago and found himself walking into the midst of a political protest. An angry and militant young woman thrust a mimeographed sheet into his hands, shouting 'Fascist Pig!' When Stansky pointed out that the sheet was blank and had not printed properly, her tone completely altered. 'I'm so sorry', she said in cultured tones, as she politely offered him another. There will never be a revolution in this country, Stansky thought to himself, with both resignation and admiration, as he left.

This is a theme he has chronicled from the early nineteenth century to the middle of the twentieth. In *London's Burning* (1994), he and Abrahams wrote about British art and artists during World War II, concentrating in particular on three outstanding figures: Henry Moore and his drawings of the Underground shelters; the documentary film-maker Humphrey Jennings, director of *Fires Were Started*; and Benjamin Britten and the creation of *Peter Grimes*. Each artist, in his own way, tried to encapsulate the anxieties of ordinary people under extreme pressure; yet each was also concerned to portray a sense of stiff-upper-lip resignation in the face of apparently insuperable odds. Nor was this art itself truly revolutionary.

For all their undoubted genius, Britten and Moore, like Forster
or even Virginia Woolf, were essentially working within an
accepted idiom – at least as compared with the real radicalism
emanating from the continent.

In late 1910, Roger Fry assembled an exhibition of 'Post-
Impressionists' in London, an event that Virginia Woolf
evidently had in mind when she later recalled that 'on or about
December 1910' human character changed. Stansky, in a book
using Woolf's phrase as its title, takes the exhibition as his
focus for an exploration not only of early Bloomsbury but also
of British art and intellectual life at the time. These were the
years of early European Modernism, of Picasso's *Demoiselles
d'Avignon* and Stravinsky's *Sacre du Printemps*. Modernism
may have entered British cultural life via the conduit of
Bloomsbury, Stansky acknowledges, but it was much modified
and even neutralized in the process. In England, even the most
radical artists tend to be middle-class figures, more concerned
with how to come to terms with society than with transforming
it. But did not Lytton Strachey and Virginia Woolf mock British
pretensions? Yes, he admits – but they were able to do so out
of a sense of security which they obtained from their place in
a social (and class) system they never challenged. 'England',
writes Stansky:

> … seems incapable of producing a genuine avant-garde – revolt
> itself is domesticated, or is presented in domesticated forms. One
> might argue that the great strength and weakness of England is
> the domestication of the extreme.

'Reform from within', says Stansky, has always been the English
way; radicals are regularly co-opted and nowadays given life
peerages. An incurable and affectionate Anglophile, with
dashes of Anglophobia, he says that the British seem to regard
the legacy of their past like a much-loved old sock: so often
darned over the years that by now it retains little of the original
– yet no one is prepared to jettison it for something better.

The 'Radical Domestic', a phrase borrowed from the art historian Christopher Reed, sums up Stansky's view of many of the great figures of the British political, literary and artistic past, and he adopts it as the subtitle of an anthology of his essays (*From William Morris to Sergeant Pepper*) published in 1999. The volume contains engaging visits to old friends – Morris, various Bloomsburyites, Orwell & Co. – as well as encounters with Nancy Astor, Oswald Mosley, Chaim Weizmann, Isaiah Berlin and the Beatles. Virtually all, in their very different ways, were domesticated radicals, tigers (or rottweilers) housetrained by English respectability.

From William Morris to Sergeant Pepper is Stansky's first book to appear since the death, in 1998, of Billy Abrahams, to whom it is dedicated. Some of the essays have a faintly valedictory feel to them, as when Stansky sums up how he came to be drawn to his kind of intellectual history-cum-biography, and why he has left more theoretically based approaches to others. But this is not so of all of them. Towards the end of this collection he has a group of pieces in which he considers how far it has been possible to be both Jewish and English – the subject of a forthcoming book.

In his new work, as in so many of his past publications, Stansky will look at powerful, influential figures on the edges of the British establishment who remained, or were kept – or maybe simply felt – subtly outside its top ranks. This time, the insider-outsiders are Philip Sassoon and his sister Sybil (cousins of the poet Siegfried). The Sassoons were a distinguished Anglo-Jewish family with exotic roots going back to India and Mesopotamia (Iraq).

Sir Philip Sassoon (1888–1939), educated at Eton and at Christ Church, Oxford, was a minor politician who became General Haig's Secretary during World War I, Parliamentary Secretary to Lloyd George, then the Tories' Under-Secretary of State for Air and, finally, Commissioner of Works in 1937–39. A wealthy connoisseur of the arts and artists, Philip threw lavish parties for the famous and fashionable in his Park Lane mansion (later demolished to make way for the Playboy Club) and his home at Trent Park (now part of Middlesex University). At his summer residence at Port Lympne, near his constituency of Hythe (now preserved as one of John Aspinall's Zoos), Sassoon would entertain the Prince of Wales and the Duke of York, Bernard Shaw, T.E. Lawrence, Lloyd George and Charlie Chaplin. Churchill, a frequent guest, often relaxed there with his easel and paints, while Rex Whistler contributed decorative murals.

As for Sybil, she became the Marchioness of Cholmondeley (and chatelaine of the Walpole mansion in Norfolk, Houghton Hall). Renowned as an automobile connoisseur and muse to numerous painters, poets and musicians, she lived on into her mid-nineties.

Did Philip and Sybil become fully accepted in the top echelons of 'society'? If so, what sort of accommodations were made, on either side? 'We really don't have a Jewish problem in England', says an old Salisbury-type Tory peer whom Stansky quotes in one of his essays. 'They're not really Jewish here in England, the Jews.' And then the old buffer adds: 'Of course, they're not really English either.'

How English were the Sassoons? How English did they want to be? How far was their Englishness compatible with their Jewishness? Today, it is fashionable to assert pride in having a multiple identity, in flaunting 'ethnicity'. But in the 1920s and 1930s?

The Sassoons were insider-outsiders writ large. They thus provide a perfect mix of so many of the themes that have intrigued Peter Stansky, and enlivened his writings, for 40 years. 'Being English' is the tentative title of the new book. I hope he sticks to it, with its gently enigmatic suggestion that 'being British' was something that people – even those very near the top of the pile – always felt that they had to work at. In a way, the phrase could stand for Stansky's entire *oeuvre*.

EPILOGUE

Peter Stansky writes:

Peter Stansky's study of Philip and Sybil Sassoon appeared in April 2003 as *Sassoon: The Worlds of Philip and Sybil.* Since then he has been at work on a short study of the first day of the London Blitz, 7 September 1940, which he hopes will be published shortly. After that, he is considering returning to the subject of Julian Bell as so much more material has become available since his and William Abrahams' *Journey to the Frontier* was published in 1966. In it, in the spirit of the present interview, he may incorporate appropriate autobiographical aspects of the many years he has spent in the Anglo-American world.

Natalie Zemon Davis

BIOGRAPHY

Natalie Zemon Davis was born in Detroit, Michigan in 1928 and after high school years at Kingswood School Cranbrook, attended Smith College for her BA (1949). There she did her Senior thesis on the rationalist Renaissance philosopher Pietro Pomponazzi, was active in 'progressive' student politics, wrote college songs, and met and married her husband, the mathematician Chandler Davis. She received her MA in history from Radcliffe College, Harvard in 1950, and then followed her husband to the University of Michigan, from which she received her PhD in 1959.

While writing her dissertation on 'Protestantism and the Printing Workers of Lyon: A Study in Religion and Social Class', she also gave birth to three children. She has taught at Brown University, York University (Toronto), the University of Toronto (1963–71, first in Political Economy and then in History), the University of California at Berkeley (1972–77), and Princeton University (1978–96), where she became the Henry Charles Lea Professor of History and in 1990 succeeded Lawrence Stone for four years as the Director of the Shelby Cullom Davis Center for Historical Studies.

She has held several posts as a visitor, including in 1994–95 as the Eastman Professor at Balliol College, Oxford. She is currently Professor Emerita from Princeton and associated with the University of Toronto as Adjunct Professor of History and Anthropology, Professor of Medieval Studies, and Senior Fellow in Comparative Literature.

Over the years she has taught courses in Early Modern European social and cultural history, Early Modern France, the history of women and gender (at Toronto, Berkeley and Princeton she helped found programmes in the study of women), Jewish history in the Early Modern period, and history and film. Partly inspired by her role as historical consultant for the film *Le Retour de Martin Guerre* (1982), she became interested in integrating anthropological and literary approaches into those derived from social history. In her books and articles, she has been especially concerned to get at the lives and values of artisans, peasants, and women, and to analyse their reaction to other social groups, and to power, property and authority.

Among other editorial and professional activities, she has served as President of the American Historical Association (1987) and as Vice-President of the International Commission of Historical Sciences (1995–2000). Thinking of her own world and that in which her grandchildren will become adults, she has continued her engagement with politics and the antiwar movement, if not quite with the same hopes that she had in her student days.

PRINCIPAL PUBLISHED BOOKS

Society and Culture in Early Modern France (1975)

The Return of Martin Guerre (1983)

Fiction in the Archives: Pardon Tales and their Tellers in Sixteenth-Century France (1988)

Women on the Margins: Three Seventeenth-Century Lives (1995)

Slaves on Screen: Film and Historical Vision (2000)

The Gift in Sixteenth-Century France (2000)

L'histoire tout feu tout flame: Entretiens avec Denis Crouzet (2004)

Trickster Travels: A Sixteenth-Century Muslim Between Worlds (2006)

PROFILE, October 2002

What is history? What is it about and how should it be portrayed? Such questions are much in the air these days. But few have examined them more consistently and imaginatively than Natalie Zemon Davis.

Widely revered as (variously) a leading historian of Early Modern France, a left-leaning intellectual who helped pioneer the shift from social to cultural history, and one of the great iconic figures of feminist history, Natalie Davis is not 'simply' any of these. The sheer versatility of her skills, and her capacity to incorporate multiple meanings, defy simplistic labelling. Like a jeweller turning a diamond this way and that in different lights, Davis insists on the multivalent meanings of the historical record. If you come across (say) an early edition of the essays of Montaigne, she insists, check not only its contents but how and by whom it was printed and bound, who bought it from whom and who gave it to whom, what the inscription says and what the handwriting is like, and which pages are particularly frayed. You may not have hard and fast evidence to answer all the questions that arise; but, given all the other things you know – be brave, use your imagination. 'What I offer you here is in part my invention,' Davis acknowledges in the introduction to her most famous book, *The Return of Martin Guerre*, 'but held tightly in check by the voices of the past.'

Martin Guerre was a sixteenth-century French peasant who deserted his wife and family to become a soldier of fortune. A few years later 'Martin' returned from the wars and took up again with his wife – until the 'real' Martin returned and the man living in his place was tried and executed as an impostor. Davis was consultant to the film (starring Gérard Depardieu), and her ground-breaking book, first published in 1983, has been translated into some 20 languages. Meanwhile, the Martin Guerre story has ridden off into all sorts of new directions, among them the film *Sommersby* and a musical version.

Evidently, Davis had touched upon a story with profound reverberations for our own times. And not only in Martin Guerre. Impostorship, uncertain identity, multiple portrayals: these themes run throughout her work.

Their roots go back to her childhood. Born to a prosperous, liberal-leaning Jewish family in Detroit in 1928, Natalie Zemon grew up straddling different worlds. An all-American girl, she became increasingly conscious of her European ancestry. Attending a private girls' high school, she'd go to Christian chapel but cross her fingers lest her Old Testament God be angry with her. As a politically active undergraduate at Smith College after the war, she gravitated towards the radical 'Progressivism' of Henry Wallace just as the national mood was swinging towards the anti-Communist Right. A History major, she loved reading European (especially French) literature, thought about working in film – and went to a Harvard summer school to study the philosophy of science.

In general, Natalie thrived as she bridged her disparate worlds. But the foothold faltered. At Harvard, she met and married a young (non-Jewish) mathematician, Chandler Davis, receiving opprobrium, especially from her mother, for marrying 'out', while the political radicalism she and Chandler shared brought the young couple into conflict with the House Un-American Activities Committee. The HUAC confrontation led to the withdrawal of Natalie's passport, which distressed her deeply as it put a (temporary) end to the PhD research she was undertaking in Lyon. But there were beneficial by-products. Pregnant with her first child, she realized it was perhaps no bad thing, at least temporarily, to forego transatlantic commuting. Also, living in the New York area, she began to encounter some of the incomparable rare book collections on her doorstep.

Davis was a 30-year-old mother of three before she completed her PhD, and she held teaching posts at Brown, York (Toronto), the University of Toronto and at Berkeley before she published her first book. When it came, it was a collection of highly researched and tightly compressed essays (several of them published earlier) under the almost blandly academic title *Society and Culture in Early Modern France*. But it was a debut book with a difference. For between its respectable covers, Natalie Davis concealed a series of little bombshells as, in essay after essay, she contrived to enter the minds of ordinary people, the 'menu peuple', so often left out of the history books. What was it like, she asked, to be a printworker, derided as a 'scold' or accused of a capital crime in small-town France at a time when Reformation ideas were beginning to take hold? How did the wider processes of history interact with the personal and the individual – particularly when the individuals were often illiterate and left little formal documentation?

Here was a historian able to use the insights of anthropology and ethnography – one, moreover, not afraid to speculate when 'proof' was unavailable. But even more striking than her methodological ingenuity were some of her conclusions. In a number of essays, notably one entitled 'Women on Top' (long before the phrase became a cliché), Davis examined ritual occasions when those lower down the social hierarchy were temporarily permitted to subvert the rules and mock their supposed betters. A period of calculated 'Misrule' was a feature of most societies in Early Modern times, and had generally been regarded by historians as a kind of social safety valve – the historical counterpart of Speakers' Corner. What Davis found, especially when examining rituals permitting cross-dressing, was that such occasions could, on the contrary, prompt participants to new ways of thinking about traditional social and sexual hierarchies. Women, far from being on the receiving end of history, had, it seemed, sometimes been able to use such rituals of social engineering to their own betterment. The very subtlety of Davis' message, and the impeccable scholarship with which it was delivered, added to its weight.

Already something of a heroine to feminist intellectuals, Natalie Davis, by now a professor at Princeton, was soon to become one of the most widely read historians of her generation. When she first came across accounts of the Guerre story (notably by Jean de Coras, one of the judges of the court case), she thought: 'This story would make a great movie.' By coincidence, at that very time, the Depardieu film was being set up and Davis was engaged as historical consultant. As she helped the actors (including many from the local population) think themselves into their characters, Davis realized that she was participating in a direct 'dialogue with history', an event that paralleled the one they were all struggling to portray, as members of a tight-knit community began to imagine that they were other than they appeared. Furthermore, as the film-makers inevitably smudged some of the historical detail, Davis decided to write a book on the Guerre story and found herself reflecting further on the nature of historical invention. What is historical truth? Did Martin Guerre's wife Bertrande 'know' for sure that the man with whom she shared her bed was not her husband? If she did – how can we know?

Famously, and controversially, Davis 'invented', that is surmised. On the basis of her intimate knowledge of not only all the historical sources but also the location and its modern-day denizens, she was able to portray, like a novelist, the day-to-day texture of life in Martin's part of France – and then to show how someone like Martin would have 'dreamed of life beyond the confines of fields of millet, of tileworks, properties, and marriages'. Did Martin and the man who later impersonated him ever meet? Probably not. But that does not stop Davis picturing the scene that might have occurred if they had, a device that neatly enables her to pick out some of the detail each might have noticed about the other. As for Bertrande, local lore insisted there is no mistaking 'the touch of the man on the woman', so she must have known that the man she took to be her husband was not Martin. Did she not feel guilty at her complicity? Perhaps. But Davis shows that Protestant ideas were beginning to become fashionable in this part of France so that, while Bertrande doubtless felt guilt, she might not have felt obliged to confess as a sinner. 'It is possible,' Davis concludes, 'even probable, that the new Martin and Bertrande ... were becoming interested in the new religion, in part because they could draw from it another justification for their lives.'

This is breathtaking stuff. But is it history? Not in the narrow Gradgrind sense, perhaps; the 'facts' aren't there in the record. But, as Davis points out, the job of any historian is to examine the available evidence and then to make intelligent and informed conjectures. That means knowing not only all the 'hard' evidence, such as the documents and artefacts people left, but also their psychological processes: their hopes, their fears, and what they understood by words and concepts ('sin', 'adultery', 'lord of the household') that have taken on a different hue over the centuries.

Like a preacher, Davis loves to recount a story, tease out the detail, make inferences and where appropriate incorporate her own experiences and persona into what she has to say. Unlike most preachers, however, she tends to avoid clear-cut conclusions, preferring (relishing, one feels) an element of ambiguity. Thus, *Martin Guerre* ends, not as you might expect with an exegesis about impostorship and historical truth, but with a section on those who first documented the story (among them not only the judge, Coras, but also Montaigne who wrote a contemporary commentary) – each of whom has his own perspective on the story. Davis believes that, by allowing an element of fabrication, or 'creative fiction', into her writing, she has probably come closer to the truth than anyone else who has written about what remains a supremely enigmatic historical episode.

There is an element of storytelling – of 'fiction', indeed – in much of her writing. Her next book was actually entitled

(provocatively you might think) *Fiction in the Archives*. In this
she looked at letters of remission in which people in sixteenth-
century France begged to be pardoned after having been found
guilty of capital crimes. What interested Natalie Davis was
the way such letters would be crafted, shaped, moulded and
sculpted to enable the writer to put the best possible 'spin'
(as we would now say) on the story of the crime. The very
fabrication of such letters, says Davis, provided new insights
into the way people thought at the time. In *Women on the
Margins*, similarly, Davis takes off from stories, in this case the
lives of three seventeenth-century women – one Jewish, one
Catholic and one Protestant – each of whom left a somewhat
'fabricated' record. All three were women of some substance,
yet 'on the margins' in the sense that they crossed boundaries
of geography, politics and culture: the Catholic went out to
New France to bring Christ to the Canadian Indians, while
the artistic and scientific interests of the Protestant took her
as far afield as Suriname.

As Davis pursued her three women hither and yon (and there
is a wonderful sense of place in each of the three narratives),
she sensed herself also traversing new intellectual frontiers.
Here was a book in which the entire cast consisted of women
– a book, moreover, of comparative history that took Davis for
the first time beyond the confines of France. The Jewish woman
was from Hamburg and this required Davis to read documents
in Yiddish, the language of her forebears, and, for the first time
in her life, to spend extended periods in Germany. While Davis
largely lets her characters weave their own tapestries, leaving
us to draw what conclusions we may, there is no mistaking the
intensity of her personal involvement with her subject matter.
Indeed, in an extraordinary prologue, she imagines the women
meeting to discuss the book – and rounding on the author
for what they see as her misrepresentations of them. 'Let me
explain', says Natalie as she steps from the shadows to join
them. 'You have a lot of explaining to do', the women riposte.

If *Guerre* reads at times like a novel, the prologue to *Women on the Margins* reads like a filmscript.

When I first met Natalie Davis some years ago, she talked animatedly about her desire to work again in film. A movie option on *Women on the Margins* was taken up, but nothing materialized. But her next book, *Slaves on Screen*, contained a string of chapters on several famous feature films about slaves, among them the Kirk Douglas movie *Spartacus* (directed by Stanley Kubrick), Gillo Pontecorvo's *Burn*, Steven Spielberg's *Amistad*, and *Beloved*, based on the novel by Toni Morrison (a friend and colleague from Princeton). What, asks Davis, is the nature of the historical 'truth' available to the film-maker? Why should we assume that a conventional history book, in prose form, is necessarily better able to capture and communicate aspects of the past than a partly fictionalized film? Film, by its capacity to reproduce the visual imagery and passions of the past, can tell an ancient story with a *vraisemblance* unavailable to the writer (a theme on which she elaborated in an address to the British Academy earlier this year). Davis is adamant, however, that film-makers, like academic historians, should be honest about their intentions and the nature of their evidence. Thus, she praises Pontecorvo for making it clear that his grainy, documentary-style *The Battle of Algiers* was made with actors and contained no authentic newsreel or documentary footage, while she has no truck with those who, affecting to present history on the screen, distort what they know to be the truth. But within these constraints, Davis believes film 'can be both good cinema and good history'.

I asked Natalie Davis about other historians she admired or who were important influences upon her. She talked warmly of contemporaries, like Emmanuel Le Roy Ladurie and Carlo Ginzburg, who, like her, were among the first to absorb insights from cultural anthropology in their writings on the past. If she has a hero, it would be Marc Bloch, the great French (and Jewish) historian who was executed by the Gestapo, while her most recent book, *The Gift in Sixteenth-Century France*, was partly inspired by the work of another prewar French (Jewish) writer, Marcel Mauss.

The Gift took Davis back to sixteenth-century France and is packed with stories and instances. But, unusually for Davis, the book is highly schematic, structured by concept rather than story. There are sections on the nature of gifts and giving at birth, marriage and death or during the seasons of the year and the Christian calendar, gifts that go wrong (bribes, contested wills, deceptive sales), the power relationships arising from gift giving and receiving, gifts across social boundaries (royal bounty, tips, alms), and gifts to and from God. It is an astonishing book, dense in texture and not always easy to read. But you emerge reflecting that just about every transaction contains an element of emotion-laden giving and receiving.

A brisk and vigorous 73, Davis continues to read and write and think – and talk – with an intensity and energy that would be impressive in a woman half her age. She is now in the early stages of a major new project on 'Cultural Mixture' (the topic of an address at last summer's Anglo-American Conference in London), which will consider the lives of a number of people from earlier centuries who crossed traditional thresholds. The stories are rich and colourful, and Davis held me in thrall, like the Ancient Mariner, as she told me of a Dutch-Scottish soldier in Suriname; a Romanian-Jewish linguist living in Paris – and of a Muslim who was born in Granada shortly before the expulsion of 1492 and raised in Fez who travelled across north Africa, as far south as Timbuctou, across Europe to Istanbul, was kidnapped by Christian pirates, handed to Pope Leo X for baptism and went on to become a writer and teacher in Italy under the name of Johannes Leo Africanus.

As Davis works these stories towards book form, she will doubtless find herself yet again at the vanguard of those whose presentation of the past helps us come to terms with the struggles and preoccupations of our own times – postcolonial guilt, racial prejudice, globalization, Christian–Islam perceptions, immigration and identity politics and the rest. She and I started to talk about these issues, when I suddenly realized there was a more immediate struggle to confront: the dense traffic on the Euston Road. I had promised to run Natalie to the British Library where some rare documents awaited her. My last view of her was of a dynamic, compact figure, her thirst for intellectual adventure clearly unquenched, as she marched towards yet another threshold.

EPILOGUE

Natalie Zemon Davis writes:

In the last few years I've continued a process that began when I wrote *Women in the Margins,* specifically, the sections on the encounters between the Ursuline Marie de l'Incarnation and her Amerindian converts and between the entomologist Maria Sibylla Merian and her African slave informants. I started to resituate myself as a European historian. Trying to understand the world from different positions within Europe – different social, religious, or gender positions – was not enough. I really had to move beyond those boundaries entirely. My current work on cultural crossings tries to do just that. The research on Suriname is still under way; the last few years I have concentrated on the figure known to Europeans as 'Leo Africanus', but whom I soon came to call by the name he had in Granada and Fez, al-Hasan al-Wazzan, or by the name he acquired during his seven years as a Christian in Rome, Giovanni Leone – Yuhanna al-Asad, as he wrote it in Arabic. The book is now finished: *Trickster Travels: A Sixteenth-Century Muslim Between Worlds*. I feel lucky to have had the chance to spend those years learning about Islam in its various forms, North African life, and the many genres of Arabic writing. Trying to see the world through his eyes allowed me to find not only differences between North Africa and Europe, but also analogies, as with the trickster figure. And Yuhanna al-Asad's doubts about would-be world-conquerors, whether Ottoman sultans or Holy Roman emperors, revealed an Islamic sensibility speaking both to his own time and to our own.

Linda Colley

BIOGRAPHY

Linda Colley graduated from Bristol University with First Class Honours in history in 1972 and completed her PhD at Cambridge University five years later. The first female Fellow of Christ's College, Cambridge, she moved to Yale University in 1982. Her first book, *In Defiance of Oligarchy: The Tory Party 1714–1760* (1982), challenged the dominant view by arguing that the Tory Party remained active and potent during their years out of power. *Britons: Forging the Nation, 1707–1837* (1992), which won the Wolfson Prize for History, shows how the inhabitants of England, Scotland, and Wales came to see themselves as British over the course of the eighteenth century. In 1998 Professor Colley left Yale to accept a Senior Leverhulme Research Professorship in History at the London School of Economics. Supported by the award, she spent the next five years researching the experiences of the thousands of Britons who were taken captive in North America, South Asia, and the Mediterranean and north Africa between 1600 and 1850 as the British Empire expanded. *Captives* (2002), the result of this research, uses captivity narratives to investigate the vulnerability of the empire, the complex relations between the imperialists and the societies they sought to invade, and the flexibility of individual identity. She is also the author of *Namier* (1989), a reappraisal of the Polish-born historian Lewis Namier. Professor Colley writes for British and American periodicals and newspapers, including the *Guardian*, *The*

Times, the *New York Times*, the *Times Literary Supplement*, and the *London Review of Books*. In 1999 she delivered the Prime Minister's Millennium Lecture at 10 Downing Street. Among other public lectures, she has delivered the Trevelyan Lectures at Cambridge University (1997), the Wiles Lectures at Queen's University, Belfast (1997), the Ford and Bateman Lectures at Oxford (1999 and 2003), the Nehru Memorial Lecture at the London School of Economics (2003), the Lewis Walpole Memorial Lecture at Yale (2000), and the Carnochan Lecture at Stanford (1998). In 1999 she was elected a Fellow of the British Academy. Professor Colley joined Princeton University in 2003, where she is now the Shelby M.C. Davis 1958 Professor of History.

PRINCIPAL PUBLISHED BOOKS

In Defiance of Oligarchy: The Tory Party 1714–1760 (1982)
Namier (1988)
Britons: Forging the Nation, 1707–1837 (1992)
Captives: Britain, Empire and the World, 1600–1850 (2002)

PROFILE, January 2003

> 'Great historians tend to be called great not because their writings come as a total revelation, but rather because they address and confirm in some way preoccupations that already exist.'

Linda Colley was writing about Sir Lewis Namier, a Polish-Jewish immigrant who, while Britain was undergoing Depression, war and loss of empire, documented the lives of eighteenth-century English landowners in apparently terminal decline. Reading Namier, wrote Colley in 1989, 'is one of the best introductions to this century's insecurity, alienation and angst'. Colley, herself an eighteenth-century specialist, published a book on the Tory Party under the early Hanoverians and another on Namier. Then, in *Britons* (1992) and *Captives*

(2002), Colley took careful aim and bagged a brace of prize topics each packed with contemporary resonance. She has not only 'addressed and confirmed' contemporary preoccupations. She has seen them coming.

The core of Colley's *oeuvre* lies in the historical development of a sense of British national identity, nationhood and nationalism, and the pride and prejudices to which these have given rise both at home and abroad. In 1999, Tony Blair invited her to deliver a lecture at Downing Street on the future of 'Britishness'. If the Prime Minister and his guests had anticipated earnest guidelines about how to capitalize upon national identity in the years to come, they were in for a big – but stimulating – disappointment.

'What will Britishness signify a century from now?' Colley asked dutifully. Her answer? That it may turn out to be 'not very much', but that this may not matter. We all have multiple identities, she reassured the assembled Downing Street guests, saying how she herself was part Welsh, part Irish, part English, had recently spent 16 years in the USA and was currently dividing her time between a terraced house in a predominantly Bangladeshi part of London's East End and a cottage in the heart of rural Norfolk. At a time when it was politically estimable to label oneself 'British' (or 'Welsh' or 'Scottish') but not 'English', Colley made an eloquent plea to her distinguished audience to downplay the very issue of national identity, to allow people whatever mix of identities they choose – and to concentrate instead on questions of shared citizenship.

Born in Chester in 1949, Linda Colley's earliest memories include being shown the historic features of her home town. Her mother's family was Welsh and her father an Englishman with Irish antecedents whose job in the Customs and Excise required the family to move from Chester to Hull, Birkenhead and Cardiff. She went on to read history as an undergraduate at the University of Bristol, home of bright girls whose male counterparts had been swallowed up by Oxbridge.

At Bristol, Colley's interest in the eighteenth century was aroused by John Cannon, a former Namier pupil and an imaginative teacher who used slides in his lectures and incorporated art and culture as well as politics into his teaching. Cannon obviously did a good job, for Colley went on to Cambridge to continue her researches on the eighteenth century: an era, she says, whose sources are abundant but not such as to overwhelm ('God's century to study!' she rhapsodises). Her doctoral dissertation on the Tory Party during its period of eclipse under George I and George II became the basis of her first book, *In Defiance of Oligarchy: The Tory Party 1714–1760*.

Colley's PhD supervisor was Sir John Plumb, Master of Christ's College, Cambridge. Plumb brought her to Christ's where she became the college's first female Fellow and one of a loose circle of distinguished Plumb protégés who, at one time or another, were also to include the late Roy Porter, Simon Schama and David Cannadine, whom she went on to marry. By Colley's account, Jack Plumb was an exceptionally laid-back supervisor but a powerful patron ('as befits someone who wrote on Walpole!'). It was partly through Plumb's advocacy that she was offered a teaching post in British History at Yale University. Before too long, Cannadine was doing much the same at Columbia and, for many years, this historical couple famously commuted at weekends between New York and New Haven before returning together to London in 1998.

As a specialist in British history at a big Ivy League university, Colley could have found herself an isolated figure, drowning in an ocean of Americana. In fact, her years at Yale provided her with draughts of fresh intellectual air, all the more welcome after the hothouse of Cambridge history. Far from allowing her interests to narrow, she found her new transatlantic filter bestowing an increasingly international perspective. Thus, when invited to contribute to a series of volumes about famous historians, she turned to a figure whose personal cosmopolitanism was as interesting as his scholarship.

Lewis Namier, born Ludwik Bernsztain vel Niemirowski in Poland in 1888, had witnessed the loss of his ancestral legacy and lands. Yearning for a new stability he was never to find, he developed two intellectual preoccupations clearly related to his own troubled life and background: Britain's loss of the American colonies in the late eighteenth century, and the apparently inexorable rise in the nineteenth of Germany. Deeply suspicious of ideology and keen to minimize its presence in the study of history, Namier saw himself as a political historian in the Rankean tradition, a positivist to whom the wider picture is the sum of its multiplicity of component facts. Hence Namier's preoccupation with the social attributes of obscure eighteenth-century English MPs (but not with the ideas by which they purported to be inspired). Namier was also a committed Freudian. While not applying psychoanalytic methods to the subjects of his studies, he believed with Freud that if you wanted to understand society you had first to study the individuals who composed it. Nobody had come to British history from anything like Namier's exotic provenance. People compared him with Conrad; but even Conrad had not presumed to write about the minor English landed gentry.

Sceptics – and there were plenty – regarded Namier as a dry-as-dust cataloguer of long-dead nonentities, toiling over his never-to-be-completed History of Parliament project. 'Why bother?' they asked one another, as Namier added a few more ants to the heap. Colley points out, however, that what Namier was aiming to create was a portrait of the English ruling class over time as reflected in the changing membership of the House of Commons. He himself would work on the eighteenth century; others could tackle the periods before and since. Namier's was thus a large-minded and visionary project. It was also a pioneering example of 'prosopography', the (now common) use of multiple biography to create a portrait of a bygone age.

In addition, Linda Colley insists, Namier helped spearhead the reaction against 'Whig' history, the interpretation of the English past that claimed to document a more or less unwavering line of (Whig-inspired) progress towards the achievement of ever greater liberty. This was a view Namier demolished. Where Whig historians had portrayed George III, for example, as an unconstitutional monarch whose corrupt Tory administration strove in vain to deny freedom to the American colonists, Namier humanized the King, revealing him to have been merely stubborn and weak. The governing elite, Namier demonstrated, was thoroughly fragmented, its members – including Whig no less than Tory – being motivated more by opportunities for individual gain than by ideology.

Colley is not uncritical of Namier, a man embattled by his own conflicts and contradictions. But, in certain respects, she judges, 'We are all Namierites now'. In Colley's own books, from her early work on the eighteenth-century Tory Party to *Britons* and *Captives*, she too has investigated the lives of countless individuals – where they came from, how they were educated, their kinship patterns, what they earned, where they went, what they said and believed – and has used these as the bricks and mortar with which to build the larger edifice.

Britons , ten years in the making, was researched and written on both sides of the Atlantic and shows how, during the century or so after the Act of Union with Scotland in 1707, people from all over these islands gradually began to think of themselves as (among other things) citizens of Britain. The book is organized around certain topics that, Colley argues, helped generate a sense of British national cohesion. Thus, she writes about war, profits and Protestantism, all forms of social cement during a century of conflict with France, and about the British monarchy which, despite the loss of the American colonies and unlike its French counterpart, survived. *Forging the Nation* was the subtitle of a book which opens with the text of 'Rule Britannia' – written in 1740 by (significantly) a Scot.

When Colley was first developing her ideas, British historiography, moving out of its consensual, 'Whiggish' phase, was much influenced by writers like E.P. Thompson and Christopher Hill who had emphasized radicalism, resistance, conflict and confrontation. Colley wondered if the pendulum hadn't swung too far. If there was so much anger and rebelliousness among ordinary people in the eighteenth century, how could industrialisation have taken hold so firmly or the nation have prosecuted so many successful wars? Wasn't there a degree of cohesion as well as conflict, of patriotism as well as protest?

There was an element of personal quest to her work too as, settling into life across the Atlantic, Colley found herself addressing the issue of national identity. Americans had long been fascinated by the topic; the Yale library shelves heaved under the weight of books about what it meant to be 'American'. Yet there was virtually nothing on the historical nature of 'Britishness'. Colley was further stimulated by shifts in the political map back home as the Falklands War, the defeat of the miners' strike, ambivalence towards the European Community, growing support for devolution in Wales and Scotland and early moves towards an Irish peace process all added further point to her endeavours. When *Britons* appeared, it found a ready readership and made its author everyone's first-choice pundit on our national destiny.

Including, a few years later, the new Prime Minister. By the time of her Downing Street lecture, Colley and Cannadine had returned to Britain – he as Director of the Institute of Historical Research, she with a five-year Leverhulme Research Professorship at the London School of Economics, which gave her the time and wherewithal to pursue her next big project.

Captives is the complement and counterpart to *Britons*. In *Britons*, the great 'Other' against whom many British people define themselves is the French. In *Captives* it is the world, or at least those non-European peoples with whom Britons engage and by whom some of them are captured. You might not think that much of significance would be revealed in a book that tells of a handful of British sailors and soldiers, and the odd missionary or military wife, who landed up in the hands of Barbary pirates, North American Indians or Afghan tribesmen. We are all outraged when one of 'ours' is made a hostage of 'theirs'. Think of Jimmy Carter's flawed attempt to free the American diplomats held in Teheran, or of our own Terry Waite. Or of the fun Mozart has, in *Die Entführung aus dem Serail*, when his two maidens in distress (one of them an English girl proclaiming her love of liberty) are rescued from Pasha Selim by their resolute lovers. But what light can such tales, however emotionally laden, be made to throw upon the central historical drama?

In Colley's hands, a great deal. She certainly has not made things easy for herself. Where *Britons* concentrated on one country, with sources in (mostly) one language, over a period of 130 years, *Captives* covers a quarter of a millennium and goes global. As in *Britons*, one of Colley's principal concerns is to reveal the interconnections and mutual perceptions of people predisposed to regard each other as alien. In *Britons*, one of the most striking chapters is entitled 'Peripheries'; in *Captives*, stories from the peripheries are, so to speak, central.

Richly and evocatively illustrated, the book interweaves three strands. Crudely, it could be read as a more or less chronological account of the early years of British imperial history. Thus, Colley starts with the erection and destruction of a settlement built by the British in Tangier in the last years of Charles II and ends with a saga of army officers held in Afghanistan shortly after the accession of Queen Victoria. There is also a geographical structure to the book, whose three principal sections cover respectively the Mediterranean, North America and the Indian sub-continent. And interwoven between all these are Colley's captives, a *dramatis personae* whose names and narratives gradually imprint themselves upon the reader as in a good novel. People like Peter Williamson, captured by American Indians in the 1750s, and Elizabeth Marsh who, seized by Moroccan corsairs, later wrote titillatingly of her encounter with an elegant Moroccan prince.

Many of Colley's concerns come together in *Captives*. The ghost of Namier would doubtless allow a wan smile at the way Colley constructs her big picture from numerous individual instances. The book is also an assault on what Colley regards as the still somewhat 'Whiggish' approach to British imperial history that looks back to recount an epic trajectory of inexorable rise and fall. That's not how things looked at the time, she says forcefully, for example to a foot soldier in North America during the Seven Years' War or a working-class girl living in a series of military camps in India a few years later. Her pages are packed with the stories of bewildered individuals who, finding themselves in difficulties on a variety of far-flung frontiers, struggle to adjust to their immediate situation.

This is neither a history to be jingoistically proud of, nor one simply to apologize for, says Colley. It is not, indeed, a single story at all, but rather a vast network of histories packed with every gradation of human intolerance, cruelty, compassion and kindness. Individual Britons, held by foreign forces sometimes far richer and more imperious than their own, were as often the victims as the perpetrators, more frightened than fearsome.[1] Counterpointing their personal narratives against the wider story, Colley builds what amounts to an 'alternative' view of the early centuries of British imperial history.

---

[1] *Linda Colley writes:* This needs qualifying. My concern was not to present Britons as 'victims' as opposed to those they were invading. I was endeavouring to document what Stephen M. Walt has recently written: namely, that it has always been 'extremely difficult to project power across water and onto a foreign shore'. I am not seeking to detract from the sufferings of the invaded, but I am concerned to explore the compromises, confusions and agonies that empire can also inflict on its exponents.

Captives has further reverberations for our own times, too, as when Colley demonstrates how, at least until around 1750, British encounters with the Islamic world included a strong dose of respect (as late as 1801 one British Major reported the all-powerful Turks as 'invariably men of tall stature who appeared to look down on us'). As British power burgeoned, respect for the 'Other' correspondingly dwindled. Today, the British Empire, like the Mughal and Turkish, the Spanish, Austrian and French, is no more. But, as Colley surveys the powers exerted in our own time by India, China, Russia or the United States, she insists that Britain's empire should be seen for what it was and understood comparatively alongside those of others – past and present.

In her Downing Street lecture, Colley mentioned that she had heard it said that 'New Labour' was not interested in history – adding, rapidly, that she would hate to think this could possibly be true. To Colley, the past is not a deadweight impeding progress. On the contrary, it can become a living guide to the future – but only if it is not muffled by myth and misconception. She cites the common view that this 'island nation' has always held aloof from the continent. Nonsense, she says, reminding us that, while Britain has often fought against continental powers, it has usually done so in alliance with other continental powers.

'A clearer knowledge about the productive way our past has been intertwined (rather than in conflict) with that of continental Europe', Linda Colley proclaims, 'would ease many people's doubts and fears.' An insight I trust she confided to Tony Blair.

EPILOGUE

Linda Colley writes:

At present I'm working on a book provisionally entitled *The Ordeal of Elizabeth Marsh: A Global Life and Death* to be published by HarperCollins in 2007. This is an attempt to write a biography across all kinds of boundaries. It takes an unknown woman, Elizabeth Marsh (1735–1785), who travelled further than any other woman of her time is known to have done, and further too than most of her male contemporaries, and whose life and death also intersected with a succession of global trends and developments. I am also continuing to encourage new work on captives. There were two international conferences devoted to the subject in 2005 alone. And I want in the near future to develop a series of conferences and seminars at Princeton that will examine the phenomenon of empire in the past – and perhaps in the present – in a comparative way. In 2006 I also delivered an updated version of my Millennium Lecture on Britishness in the Twenty-first Century to the Fabian Society.

Orlando Figes

BIOGRAPHY

Orlando Figes was born in London in 1959. He studied History at Gonville and Caius College, Cambridge, graduating with a double-starred First in 1982, and then went on to do a PhD in History at Trinity College, Cambridge. In 1987 he was appointed a University Lecturer in the History Faculty at Cambridge. His first book, *Peasant Russia, Civil War: The Volga Countryside in Revolution, 1917–1921*, was published in 1989. It was an important book for its extensive use of Soviet archives, which had not been used before in this contentious area of study by any historian outside the Soviet Union. *A People's Tragedy: The Russian Revolution, 1891–1921*, was published in 1996. It won the Wolfson History Prize, the NCR Book Award, the W.H. Smith Literary Award, the Longman/ *History Today* Book of the Year Award and the Los Angeles Times Book Prize. It has been translated into more than a dozen languages. In 1999 Figes was appointed Professor of History at Birkbeck College, University of London, a post which he still holds today. In the same year he co-authored with Boris Kolonitskii *Interpreting the Russian Revolution: The Language and Symbols of 1917*. His next big book was *Natasha's Dance: A Cultural History of Russia* (2002) which has also been translated into many languages. Figes is a regular contributor to the *New York Review of Books* and to other international journals and newspapers. He appears frequently on TV and radio and has written several TV history documentaries. In 2004 he wrote and presented *The Tsar's Last Picture Show* (BBC 4) about the life of the photographer Sergei Prokudin-Gorsky. He lives in Cambridge and London.

PRINCIPAL PUBLISHED BOOKS

Peasant Russia, Civil War: The Volga Countryside in Revolution, 1917–1921 (1989)
A People's Tragedy: The Russian Revolution, 1891–1924 (1996)
Interpreting the Russian Revolution: The Language and Symbols of 1917 (with Boris Kolonitskii) (1999)
Natasha's Dance: A Cultural History of Russia (2002)

PROFILE, April 2003

Orlando Figes is unafraid of thinking big. *A People's Tragedy*, his (nearly) 900-page study of the Russian Revolution from the 1890s to the mid-1920s, is, he says, 'the first attempt at a comprehensive history of the entire revolutionary period in a single volume'. His recent book, *Natasha's Dance*, is a richly textured cultural history of Russia from the time of Peter the Great to that of Brezhnev. Like Tolstoy, Figes seeks to integrate the public and the private, the panoramic and the personal, and he writes with great flair (for which he acknowledges the influence of his mother the novelist Eva Figes) whether about princes, priests, poets and peasants, or about Tsarism, Revolution and Civil War. It is bold for an academic historian to opt for such broad horizons. It is also risky (as Figes discovered last autumn when the victim of a notoriously mean review of *Natasha's Dance* in the *Times Literary Supplement*). So is the Professor of History at Birkbeck College, London, planning to retreat into a more conventional academic shell? That is not the Figes style.

Orlando and his sister, the writer Kate Figes, were brought up by their mother in a bookish home in northwest London. Orlando, born in 1959, was always an omnivorous reader

('I jumped straight from Topsy and Tim to Tolstoy!'). From
William Ellis school he went to Cambridge where, the son of
a German Jewish refugee, he gravitated towards Central and
East European history, taking supervisions from Peter Burke
and Norman Stone. Under Stone's tutelage, Figes wrote an
undergraduate dissertation on a left-leaning German Jewish
contemporary of Marx and Heine (for which Stone sent him
off to talk to Isaiah Berlin). Later, when Figes set out to do his
PhD, Stone nudged him away from the arcanae of German-
Jewish philosophy. 'You need something you can get on with
even when distracted by love or a hangover,' said Stone in
his down-to-earth way, 'something practical, like counting
Russian peasants.' Thus was born what became Figes' first
book, *Peasant Russia, Civil War: The Volga Countryside in
Revolution, 1917–1921*.

Figes' research was undertaken in Moscow during what was
still the Soviet era. Much of the Volga region itself was 'closed';
the nearest he got to the areas he was studying was when he
slipped onto an overnight train and enjoyed an illegal away-
day in Samara (then known as Kuibyshev). Back in Moscow, he
had excellent contacts, among them two outstanding scholars
of Russian agrarian history. But the bureaucracy made things
difficult. As a foreign student, Figes was housed apart from his
Russian confrères, made to study in a separate reading room in
the library and denied access to the official catalogue. Archives
were revealed sparingly and the librarian was presumed to be
a KGB plant. Figes needed subterfuge to identify and prise out
the documentation he needed. When fobbed off with a handful
of useless archives, he would spend half a day pretending to
work his way through them in order to demonstrate that he
was not planning to give up. Banned as a foreigner from the
canteen, he found that one place he could talk to Russians
was in the toilet area – a facility they shared – where he and
they, nipping off for a smoke, would chat about what they
were working on. On a good day, he'd emerge from these

visits armed with information on new archive sources which
he would promptly order.

The focus of Figes' study was the relationship between the
peasants and the Bolsheviks during the Revolution and Civil
War. The Bolsheviks could not have attained power if they had
not first gained the allegiance of the peasantry. How did the
peasants of the Volga region and the local Bolsheviks regard
each other? It was a crucial question. The big breakthrough
came when Figes managed to obtain the papers of the *Volost*-
level Soviets, enabling him at last to get to grips with the
dynamics of village politics as Bolsheviks gradually took
control and steered peasant revolt towards revolution.

Peasant Russia, Civil War, published in 1989, established
Figes as an impressive young scholar, capable of presenting the
results of thoroughgoing research with a fluent pen. Buoyed
by the book's reception, he contemplated a second. By now a
Fellow of Trinity and Lecturer in History at Cambridge, Figes
felt he had the security, and the maturity, to assay something
on a grander scale – the more so as an Aladdin's cave of
archival material opened up following the collapse of the Soviet
Union. Why stick to the Volga region, Figes wondered? Or
to the terminal dates of his first book? You could only really
understand the Russian Revolution, he felt, if you went back
well into Tsarist times and pursued the story until around the
time of the death of Lenin.

I first read *A People's Tragedy: The Russian Revolution,
1891–1924*, around the time of the death of Princess Diana.
As I struggled to understand the wave of public grief sweeping
Britain and the impact it had on the comportment of the
royals, I was absorbed by the way Figes showed how peasant
opinion, such an intrinsically inchoate force, gradually took
form in pre-revolutionary Russia, made itself felt and fed into
subsequent historical events. Figes peppers his narrative with
evocative insights into peasant life in the remote provinces,
and demonstrates again and again how impenetrable the

countless communities of the Russian hinterland had always been to those in Moscow or Petersburg. Figes does not argue that the Russian Revolution was merely a 'peasants' revolt' or the result of anything so simplistic as the 'general will'. Nor does he eschew the traditional emphasis on political ideologies and personalities such as the appeal of Communism, the misjudgements of Kerensky or Kornilov or the part played by Bolshevik planning or Tsarist incompetence (and vice versa). But in Figes' account, centre stage is frequently occupied by the ordinary people of Russia, especially of peasant Russia, who, collectively and sometimes individually, are actors in the drama, not passive props.

The book is packed with personality and incident. Figes homes in on a small, recurrent cast of characters, among them an obscure peasant reformer, an aristocrat (Prince Lvov), the patriotic Tsarist general Brusilov who later changed sides, and the writer Maxim Gorky who was close to Lenin but despaired of much that the Revolution effected. All found their lives intersecting with the larger picture, and each saw events turning out very differently from the way he had hoped or expected. Figes' intention is to convey a heightened awareness of the fortunes and misfortunes of the Russian people as a whole as perceived by those who were alive at the time. Thus, he is at pains to communicate a sense of the chaos, the riderless horse, the chance that so often drove events. And the sheer absurdity. We catch a glimpse of Lenin attending a secret meeting in a wig that keeps slipping off; or Alexandra Kollontai, the new People's Commissar of Social Welfare, turning up at the old Ministry of Welfare but being politely barred entry by the liveried doorman.

It is often maintained that history is returning to 'grand narrative' and *A People's Tragedy* is quoted in evidence. But the book is adduced as evidence for other trends, too. Some critics proclaimed *A People's Tragedy* light on analysis, while Richard Evans has noted that Figes' book, with its interweaving of the

micro and the macro, 'could not have been written without
the theoretical and methodological impact of postmodernism'.
Figes, faintly amused and perhaps flattered at the labelling
his work has attracted, shrugs off the suggestion that he
was consciously following or avoiding any historiographical
agenda. The job of the historian, he says disarmingly, is not to
impose meanings but to suggest them – and to leave readers
to reach their own conclusions. This they have done. To
Figes' evident delight, a large postbag reveals that readers of
A People's Tragedy have drawn a wide variety of messages
from the book.

They are beginning to do the same with *Natasha's Dance*.
Covering three centuries, this is history on the grand scale.
Broadly chronological, *Natasha's Dance* can be read as an
account of Russian culture from the foundation of St Petersburg
in the early eighteenth century through to Akhmatova,
Prokofiev, Nabokov and Stravinsky. There is scarcely a poet
or painter, designer, director, composer or choreographer of
note Figes does not cover.

We begin in the West with the erection of Tsar Peter's
avowedly European capital, then move deep into the Russian
heartland, through the greater informality of Moscow, the
sanctity of the Russian family and Orthodox church, across the
supposed Slavic and Asiatic origins of the Russian soul – and,
finally, out of Russia altogether, with a chapter on Russia and
Russians abroad. This geographical peregrination is also of
course a spiritual one as generations of artists and artisans,
struggling to identify the 'true' Russian character, seek its roots
in a sequence of myths increasingly at odds with the European
legacy from which, at the same time, they gain sustenance.
Thus, at the beginning of the story, we encounter eighteenth-
century aristocrats who think it important to speak French,
savour the latest Italian music and dress in English fashions
and fineries. By the twentieth century, sophisticated figures like
Diaghilev, Bakst, Chagall and Stravinsky apotheosize the myths

of an altogether more primitive, Eastern or Slavic 'Russia-of-the-mind', one characterized by onion-domed churches, matrioshka dolls, peasant songs, wooden houses and magic firebirds.

Figes uses the word 'culture' in both its traditional sense (meaning 'high art'), and in its anthropological sense to refer to people's beliefs and behaviour. He writes about not only the great canon of literature, music and art but also about the customs of daily life, about food and drink, weddings and funerals, the brutality within many Russian marriages, the centrality of nanny in traditional households. Indeed, he sees the two as inextricably linked. Thus, Tolstoy feared death and wrote incomparable descriptions of it. Nanny is featured in works of high art such as Pushkin's (and Tchaikovsky's) *Eugene Onegin* as well as in folk myths and in the record of countless lives.

In a nation lacking a tradition of free speech and a free press, serious political and philosophical debate was often conducted through artistic allegory. Elsewhere, says Figes, artists might reflect or express aspects of the nation; in Russia, they have been in the vanguard of its formation. When Tolstoy (in *Anna Karenina*) wants to consider the agricultural reforms required after the liberation of Russia's serfs, he puts his own arguments into the mouth of his alter ego, Levin. And when he describes an aristocratic girl, Natasha Rostov, visiting a peasant's hut and instinctively picking up the rhythms of a folk dance (hence the title of Figes' book), he is portraying not only the girl's unspoiled charm but also the deep bonds that he believes have always united Russians regardless of class or background.

It is this supposed lineage of Russian culture over time that interests Figes in *Natasha's Dance*. Hence his focus on certain families (the Sheremetevs, the Volkonskys) or objects and places (the Bronze Horseman statue, the Optina Pustyn monastery, the Fountain House in St Petersburg) with long-term resonances. Prominent individuals also reappear from time to time (Gogol, Pushkin, Stasov, Chekhov, and so on), their significance transcending Figes' thematic divisions, and the reader might occasionally be troubled by a sense of déjà vu, or by passages some experts have claimed to be derivative or inaccurate. But this is a small price to pay for a wonderfully informative and readable book of breathtaking ambition. The multifaceted quest for that elusive cultural grail, the true nature of 'Russianness', was never so vividly illuminated.

Towards the end of *Natasha's Dance*, Figes describes how artists such as Meyerhold and Akhmatova were forced to tread through the poisonous undergrowth of Stalinism as they strove to express the inexpressible, while others sought a degree of freedom abroad. Of those who remained in Stalin's Soviet Union, some survived, many were murdered. It was all so arbitrary. Were Eisenstein or Shostakovich wrong to adjust their art to the dictates of a tyrant whom Mandelstam described as 'the Kremlin mountaineer, the murderer and peasant-slayer'? They lived, but Mandelstam perished; it could so easily have been the other way round.

Figes writes with insight about those dark years, a topic he plans to pursue in his next project: a study of 'private life' during the Soviet era and, especially, under Stalin (working title: *The Great Fear*). Many books describe the externals of the Terror – the accusations, trials, enslavements and killings. But what interior accommodations did people have to make in order to live in a moral vacuum? What was it like living in a state of permanent fear? What kind of ethic did you adopt, knowing your children or spouse might be informing on you? How could you be sure you were not one of the guilty?

In a sense, this should be easy to research; anyone in Russia over the age of 60 is a potential interviewee. But how easily or accurately will people talk about an era still too close for comfort? How representative would their testimony be and how could it be corroborated from archival sources? As Figes reflects on his forthcoming voyage into the lower depths, a host of methodological problems springs up.

Meanwhile, he has a more manageable project in his sights: a history of the Crimean War. What Figes plans to do is to reinstate the ideological and religious tensions between Russia and the Ottoman world, epitomised by competing Orthodox and Muslim claims in the Holy Land. In today's world, riven by ideological conflict and in palpable need of understanding of the historical role of Islam, this could prove to be the right book at the right time.

As for *The Great Fear*, Figes remains sanguine, and humbled, by the immense challenge it presents. 'It's probably the hardest thing I shall ever do', he says. And he is profoundly conscious that – like those who have tried to comprehend the world his mother had to flee – he is embarking upon a journey that will take him into the very heart of darkness.

EPILOGUE

Orlando Figes writes:

The book on private life in Stalin's Russia will be published by Allen Lane in 2008. It will not be called *The Great Fear* (but I am not saying what the title is). The book is based on a large oral history and archival project in Russia which I have been able to complete thanks to two major grants from the Arts and Humanities Research Council, and another from the Leverhulme Trust. In collaboration with the Memorial Organization in Moscow, St Petersburg and Perm, the project has recovered nearly 200 family archives (photographs, letters, diaries, memoirs, artefacts, and so on) amounting to a total of several million words and thousands of photographic images. These archives are supplemented by extensive interviews with surviving relatives. The archive will be put online in 2009. It represents the biggest collection of primary materials relating

to family and personal life in the Stalin period, and will become
a major resource for all historians of Soviet Russia, private life
and dictatorship.

Felipe Fernández-Armesto

BIOGRAPHY

Felipe Fernández-Armesto was born in London in 1950, of Anglo-Spanish parentage, and attended school in England. He was a *Libre-oyente* (non-examination student) at the University of Salamanca, and an undergraduate and doctoral student at Oxford (First Class Honours, Final School of Modern History 1972; MA 1976; D.Phil. 1977). He was awarded an Honorary D.Litt. from La Trobe University in 1997. He became a journalist, then a schoolmaster before embarking upon a long apprenticeship in temporary and part-time university jobs, notably at Warwick University and the University of Buckingham. He has been a Fellow of St Antony's College, Oxford (1981–90); a member of the Modern History Faculty, Oxford (1983–2004); a Professorial Fellow and Professor of Global Environmental History, Queen Mary, University of London (from 2000; Visiting Professor from 2005) and Prince of Asturias Professor in the Department of History, Tufts University, from 2005. He has delivered courses in global, environmental, Spanish and Atlantic history, and has supervised many Masters' and doctoral students. He has had posts as Visiting Professor and Fellow along the way at the John Carter Brown Library, Brown University, Warwick University, the University of Minnesota and the Netherlands Institute of Advanced Study in the Humanities and Social Sciences. He is a Fellow of the Society of Antiquaries of London, and the the Royal Historical Society and the Society of Arts, and a Life Member of the American Historical Association.

His journal articles have been widely syndicated, mostly originating in Spanish and British national newspapers, and he has had many television and radio appearances, including as a regular presenter of *Analysis* on BBC Radio 4 and a frequent guest presenter on *Leviathan* on BBC 2 television. His screenwriting includes CNN's ten-part series, *Millennium*. He was awarded the Caird Medal (National Maritime Museum) in 1997, the John Carter Brown Medal in 1999, the IACP Prize for best food-writing in 2002, the Premio Nacional de Investigación (Sociedad Geográfica Española) in 2003, and the Premio Nacional de Gastronomía in 2004. He is married to Lesley Hook and has two sons, Sebastian and Federico.

PRINCIPAL PUBLISHED BOOKS

The Canary Islands after the Conquest (1982)

Before Columbus: Exploration and Colonisation from the Mediterranean to the Atlantic, 1229–1492 (1987)

The Spanish Armada: The Experience of War in 1588 (1988)

Edward Gibbon's Atlas of the World (1991)

The Times Atlas of World Exploration (General ed.) (1991)

Barcelona: A Thousand Years of the City's Past (1991)

Columbus (1991)

Columbus on Himself (1992)

The Times Guide to the Peoples of Europe (ed.) (1994)

The European Opportunity (1995)

The Global Opportunity (ed.) (1995)

The Times Illustrated History of Europe (1995)

Millennium: A History of the Last Thousand Years (1995)

Reformations (with Derek Wilson) (1996)

Religion (1997)

Truth: A History (1997)

Civilizations (2000)

Food: A History (2001)

Ideas (2003)

The Americas: A History of the Hemisphere (2003)
Shifting Communities and Identity Formation in Early Modern Asia (ed. with L. Blussé) (2003)
So You Think You're Human: A Brief History of the Concept of Humankind (2004)

PROFILE, July 2003

Felipe Fernández-Armesto's published bibliography, if printed in its entirety, would take up half this article. Helpfully, many of his books have one-word titles. But the brevity of the titles often belies the immense ambition of the projects they are chosen to encapsulate. 'I only do one planet', replies this self-confessed agent provocateur when asked about his field. And his period? 'From primeval slime to the future.'

Felipe was born in Britain in 1950 to a Spanish father and English mother, both of them journalists. His father is still recalled affectionately by old-timers in Spain for having filed sympathetic reports to the leading Barcelona paper *La Vanguardia* from wartime Britain (where he was also, it seems, doing intelligence work for the Allies).

The household was Anglophone, but Felipe soon felt the pull of his Spanish name and ancestry. His Oxford doctoral dissertation was a study of the Canary Islands in the years immediately after Columbus, for which he drew on a mass of surviving notarial archives. Arcane, specialized stuff? Perhaps. But far from constricting his islanders within a narrowly academic coastline, Felipe contrived to give them an extensive waterfront, revealing aspects of their social and economic life, agricultural methods, governmental and judicial systems, faith and mores. The result (as he says in the preface to the later published version) was 'the first attempt comprehensively to depict the society of a Spanish overseas colony in the sixteenth century'. Moreover, it was written in a style that, while making due obeisance to the formalities required of an aspiring young academic, gave notice of a writer prepared to risk the arresting phrase, the big idea, the bold generalization – including the impossibility of generalizing. The Canaries (he concluded with a characteristic flourish) did not provide an archetype of Spanish colonial development; rather, they were 'a crucible into which ingredients were flung at random, as though by a sorcerer's apprentice, not by a laboratory technician'.

When I first met Fernández-Armesto a dozen or more years ago, he had done a stint as History Master at Charterhouse and as a Lecturer at Warwick and was a Fellow of St Antony's, Oxford. He had already produced a succession of books and articles on the history of Spain and its interactions with the wider world, all of them suggesting a writer keen to expand his horizons and perhaps his audiences. The journalistic heritage gave him a good eye for a centenary and his early *oeuvre* included books on the Spanish Armada timed for the 400th anniversary (1988), followed by a biography of Columbus and a history of Barcelona, both published as Spain geared up for the quincentenary – and Barcelona Olympics – of 1992. Then, as the mother of all anniversaries loomed, he published *Millennium*. The transformation from Hispanicist to Globalist was complete.

There is of course an element of playful posturing to Fernández-Armesto's boast that he 'only does one planet', as there is to many of his deliberately provocative bons mots. But in *Millennium* the word becomes flesh, as it were. It is true that we travel through merely the last 1,000 years or so (as in *Barcelona*). But the journey is of truly global scope. One boards the millennial magic carpet with some trepidation, or at least I did. For this is a voyage that will dazzle and bewilder as we swoop down into the Maya Renaissance, the myths and markets of early Islam, the conquests of Timur or the exploratory voyages of the Chinese navigator Cheng Ho. Europe is not ignored. But Fernández-Armesto suggests that anyone looking back from some futuristic galactic museum will probably see our much-vaunted Western culture – the Renaissance heritage, the hegemony of North America – as a brief episode that soon gave way to resurgent Islam or the culture of the Pacific Rim. Most historians regard the past from the perspective of the present. Here is one who tries to do so from an imagined future.

Millennium begins with 'The Tale of Genji', written 1,000 years ago. For primeval slime, you have to turn to *Civilizations*. Few books in recent times have been as ambitious. This is not a chronological romp through the rise and fall of Ancient Egypt, the Greeks and Romans & Co., nor a narrative illustrating the eventual triumph (or decline) of the West. Instead, daringly, *Civilizations* takes as its basic structure the world's great ecologies, the 'glutinous natural environment with which societies are surrounded'. Thus, we start in the polar ice and tundra, move on to grasslands, thence to rain forests and marshes, then uplands, seaboards and maritime civilizations. All human life is there, and much else besides. The approach also helps suggest links across time and place – between bog peoples of Europe or of New Guinea, the Olmecs practising agriculture in swampy Mesoamerica and those enjoined by Mussolini to drain the Pripet Marshes. You won't find the Aztecs and Incas in a chapter on South America; rather, they take their place alongside Ethiopia and Tibet in a section on highlands and mountains. Phoenicia and Scandinavia are considered together; both civilizations, after all, developed the way they did in part because of a long but narrow coastline. This is not to suggest that all civilizations are determined by their ecologies. Just that the natural environment provides an influential backdrop that historians too often ignore.

I said just now that all human life is there. Except that, of course, it isn't. It couldn't be. No historian is omniscient and, in any case, a book containing everything would be an encyclopaedia, and Fernández-Armesto does not write encyclopaedias. So what does he include in these big books and what does he leave out?

In general, he has a predilection for the rills and runnels of the past, the tributaries of history rather than what you might consider to be its mainstreams. In *Millennium*, he offers more on the thirteenth century in Tunis than Paris, more on the sixteenth in Siberia than Moscow. He writes of the fall of Makassar in 1660, but not of the restoration of Charles II in London that same year. *Civilizations*, similarly, visits Polynesian and Scythian culture, and even the Dawadar people of Fezzan deep in the interior of Libya. But the Italians scarcely make an appearance. Nor will you find much about Elizabeth I, Napoleon or Bismarck. This is partly because Fernández-Armesto takes it that mainstream Western history is already well enough known. But he is drawn towards what you and I may think of as the margins and frontiers for other reasons too. Civilizations and cultures, he says, are the tectonic plates of world history. It is at their frontiers that they confront each other most profoundly, bringing about the deepest historical shifts.

Seismic shifts are notoriously unpredictable. Sometimes, history happens very fast, 'like a snake darting between stones' (Fernández-Armesto cites the dissolution of the Soviet Union as a recent instance). Until not long ago, he recalls, it was de rigueur for historians to adduce long-term causes when explaining great cataclysmic events. Nowadays, in what Fernández-Armesto considers a major intellectual revolution of our times, these lengthy causal chains are increasingly revealed to be composed of brittle links as scholars allot ever-briefer timespans to their explanations of, for example, the origins of the English Civil War, the French Revolution or World War I.

Sometimes, the causes are there, but not the effects; the tectonic plates of history meet and rumble – but the earth trembles rather less than one might have expected. Take the Crusades, for example, a series of episodes scoured by generations of Western historians for evidence of the vitality of medieval Christendom. The galactic museum-keepers of the future, Fernández-Armesto suggests, will hardly bother with the Crusades, 'a flea bite on the hide of Islam'. Or consider those epic voyages of Cheng Ho between 1405 and 1433. Where Columbus, later on, had three vessels on his first expedition, Cheng Ho had sixty-odd; Cheng's seventh and final voyage took his fleet some 12,000 miles. Much of Asia and East Africa were there for the taking had China wished to acquire a seaborne empire. But she chose not to do so, in what Fernández-Armesto regards as 'one of the most remarkable instances of collective reticence in history', leaving the way open to the later depredations of the European powers.

As for the great age of European expansion that followed, this was 'no outpouring of pent-up dynamism'. On the contrary, it was 'launched from the insecure edges of a contracting civilization' which the galactic museum-keepers will probably regard – if at all – as 'stagnant and introspective'.

The way you perceive the past depends in part upon your perspective. But this does not mean that there is no such thing as historical truth, that it is merely a construct of the historian. In a striking metaphor, Fernández-Armesto says that history

> is like a nymph glimpsed bathing between leaves: the more you shift perspective, the more is revealed. If you want to see her whole you have to dodge and slip between many different viewpoints.

This is from *Truth*, a lengthy essay, really, in which Fernández-Armesto attempts to reconcile various kinds of truth that may seem *prima facie* to be mutually inconsistent. Published in 1997, it springs from a desire to refute the extreme relativism of postmodernism, while acknowledging that, for the historian, there can be no single, simple 'truth'. As a committed Roman Catholic (and co-author, with the Evangelical Protestant Derek Wilson, of a study of the Reformation and its worldwide ramifications), Fernández-Armesto recognizes that there are certain kinds of truth that one accepts from authority. But other kinds of truth are recognized in other ways: through the exercise of reason, for example, or through the senses. Historians, he says, in a typical piece of euphonious hand-wringing, 'are priests of a cult of truth, called to the service of a god whose existence they are doomed to doubt'.

To some extent, books like *Truth* and *Food* (published in 2001), and indeed his bigger books, are all prequels, sequels, tryouts or spin-offs of each other, part of a single giant enterprise. Passages from *Truth* or *Millennium* turn up again in *Civilizations*; dishes that were fresh in *Civilizations* are warmed up for *Food*. But then, a section on grasslands beds down as well in a book about natural ecologies as in one on the history of food, while the Egyptian pyramids are as germane to a discussion about civilizations that arise in sandy deserts as to one investigating the truthfulness of ancient science.

The sheer breadth of Fernández-Armesto's scholarship invites the reader to wonder about the outer limits of his research skills. On the face of it, there appear to be none; he seems to have been everywhere and read everything. In addition to written documents, Fernández-Armesto cites art, artefacts and archaeological evidence; nothing is excluded in his quest for *histoire totale*. Thus, he tells us plausibly that the mosque of Jenne is perhaps 'the most undervalued great building of the world', while Olaus' *Description of the Northern Peoples* 'is one of the world's great unacknowledged works of genius'. In *Millennium*, an image he reproduces of twelfth-century life on the Yang-tse is labelled as 'deservedly the most famous of Sung scroll-paintings', while a chapter about the Central Asian steppelands in *Civilizations* is introduced with the words: 'This is where you can feel the wind ... You can feel its sting when the dust storms invade your eyes and hair and the pores of your skin.' In the Javanese language (he informs us in *Truth*), *rasa* means both 'feeling' and 'meaning' and conveys the implicit and the tentative – like the Japanese concept of *aimae*. In *Food*,

we learn that 'the importance of molluscs as probably the first creatures herded and bred by men has never been broached, much less investigated or acknowledged'. Until now, that is.

Fernández-Armesto admits to being limited to Western European languages and also to being (like Edward Gibbon) something of an armchair traveller. But, like all good writers about other times and places, he has become expert at covering up – and, occasionally perhaps, at creating – his tracks. There are passages in his work that will enlighten, amuse, irritate, infuriate or bewilder. Perhaps (as he says of Descartes) he is 'as anxious to be original as to be right'. Certainly, much that he has written about was completely new to me, but possibly not to experts in each of the myriad topics he covers. When he does deal with a subject one knows something about, his treatment can appear a little cavalier or derivative – an inevitable concomitant, perhaps, of the enormous range of his intellectual ambition. 'One of the reasons I am attracted to these over-ambitious projects', he acknowledges disarmingly, 'is that even if nobody learns anything from reading my books, I learn a lot from writing them.'

Like many stimulating intellectuals, Fernández-Armesto is probably at his best when asking stimulating questions. Why did people, after thousands of years as hunter-gatherers, settle down and start farming? Why didn't the Chinese develop an overseas empire when they could so easily have done so? Why is ours virtually the only civilisation in history in which the rich are thin and the poor fat (a topic developed at this year's Anglo-American conference)? His next book, to be published in the UK this autumn, is an extended essay about the Americas in which Fernández-Armesto asks why, in a hemisphere where great civilisations have historically sprouted up in central and south America, supremacy over the past century or two has been achieved in the north. Will that dominance, he wonders, appear to future historians (not to mention galactic museum-curators) as but a short-term blip?

You may not get easy answers, but the journey is invariably stimulating. It is hard not to warm to a book that begins: 'Most western parents feel guilty about Santa Claus.' Hard not to read on when a chapter starts by telling you: 'An Oghuz Turkish woman in need of a scratch casually exposed her pudenda to Ibn Fadlan, the Caliph's ambassador, during his journey to the court of the Volga Bulgars in 921.'

Fernández-Armesto is a spirited storyteller, the sheer bravura of his language generally helping to draw the reader into the argument. He can sometimes get carried away, opting too often for words like 'emulous', 'philoprogenitive', 'lucubrations', 'cosmogony' or 'pasquinade'. And I suspect he ingested too many good menus and wine lists while writing *Food* (Cumberland sauce, he informs us, is 'based on redcurrants but succumbs to self-conscious sophistication by admitting added orange peel and port').

The showmanship is part of the presentation. With his trademark cut-glass accent, and a predilection for stiff collars, cuff-links and watch-chain, Felipe Fernández-Armesto is a compulsive communicator who wants to know everything there is to know and tell everyone else about it. He loves teaching (he is a Professor at Queen Mary, London University, Director of the Global History Programme at the Institute of Historical Research and remains a member of the Oxford History faculty), and he is also frequently called upon as a broadcaster, journalist and contributor of chapters to other people's books. He is currently completing two further short books of his own: an illustrated volume about 'ideas that have changed the world' (in which the reader will be a third of the way through before encountering the Ancient Greeks!), and an extended essay – that will draw on his cross-cultural expertise as well as his Catholicism – on the changing concept of humankind.

Like many engaging figures, Fernández-Armesto is something of a pre-emptive pessimist. 'I recommend pessimism to everybody', he writes in the epilogue to a recent collection edited by David Cannadine. 'It is the only way to indemnify oneself against disappointment ... The function of pessimism is to arm oneself against disaster.'

Maybe this is why we study the past. For, as Fernández-Armesto says, the past is the name we give to everything in our collective experience. There isn't anything that we know about that isn't in the past and therefore part of history. The only point in studying anything is to enhance life and prepare for death. So we have to go on studying history – because it's all we have.

EPILOGUE

Felipe Fernández-Armesto writes:

Since Dan Snowman's perceptive interview, I have persevered in the faults he detected. I still prefer to be original than right because a fertile error does more for the world than a boring fact. I still subject audiences and readers to torrents of novelty. I still like the strange and new for their own sake. I still eat a lot of my research material and over-write about it (despite the purple-sprouting prose in which Dan caught me out, I recently won the IACP prize for best food-writing and Spain's Premio Nacional de Gastronomía). I haven't been able to resist opportunities in journalism, and now write regularly for three Spanish papers and for the *Times Higher Education Supplement*. In other respects, I have moved on a bit, to be Prince of Asturias Professor at Tufts, where it is a condition of my Chair that I teach some Spanish history; but I still belong to Queen Mary, University of London, where I have my doctoral students and return periodically. The Prentice Hall Seminar Series in Global History, which I used to run at the Institute of Historical Research, now meets at Tufts, where my colleagues and I are launching masters' and doctoral programmes in global history. Since Dan's piece, I have published a strange assortment of new books. *Ideas* was a commission from Dorling Kindersley, who, having specialized in books for children, want to keep the allegiance of their readers as they grow up. This book tackles the history of ideas idea by idea (with not more than 500 words on any one of them). It is unusual, too, in beginning with the Palaeolithic (and even with some speculations about pre-human hominid thinking – a subject which has since become fashionable). You only get to the ancient Greeks when you are a third of the way through the book. *The Americas* is a concise attempt to look at the hemisphere whole – instead of treating Anglo-America and Latin America discretely in the usual way. I think the effects are illuminating. *So You Think You're Human* is a little essay sketching the outlines of a major untold story: how we came to have the broad concept of humankind which enables strangers to recognize each other as fellow-humans despite the chasms of culture and appearance that separate us. I trace, too, a narrowing 'animal frontier' – a story of the progressive exclusion of animals from a moral community which has become exclusive to one species. And I argue that these stories are not over: the present limits of our concept of humankind will change.

I have two big books in the press: *The World: A Global History* is a textbook commissioned by Prentice Hall for US students, in which I try to break the textbook mould and deal with the entire world – or as much of it as possible – in every chapter, instead of arranging the material along regional or cultural lines. The emphasis is on environmental history and the history of cultural exchange. *A Girdle Round the Earth* (US title: *The Pathfinders*) is a global history of exploration, beginning with the migrations of *homo erectus* and ending in Brazil in the 1990s: I see explorers as laying the infrastructure of global history – the routes by which sundered cultures re-established contact and reversed the long history of cultural divergence that dominated most of our past, substituting the reconvergence we are now experiencing.

Three projects engage my current research. I have found something new and, I think, important, to say about Vespucci in a short biography which (as I write these lines in October 2005) is nearly finished. I am at work on a study of Creole languages, especially in slave communities, in the Early Modern New World, starting with Negerengels, about which many fascinating early sources survive. This work will be the subject of the Schouler Lectures at Johns Hopkins in 2008. Finally, taking advantage of the fact that I now hold the Prince of Asturias Chair, I have started work on a history of Spanish civilization, so the trajectory Dan described in his piece about me will, one day, come full circle.

Lisa Jardine

BIOGRAPHY

Lisa Jardine CBE is Director of the Arts and Humanities Research Council's 'Centre for Editing Lives and Letters', and Centenary Professor of Renaissance Studies at Queen Mary, University of London. She is a Fellow of the Royal Historical Society, the RSA and the English Association.

She is an Honorary Fellow of King's College, Cambridge, and holds honorary doctorates from the University of St Andrews and Sheffield Hallam University. She is a member of the Council of the AHRC and chairs its Museums and Galleries Committee. She is a Trustee of the V&A Museum and sits on the Council of the Royal Institution and the Michael Faraday Prize Committee of the Royal Society.

Professor Jardine read mathematics at Newnham College, Cambridge, where she changed to English in her final year. While there she became Senior Treasurer of Footlights at the invitation of Emma Thompson and Simon McBurney. She completed her PhD at Cambridge on the scientific method of Sir Francis Bacon.

From 1971 to 1974 she was a Senior Research Fellow at the Warburg Institute in London. In 1975 she became a Teaching Fellow of King's College, Cambridge, and in 1976 the first woman Fellow of Jesus College, Cambridge.

From 1976 to 1989 Lisa Jardine was a lecturer in the Faculty of English at the University of Cambridge, becoming Reader in Renaissance Studies in 1989. In October 1989 she moved to London, to become Professor and Head of Department at

Queen Mary College, now Queen Mary, University of London. She was Dean of Arts at QM from 1993 to 1996. She has held visiting Professorships in the History Department at Princeton University and at Johns Hopkins University, where she was the John Hinkley interdisciplinary professor in 1997–98, combining her interests in English, History and History of Science.

Professor Jardine writes and reviews for the major UK national newspapers and magazines and for the *Washington Post*, and has presented and appears regularly on arts, history and current affairs programmes for TV and radio. She judged the 1996 Whitbread Prize, the 1999 Guardian First Book Award, the 2000 Orwell Prize and was Chair of Judges for the 1997 Orange Prize and the 2002 Man Booker Prize.

She has published over 50 scholarly articles in refereed journals, and 17 full-length books, both for an academic and for a general readership. She is currently working with Dr David Colclough, preparing the *Sylva Sylvarum* and *New Atlantis* volume for the *Oxford Complete Francis Bacon*, and with Professor Tony Grafton on completing *Reading in the Renaissance*, a book-length study of the marginalia of Gabriel Harvey. She is writing a single-authored book on Anglo-Dutch influence in the seventeenth century, entitled *Going Dutch*.

She is passionately interested in education from cradle to grave. She was Chair of the Governors of Westminster City School, an inner-city state boys' school in London, and is now a Foundation Governor of St Marylebone School for Girls, an inner-city London state girls' school. She is active in debates about History and English in the National Curriculum.

Lisa Jardine is married to architect John Hare and has three children.

PRINCIPAL PUBLISHED BOOKS

Francis Bacon: Discovery and the Art of Discourse (1974)

Still Harping on Daughters: Women and Drama in the Age of Shakespeare (1989)

From Humanism to the Humanities: Education and the Liberal Arts in Fifteenth-and Sixteenth-Century Europe (with Professor A.T. Grafton) (1986)

What's Left? Women in Culture and the Labour Movement (with Julia Swindells) (1989)

Erasmus, Man of Letters: The Construction of Charisma in Print (1993) (winner of the Bainton Book Prize)

Reading Shakespeare Historically (1996)

Worldly Goods: A New History of the Renaissance (1996)

Erasmus: The Education of a Christian Prince, for Cambridge Texts in the History of Political Thought (ed.) (trans. N.M. Chesire, M.J. Heath and L. Jardine) (1997)

Hostage to Fortune: The Troubled Life of Francis Bacon (with Dr Alan Stewart) (1998)

Ingenious Pursuits: Building the Scientific Revolution (1999)

Global Interests: Renaissance Art between East and West (with Dr Jerry Brotton) (2000)

On a Grander Scale: The Outstanding Career of Sir Christopher Wren (2002)

Robert Hooke: London's Leonardo (with J. Bennett, M. Cooper and M. Hunter) (2003)

The Curious Life of Robert Hooke: The Man who Measured London (2003)

The Awful End of Prince William the Silent: The First Assassination of a Head of State with a Hand-gun (2005)

PROFILE, October 2003

'I have never understood the difference between the arts and the sciences, or felt the need to choose between them.'

The sentence could have come from Dr Jacob Bronowski, the Polish-born mathematician, scientist, television Brains Truster, presenter of TV's *Ascent of Man* and expert on the poetry of Blake. In fact, it comes from his daughter, Lisa Jardine, whose writings are peppered with statements to the effect that intellectual boundaries are for crossing.

As you read Jardine's work or spend time in her company, you get a firm impression of someone – like Erasmus or Bacon – unconfinable within conventional borders. In an early, feminist study of Shakespeare, she identifies herself with those scholars 'who struggle to position ourselves between the disciplines of history, cultural studies, and text criticism'. Various universities have made her professor of History or of English. But London University's Queen Mary probably have it right, pinning her down as their Professor of Renaissance Studies.

Except that I doubt whether this energetic, intellectually omnivorous Renaissance woman is ever fully pinned down. Jardine's conversation bubbles with exhibitions she's just reviewed, novels she's just read (she was Chair of last year's Man Booker Prize jury), radio and TV programmes she's been asked to present or appear on, conferences she's shortly to address, committees she sits on, grants she is applying for, new books she'd like to write, trips she's about to make. The day we met for lunch, she'd just been to Dallas for the weekend to visit one of her sons and his family. She also talks with infectious glee about students, friends and colleagues. This is clearly someone who loves to work collaboratively, as so many of her joint-authored books demonstrate. One of Jardine's latest innovations is the annual 'Masterclass' she has set up at Queen Mary (under the aegis of the new Arts and Humanties Research Board-funded 'Research Centre for Editing Lives and Letters' that she heads) where postgraduate students, in full view of an audience, spend a day honing their textual research skills under the critical eye of a major historian.

The eldest child in a household where dinner guests in the 1950s and early 1960s included people like Aldous Huxley and C.P. Snow, Lisa was a clever little girl with a well-developed ego who sailed effortlessly through Cheltenham Ladies' College ('I was probably an obnoxious, opinionated little swot!') and thence to Cambridge. Here, doubtless to her father's delight but without his prompting, she registered to do maths. Was there any sign yet of the budding historian? Lisa remembers borrowing history books from the Boots Library as an adolescent, but points out that, in the Bronowski home, everything was fair game: history, literature, languages, politics, the sciences and the arts. All these came together when, having stumbled slightly in maths, she transferred to English for Part II and went on to do a PhD on the writings of that archetypal boundary-crosser, Francis Bacon.

A committed socialist, Jardine became secretary of the university Labour Club, and found links between her political and intellectual worlds in the inspired radicalism of Raymond Williams, whose advocacy of a more democratised culture shone through *Culture and Society* and *The Long Revolution*. At the time, Williams was (somewhat improbably) a Fellow of Jesus College, and it was here (after a three-year research spell at the Warburg Institute, and brief stints at Essex, Cornell, Girton and King's) that Jardine herself was to settle in 1976.

Her intellectual centre of gravity as a young academic was sixteenth-century Humanism, and many of her early articles are formidably learned, calling upon sources in French, Italian and Latin. She was officially a Lecturer in English. But what interested this working mother with a strong socialist-feminist conscience was the politics of the texts she read. Thus, in *Still Harping on Daughters*, Jardine tried to draw out the underlying relations of power and gender in the works of Shakespeare and his contemporaries. She wrote about shrews and scolds and tongues, considered Shakespeare's representation of 'strong' women and analysed the cultural significance of cross-dressing in his plays and the importance of inheritance laws to the status of women in Elizabethan England. Some of these themes recur in a later series of essays published as *Reading Shakespeare Historically*. In a tightly argued book about Erasmus, drawing on close study of the texts and Erasmus' own marginalia, she showed how the celebrated Humanist teacher manipulated and manufactured his own image and reputation, even to the point of systematically elevating the stature of one of his supposed intellectual forbears. Jardine's most avowedly political book, *What's Left?* (with Julia Swindells), was in part a homage to Raymond Williams, who died while it was being written. Stimulated by the oft-repeated mantra that women voted to the 'right' of men (and were keeping the Thatcher government in power), Jardine and Swindells argued that the Labour Party should develop a more inclusive culture, moving beyond its somewhat atavistic preoccupation with working men.

Fiercely independent-minded, at times combative, Jardine already felt herself to be part of an international community of like-minded scholars. In the introduction to *Still Harping on Daughters*, she took to task what she saw as the dogmatism of certain feminist American critics, while in *Reading Shakespeare Historically* she recorded the 'differences of opinion', 'head-on confrontations' and 'crossed swords' her approach had stimulated. But there is no fight so vigorous as one between comrades, and she proclaimed that she had learned far more from her intellectual bunfights with the Americans than from their 'dignified' British counterparts. I suspect Lisa Jardine would be rather a fun person to cross swords with.

For nearly 15 years, Jardine has been at Queen Mary. From here, she has produced a torrent of books which – alongside a busy subsidiary career as broadcaster and reviewer – have brought her name to a wider audience than the young researcher into the textual arcanae of Erasmus could ever have imagined. In some ways, Jardine appears to have reinvented herself. Her biographies of Bacon, Wren and Hooke, like her studies of the Renaissance and of the scientific revolution, may be substantial works of scholarship based on original textual research. But all are distinguished by an easily readable narrative style, the scholarship (and the residual politics) worn lightly.

Sometimes, like a writer of detective novels, Jardine starts with something familiar, raises questions about what it signifies, and then picks up clues from a wide variety of sources to help clinch a final verdict. Thus, in *Worldly Goods* (and again in the later *Global Interests*, co-authored with Jerry Brotton), Jardine considers some of the most famous artworks of the Renaissance. Since Burckhardt, it has been the fashion to think of the Renaissance as signifying the re-emergence of individualistic artistic creativity. Jardine proposes a different approach. Take a well-known work like the *Arnolfini Marriage* by Jan van Eyck. A sensitive portrait of a happy couple? Perhaps. But note the oriental rug, says Jardine, the lavish furniture, the rich fabrics of the couple's clothes, the ornate chandelier and the kitsch little lap dog. This painting, she concludes, is best understood as a display of the acquisitiveness of a wealthy Flemish merchant, 'a celebration of ownership – of pride in possessions from wife to pet, to bed-hangings and brasswork'. Similarly, Holbein's *Ambassadors* is 'a painting of French aristocrats, executed in England by a German artist, and replete with allusions to commercial centres in Nuremberg, Wittenberg and London, and to political exchanges between France, England, Germany, Venice and Istanbul'. The underlying message of works such as these, in other words, lies not so much in their being aesthetic masterpieces, but rather in what they reveal of the power and wealth of those who commissioned and owned them at a time of ever-widening diplomatic and trading patterns.

Jardine's 1998 biography of Bacon, *Hostage to Fortune* (written with Alan Stewart), similarly, scarcely touches on the aesthetic or intellectual qualities of Bacon the essayist and philosopher of science, and you would search here in vain for enlightenment about, for example, Mary Queen of Scots, the Shakespearean theatre, the succession of James I or the Gunpowder Plot. The monarchs and hierarchs of Bacon's day do appear, but chiefly as recipients of the stream of anxious supplications for preferment Bacon submits throughout his 'troubled life'. It was a troubled death, too, traditionally attributed to a cold this inveterate experimenter caught while stuffing a dead chicken with snow to see whether that would

preserve the flesh. Like Holmes and Watson, Jardine and
Stewart adduce strong evidence to suggest, on the contrary,
that Bacon had been ill for some time, that he was a chronic
physic-taker (or drug addict), and that he probably killed
himself by the self-administration of inhaled nitre or opiates
in a vain attempt to alleviate his suffering. *Hostage to Fortune*
('Misfortune', the authors ought perhaps to have entitled their
book) is a gripping story in close focus of a man of huge and
varied talents constantly seeking the fame and fulfilment (and
wealth) that eluded him.

A year later came *Ingenious Pursuits*, a hugely successful
book about the scientific revolution containing largely
anecdotal (and richly illustrated) chapters on some of the great
breakthroughs in seventeenth-century science and technology
in such areas as astronomy, anatomy, horology, cartography
and the identification and classification of new flora and fauna.
Here, Jardine introduces a new *dramatis personae*, a galaxy
of starry scientific savants: Newton, Boyle, Flamsteed, Jonas
Moore, Halley, Hevelius and Huygens – as well as Christopher
Wren and Robert Hooke, whose full-length biographies she
went on to produce. Surprisingly, perhaps, there is virtually
nothing about the great artistic figures of the day such as
Purcell, Dryden, Lely, Kneller or Congreve. At first blush, it
seems the scholar of Renaissance Humanism has abandoned
art and literature entirely and reinvented herself as expert on
Restoration-era science and technology. And has the feminist
firebrand of old had her claws trimmed by the flattery of the
establishment? All Jardine's recent books are about men – and
men whose private lives, or what we know about them, offer
little incentive to speculation about gender or sexism. The
'Ascent of Man' *redivivus*?

Every first blush requires a second and, on closer reading,
it becomes evident that much of Lisa Jardine's recent *oeuvre*
in fact builds on principles that have guided her from the
outset. Far from abandoning an interest in the arts, she is

at pains to demonstrate how the human and commercial interrelationships that lie behind scientific advance are similar to those that stimulate artistic creation. In both, people look at the work of other people, meet, talk, argue, correspond, raise money, judge, misjudge, interact with a constantly shifting wider environment – and use their 'ingenuity' to try to advance the things they care about. The creation of a play or painting may require different skills from the invention of a telescope or microscope. But what about the attempt to portray, and then to classify, the heavenly bodies or fossil fragments revealed by the latest scientific technology? Art or science? What of Newton's struggle to understand the principles governing the cosmos? Or the meticulous drawings of insects as seen under a microscope done by Wren and Hooke – not to mention the rebuilding of London after the Fire and creation of St Paul's Cathedral? Wren is just the kind of person Jardine particularly admires (and obviously identifies with): someone of widely varied talents 'whose enterprises regularly transgress, fearlessly and with apparent ease, the disciplinary boundaries traditionally policed under the labels "arts" and "science"'. To Wren or Hooke, 'the beauty of the interior of a dome, the patterns of nerves in the human neck or the detail of the viscera of a bee were equally compelling'.

Thus, whether in the arts or sciences, great ideas are 'the product of collisions of minds and broken boundaries'. They are also, more often than is realized, the result of collaborations. Throughout Jardine's recent books, we encounter busy big-wigs marching in and out of labs and observatories, encountering one another in elegant dining rooms, royal palaces, noble houses and interminable meetings of the Royal Society. Even the most successful collaborations can contain elements of grit and acrimony. Newton, a touchy personality (Jardine calls him 'socially dysfunctional'), nearly withdrew part of the *Principia* in response to the querulousness of Hooke and might not have completed and published the work without the constant support and encouragement of Halley. On the other hand, the ubiquitous Hooke had such a fruitful partnership with Wren – the archetypal collaborator – that you sometimes cannot be sure what was Wren's work and what Hooke's. At times, English, French and Dutch scientists were working together to develop better clocks and watches, maps and navigation charts even when their countries were at war.

There are other respects, too, in which Jardine's new books build on some of her earlier themes. The Bacon biography built upon research done long ago for her doctoral dissertation while all her latest books, like the earlier ones, contain lengthy direct quotations from the historical texts, as though to let the authentic voices of contemporaries tell their own tale as far as possible. Furthermore, these figures – like Erasmus – conspicuously struggled between old and new kinds of knowledge. Thus both Bacon, the consummate philosopher of inductive science, and Newton, the magisterial author of the *Principia*, were drawn to the quasi-alchemical power of certain drugs, while the creator of St Paul's Cathedral apparently believed he could cure his wife of thrush by 'hanging a bag of live boglice about her neck'. Such men inhabited the cusp of past and future: another intellectual 'boundary' that most people find constricting but which provided both challenge and opportunity to Jardine's host of historical heroes. Several of them, too, were deeply concerned, as Erasmus (and Shakespeare's Othello) had been, with their public reputation. Newton commissioned many portraits of himself (outsmarting his adversary Hooke, of whom there is no authenticated portrait), carefully manipulating his image as paintings, busts and medallions spread the message of his genius around the world. Wren's papers, assembled by his son and grandson, more or less airbrush the unfortunate Hooke out of the picture – which helps explain why Jardine went on to write a biography, rescuing this extraordinarily versatile man from a degree of obscurity he didn't deserve.

Looking back, Lisa Jardine says she has always enjoyed
working at different levels of the intellectual rock face at the
same time. Thus, the media don, Booker jury chair and editor
of the introduction to Charles Saatchi's 'Sensation' exhibition
is currently editing (with Amanda Foreman) a series of short
volumes for HarperCollins on great moments, inventions
or encounters that 'made history'. The deeper striation
is represented by Jardine's work, with Graham Rees, on a
multivolume 'Bacon edition' for Oxford University Press, and
her forthcoming book on published collections of Latin letters
and the stories they tell. She is also contemplating a possible book
which, by calling upon the political, economic and scientific
history of the seventeenth century and digging deep into the
records of both the Dutch and English East India Companies,
could amount to a multidimensional reinterpretation of the
'Glorious Revolution' – and, incidentally, show the inadequacy
of purely national history.

'I've always liked to try and hold large bodies of disparate
information in my head, from fields that don't usually talk to
each other, and then find the links between them', she says. To
Jardine, history is a constantly shifting dialogue between the
present and the past; like Penelope, she is constantly weaving
the tapestry – and then unravelling and reweaving it. She also
admits to a shameless compulsion to share the results of her
endeavours with as many people as possible. All in all, her
father would have been proud of her.

Richard J. Evans

BIOGRAPHY

Richard J. Evans was born in Woodford, Essex, in 1947. He was educated at Forest School, Walthamstow, London, and read Modern History at Jesus College, Oxford, graduating with First Class Honours in 1969 and winning the Stanhope Historical Essay Prize the same year. He was awarded a Hanseatic Scholarship to study in Hamburg and he completed his doctorate at St Antony's College, Oxford, in 1972.

From 1972 to 1976 he was Lecturer in History at Stirling University and from 1976 to 1989 he taught at the University of East Anglia, where he was appointed Professor of European History in 1983. In 1980 he was Visiting Associate Professor of European History at Columbia University, and in 1987 he was awarded the Wolfson History Prize and the William H. Welch Medal of the American Association of the History of Medicine for his book *Death in Hamburg*. In 1989 he moved to Birkbeck College, University of London, where he was Professor of History until 1998.

In 1990, a film about his work was broadcast by German television under the title *Mr Evans geht durch Hamburg* ('Mr Evans Goes Through Hamburg'). In 1992 he gave the principal address in Hamburg Town Hall on the centenary of the cholera epidemic of 1892, and in 1994 he was awarded the city's Civic Medal for Art and Science.

In 1996, he was awarded the Fraenkel Prize in Contemporary History for his book *Rituals of Retribution*. Since 1998 he has

been Professor of Modern History at Cambridge University
and a Fellow of Gonville and Caius College, Cambridge. He
is a member of the Government's Spoliation Advisory Panel,
advising on claims for restitution of cultural objects looted
during the Nazi era, and in 2000 was the principal witness for
the defence in the libel action brought by David Irving against
Penguin Books and Professor Deborah Lipstadt. Together with
Niall Ferguson and Stanley G. Payne, he is Editor of the *Journal
of Contemporary History*. In 2001 he acted for the National
Endowment for Science, Technology and the Arts as Mentor
to the writer W.G. Sebald in respect of the latter's grant from
the Endowment and worked closely with him on a novel about
twentieth-century Germany which was never completed, due
to Sebald's tragic death at the end of that year.

Currently he is completing a three-volume history of Nazi
Germany. He is married with two children and lives near
Cambridge.

PRINCIPAL PUBLISHED BOOKS

The Feminist Movement in Germany, 1894–1933 (1976)

The Feminists (1977)

Society and Politics in Wilhelmine Germany (ed.) (1978)

*Death in Hamburg: Society and Politics in the Cholera Years,
1830–1910* (1987)

Rethinking German History (1987)

Kneipengespräche im Kaiserreich (1989)

In Hitler's Shadow (1989)

Rituals of Retribution: Capital Punishment in Germany, 1600–1987
(1996)

In Defence of History (1997)

Tales from the German Underworld (1998)

*Telling Lies About Hitler: The Holocaust, History and the David
Irving Trial* (2002; published in the US as *Lying About Hitler*)

The Coming of the Third Reich (2003)

The Third Reich in Power, 1933–1939 (2005)

PROFILE, January 2004

Richard Evans may be Professor of Modern History at
Cambridge but that doesn't stop him receiving periodic bouts
of hate-mail and internet opprobrium. It's flattering in a way.
For Evans has emerged as one of the most prominent knights
in the field to champion the honour and integrity of history
against attack. And woe betide those on the receiving end.
Whether charging against the wilder claims of postmodernism
or of counterfactual history or, most famously, puncturing the
view of Nazi history presented in the works of David Irving,
Evans' well-honed lance can be deadly. The recent reissue of his
book *In Defence of History* includes an extensive afterword in
which Evans robustly takes on his critics from all parts of the
field and, in many cases, trounces them. His painstaking trawl
through Irving's sources in the notorious libel trial against
Deborah Lipstadt played a pivotal part in Irving's downfall.

The only child of Welsh parents who migrated to London
during the Depression, Evans was born in 1947 and raised
in the Essex extension of greater London. But his lineage is
solidly Welsh and Welsh-speaking. Memories of childhood
visits to Wales soon turn to the Calvinistic Methodist chapel
(in which many cousins were deacons) – and to the historic
Welsh ruins that intrigued him even then. Not just the famous
old castles, but also, for example, the remains of once-thriving
slate quarries with their deserted workshops, idle railway lines
and rusting machinery. One of Richard's grandfathers had
been a slate quarryman. Looking back, Evans feels his small-
town Welsh heritage helped give him a sense of 'otherness',
the inclination and capacity to ask questions about one culture
from the perspective of someone living in another.

It wasn't just bygone Wales that he heard about as he sat
at the feet of a host of older Evanses. He was gripped, too,
by tales of the recent war, of heroic derring-do by the British
(and doubtless the Welsh), and by jaw-stopping stories about

that great undifferentiated and incomprehensible mass, 'the Germans'. The picture was reinforced by the war films his schoolteacher mother took him to, featuring intrepid British servicemen with their pencil moustaches and stiff upper lips and irredeemably evil, two-dimensional Nazis. The war, too, had left abundant evidence for the future historian to examine: London bomb damage to explore, air-raid shelters to enter, gas-masks to try on.

A scholarship took the lad to Forest School in Walthamstow (where co-pupils included the future historians Richard Holmes and Charles Townshend) and thence to that perennial home of clever Welshmen, Jesus College. At Oxford, Evans learned about the Crusades from Maurice Keen, seventeenth-century England from Keith Thomas and twentieth-century Europe from Tony Nicholls (who later supervised his doctorate) and Martin Gilbert. Astonishingly, for one whose subsequent career was to depend so heavily on an ability to penetrate arcane German-language documentation, it wasn't until Evans went on to work on a D.Phil. that he learned German.

Why Germany? The student activism of the late 1960s helped focus the mind, he says. Opposition to the Vietnam War, for example, raised issues of imperialism: why does one country try and conquer another? These years also saw the early flowering of the feminist movement and, on the Right, strident calls for immigration controls and the emergence of neo-Fascism not only in Britain but also in Germany. A Damascan moment came with the visit to Oxford of Fritz Fischer, the historian who had famously undercut the view that Nazism was a twelve-year aberration by revealing, in his work on World War I, some of the deeper continuities in German history. Fischer's thesis was a bold and (to Germans) disturbing one, and the appearance of this man made a deep impression on Evans.

In the early 1970s, by now an Oxford doctoral student, Evans received funding to go to Germany to research the history of German feminism. The resulting dissertation was published a few years later as *The Feminist Movement in Germany, 1894–1933*, and was followed soon afterwards by a comparative study of women's emancipation movements in Europe, America and Australasia in 1840–1920 entitled *The Feminists*. This is inevitably something of a scamper through too many countries and histories; everywhere, it seemed, feminism tended to go through a moderate earlier phase and later a more revolutionary phase. But the two books complement each other, revealing much about the development of late nineteenth-century middle-class liberalism. Read them as a pair, and it becomes clear why German liberalism in particular was likely to fail (and why, for example, so many middle-class German women would later vote for Hitler). In Germany, unlike the USA, Australasia or much of Western Europe, the middle class was comparatively weak, while the political and religious culture emphasized such traditional values as honour, obedience to authority and the subservience of women to men.

Evans still found traces of these attitudes when undertaking his research; he recalls the incredulity of archivists in Germany (East as well as West) when told that he was studying the history of German feminism. He soon discovered that there was little serious literature on the subject – unlike the history of American feminism, for example, or the British suffragette movement, which had received considerable scholarly attention. A thread common to much of Evans' work, indeed, is that he has covered aspects of social history that are widely accepted in Britain as legitimate subjects for study – feminism, medicine and disease, crime and punishment, the underworld – but which few historians of Germany had yet tackled.

By the time the books on feminism were published, Evans was well launched into an academic career. After four years at Stirling he moved in 1976 to the University of East Anglia, becoming Professor of European History in 1983. At UEA,

Evans organized a series of conferences aimed to help create a dialogue with young German historians. A series of edited anthologies resulted, including volumes on the history of the German family, the German working class, the peasantry and the unemployed. All this while, Evans was working on what was to become his first Big Book.

As you read *Death in Hamburg* you are minded of Thomas Mann. It is a long book about the incapacity of the stubborn north German bourgeoisie to deal with the gradual encroachment of incurable sickness. As in Mann's *Zauberberg*, disease becomes the metaphor for every wider malaise, while Evans' title is of course a reference to *Death in Venice*. Evans doubtless had Camus' *The Plague* in mind, too, for he describes the approach, impact and effects of a cholera epidemic that hit Hamburg in 1892. Why Hamburg? Why then and not earlier (or later)? And why nowhere else? In answering such questions, Evans shines the bright light of his investigative skills into some of the most obscure corners of nineteenth-century European history. On the face of it a book about medical history, *Death in Hamburg* contains much about the science of sickness and health as understood in Germany at the time and the prevalent theories about the transmission of cholera and how to limit its impact. But, as in a novel, it also incorporates a series of sub-narrations about, for example, the great families and merchant traditions of the old Hansa city, the fire of 1842, the quasi-independence from Berlin that Hamburg retained after German unification in 1871, and the standards of living and general attitudes of its variegated citizenry. *Death in Hamburg* also contains a forest of footnotes and a huge specialist bibliography, while the text is liberally interspersed, *Annales*-style, with corroborative maps, graphs, diagrams and statistical tables. So exhaustively researched a project might be in danger of sinking under the load of its own documentation, but Evans' literary skills guarantee that this does not happen. From general beginnings, he gradually thickens the narrative – or sharpens the beam of his torch – as he approaches the pivotal year of 1892. Finally, having eliminated other possible causes and revealed the large holes in all the safety nets that should have impeded the onset of such an epidemic, Evans is able to point to the proximate cause of this virulent yet isolated outbreak: a cholera bacillus, brought into Hamburg by Russian emigrants en route to the USA. *Death in Hamburg* ends with the political implications and consequences of so traumatic an event: the temporary rise of the Social Democrats in Hamburg, the bourgeois fear of Communism and the calculated welcome to Nazism.

Evans has continued to investigate the life and hard times of those on the margins of society and their interactions with those in authority. One of my favourites among his books is *Tales from the German Underworld* where he pursues the fate of four colourful renegades – a compulsive forger, a vagrant woman, a confidence trickster and a fallen woman – and, through their particular stories, leads the reader into some of the wider reaches of late nineteenth-century European history. But the work that most thoroughly encapsulates Evans' multifaceted approach is *Rituals of Retribution*, a one-thousand-page history of capital punishment in Germany from before the Thirty Years' War through to our own times and the eve of reunification. Evans makes no secret of his opposition to the death penalty. But this personal interest helps illuminate his writing. So does the sheer range of topics that has attracted his vivid pen: torture and witchcraft, farewell statements and songs, mob psychology, changing attitudes to punishment and death, different forms of execution, the personality of the executioner, changing forms of cruelty and the growth of squeamishness, and the promotion of the death penalty under the Nazis until it became a state instrument of mass murder. Evans skilfully avoids the gratuitously voyeuristic while never sinking into safe but dull academicism. Building on a theoretical framework owing much to such thinkers as Foucault, Elias and Ariès, he shows how pressure for the modification or abolition of capital punishment in Germany generally coincided with an upsurge of liberal reform while a predilection for the death penalty grew when political conservatism was in the ascendant. Thus, a form of punishment traditionally regarded as arising from disinterested penal or judicial considerations was in fact (and in some places still is) primarily an instrument of state power.

It is impossible to read Evans' writings about women in Germany or official attitudes to disease, capital punishment or the 'underworld' without reflecting on how far this subject matter helps explain the later rise of Nazism. Of course, one should try not to view the past through the prism of what came later. But in the case of German history, this is hard to avoid. So it is not surprising, perhaps, that two principal themes in Evans' recent work have been the history and historiography of Nazism – and the very nature of history itself.

In 1997, towards the end of a decade as Professor of History at Birkbeck, Evans published *In Defence of History*, a short volume arising from a series of undergraduate lectures Evans had given in which he provided an update on such issues as how far history is a 'science', the nature of historical fact and causation and the kind of objectivity available to the historian. In revisiting territory familiar from the writings of Carr, Elton and others, Evans found he had to traverse a far rockier landscape than anything his predecessors could have imagined. Like many historians in the 1990s, Evans was deeply disturbed by some of the more nihilistic claims of extreme postmodernism. He was prepared to acknowledge that the past is perceived through the consciousness of the historian and mediated further by the language through which it is communicated. But that must not be a recipe for regarding all history, indeed all historical 'facts', as merely a discourse; no better or worse – or more or less true – than any other. Such ultra-relativism Evans found destructive and ultimately dangerous. Anyone who thinks the truth about the past does not matter, he writes at one point, has not perhaps lived under a regime like that of Soviet Communism where it is systematically distorted and suppressed. It was Evans' spirited defence of history, allied to his expertise in German history, that led to his most high-profile appointment: that of expert witness in the Irving trial.

Evans still meets colleagues who are surprised to hear he was an expert witness for the defence and he has to remind them that David Irving was the claimant in the case and that it was he who brought the libel case against Deborah Lipstadt, not the other way round. Lipstadt had accused Irving of falsifying his material in a sequence of apparently scholarly books in order to deny the Holocaust, to claim that the Nazis did not deliberately murder millions of Jews during World War II, and to assert that gas chambers were not used to commit this crime either in Auschwitz or anywhere else. Irving sued. The task facing Lipstadt's defence team was to pursue Irving's myriad references back to their sources, a two-year task entrusted to Evans and two assistants, and to see how far they did or didn't support the conclusions he claimed to draw from them. In *Lying About Hitler*, his book about the trial and the issues it raised, Evans summarizes some of his findings. He shows, for example, how Irving consistently misrepresented his evidence to cast doubt on the numbers killed in the Nazi camps while at the same time inflating without any solid documentary basis the numbers who perished in the Allied bombing of Dresden. Irving's intention was clearly to equate the two, says Evans, thereby implying that, while it may be regrettable that people get killed in wars, Hitler's role was not especially reprehensible. Dresden, as it were, was seen to cancel out Auschwitz.

During the trial, Evans' 740-page report was presented to the court and Evans himself underwent cross-examination by Irving who conducted his own trial. Professors of history (rather like the late Dr David Kelly) are not accustomed to the pressure of public cross-examination. But the record shows

Evans keeping his cool under (literally) trying circumstances and his testimony, written and verbal, played a key role in the ringing endorsement given by the judge to the defence. It was not only Deborah Lipstadt who won that day, Evans feels. For the judgement also represented a vindication of the view that the past had reality and that this reality was susceptible to objective study by historians and that historical truth and falsehood had demonstrable meaning.

His role in the Irving trial brought Evans considerable public prominence (and, according to the Irving website, a substantial income). It also placed him at the forefront of Nazi scholarship. Before long, the potential prominence and income were boosted further by a lucrative contract from Allen Lane to write a three-volume history of the Third Reich: big, readable volumes, the texts to be delivered at two- to-three-year intervals. Evans had written about the Nazis before; his book about the German historiography of the Third Reich, *In Hitler's Shadow*, first appeared back in 1989 and he had been teaching the subject since much earlier. But does the world need yet another narrative history of the Nazis? There are plenty of excellent short books on the subject, Evans acknowledges, but few that attempt more than a colourful summary. He admires Michael Burleigh's recent study, especially for its reassertion of the sheer weight of Nazi terror and the utter subversion of the rule of law, but Burleigh is highly selective in what he writes about. In any case Burleigh concentrates on theme where Evans is writing narrative. Evans notes that much recent scholarship has tended to categorize people as 'victims', 'bystanders' or 'perpetrators' and to pass somewhat simplistic moral judgements accordingly. His aim, rather, is to present the individual stories of Germans, important and obscure, who were caught up in the wider sweep of history and whose circumstances illustrate the enormous complexities of the choices with which they were confronted.

As I write, Evans' first volume, *The Coming of the Third Reich*, is rolling off the presses, complete with a ringing encomium on the front cover from Sir Ian Kershaw, the biographer of Hitler. By the time you read this article, the book will doubtless have been widely reviewed, I trust kindly. But I doubt whether Evans will have time to enter the lists against his critics this time, for that ruthless clock in his study is ticking away: the text of volume two is due in a year or so ...

EPILOGUE

Richard J. Evans writes:

I greatly appreciated Daniel Snowman's flattering pen-portrait of me published in *History Today* in January 2004; it's accurate and sympathetic, and I for one recognize the person he portrays. Readers may no longer remember who the Dr David Kelly was to whom Daniel refers towards the end of the piece. Kelly was a government expert on weapons of mass destruction who suffered doubts about the UK government's claim in 2003 that Saddam Hussein had WMD and was prepared to use them, and that this was why Britain went to war with Iraq. He evidently shared these doubts with a journalist and was subsequently accused of breach of confidentiality and robustly interrogated (on live TV) by a parliamentary committee, after which he committed suicide. The basic point, however, is a valid one: historians are too seldom used to playing a role in public, and my experience in the Irving/Penguin libel trial strengthened my conviction that perhaps they should be. It's regrettable, however, that Daniel Snowman has accessed David Irving's website, which contains a large number of falsehoods about me, not least in respect of the legal fees I was paid for my role as expert witness, which Irving now puts at well over three times the amount I actually earned. I continue to receive emails and letters of various kinds about the trial, over half a decade on, and I continue to be proud of my role in it. Otherwise, there is little new to report, and nothing much has changed, except that since the beginning of 2004 I have completed the second volume of my trilogy on Nazi Germany, *The Third Reich in Power, 1933–1939*, published in October 2005, and I am now working on the third and final volume, *The Third Reich at War, 1939–1945*, to be published in 2007 or 2008.

John Brewer

BIOGRAPHY

John Brewer was born in Liverpool in 1947. He was educated at Cambridge and Harvard Universities, completing his PhD in 1973. At Cambridge he was first Research Fellow at Sidney Sussex College, then Fellow of Corpus Christi and University Assistant Lecturer in History. In 1972–73 he was visiting Professor at Washington University in St Louis, and in 1976 moved from Cambridge to Yale. In 1980 he was appointed Professor of History and Literature at Harvard University and Chair of the History and Literature program. In 1987 he left Harvard to become the Director of the Clark Library and the Center for Seventeenth and Eighteenth Century Studies at UCLA, where he directed a three year research programme funded by the National Endowment of the Humanities, entitled, 'Culture and Consumption in the 17th and 18th Centuries'. He became Professor of Cultural History at the European University Institute in Florence, where he was also Chair of the Department of History and Civilisation. In 1999 he returned to the United States as a University Professor in English and History at the University of Chicago, but moved to the California Institute of Technology in 2002, where he is currently the Eli and Edye Broad Professor in Humanities and Social Science.

He has received numerous awards and fellowships, including those from the Getty, Mellon and Guggenheim Foundations, the British Social Sciences Research Council and the National

Endowment of the Humanities. His book *The Pleasures of the Imagination* won the Wolfson History Prize in 1998 and was a National Book Critics nominee in the category of criticism. He has worked extensively as a consultant to museums and galleries, including the Victoria and Albert Museum, the Tate Gallery, the Institute of Arts at Detroit, and Colonial Williamsburg. He has also often lectured in Britain, the United States, Japan, Germany and Italy. His work has appeared in German, Italian, French, Portuguese, Japanese and Chinese.

PRINCIPAL PUBLISHED BOOKS

Party Ideology and Popular Politics at the Accession of George III (1976)

An Ungovernable People: The English and their Law in the Seventeenth and Eighteenth Centuries (ed. with John Styles) (1980)

The Birth of a Consumer Society (with Neil McKendrick and J.H. Plumb) (1982)

The Common People and Politics, 1750–1800: Popular Political Participation Depicted in Cartoon and Caricature (1986)

The Sinews of Power: War, Money and the English State, 1688–1783 (1989)

Consumption and Culture in the Seventeenth and Eighteenth Centuries: A Bibliography (ed.) (1991)

Consumption and the World of Goods in the 17th and 18th Centuries (ed. with Roy Porter) (1993)

Early Modern Conceptions of Property (ed. with Susan Staves) (1995)

The Consumption of Culture: Word, Image, and Object in the 17th and 18th Centuries (ed. with Ann Bermingham) (1995)

The Pleasures of the Imagination: English Culture in the Eighteenth Century (1997)

Rethinking Leviathan. The British and German States in Comparative Perspective (ed. with Eckhart Hellmuth) (1999)

A Sentimental Murder: Love and Madness in the Eighteenth Century (2004)

PROFILE, April 2004

'In the early 1960s I left my father for my uncle.' Not literally, of course. What John Brewer means is that when he was a teenager, he deserted what he regarded as the ultra-bourgeois conservatism of his surgeon father for the more free-flowing Marxism of Uncle Leslie, a radical journalist and *bon viveur* with long hair, a fine taste in wines and a succession of debts, wives and mistresses. Any lad growing up in the Liverpool of the Beatles might have been tempted to make a similar transition. Not that John 'deserted' his father completely. On the contrary. It was Dr Brewer who first took the boy to art galleries and museums. A keen collector of antiques, Brewer *père* once wrote what became a standard guide to old clocks, evidently bringing to the study of their intricate interiors something analogous to his skills as a surgeon. His view of the past may have been tinged with what his son regarded as old-fashioned, post-imperial nostalgia. But it was he who first stimulated John's interest in the material survivals of earlier times – thereby inadvertently helping kickstart the career of one of our most innovative cultural historians.

There were schoolteachers and educationalists in the family, too, while John's mother, a nurse (who had met his father in a World War II field hospital), was a passionate reader. John became an avid reader, too, immersing himself not in *Pamela* or *Tom Jones* (those would come later) but in what were the standard texts for clever, questing teenagers aspiring to intellectual cosmopolitanism: Kierkegaard, Nietzsche, Camus, Sartre, Dostoyevsky and that cult classic of the time, Colin Wilson's *The Outsider*. An interest in Russian history led him, under the watchful eye of a benign A Level History teacher, to do some work on minorities and pogroms in late Tsarist times. So when Brewer sailed into Cambridge at the age of 18, his ambition was to become one of those accomplished, cross-disciplinary, multilingual European intellectuals he so admired, an aspiration he honed further by spending six months in Paris improving his French.

At Sidney Sussex (where the Master was David Thomson, author of *Europe Since Napoleon*), Brewer had tutorials with Derek Beales, an expert on Italian and Austrian history, and the medievalist Otto Smail, while the strongest influence during Brewer's undergraduate years probably came from the intellectual historian Quentin Skinner. 'If anything looked interesting,' says Brewer, recalling the intoxicating intellectual promiscuity he enjoyed at Cambridge, 'I'd pursue it.' It was a habit that has never left him.

In his final year, Brewer encountered Herbert Butterfield. It was Butterfield's last year, too, but he evidently still taught his Special Subject on the historiography of George III with considerable élan and provided inspiration to the young man that was to help shape the rest of his career. Brewer immersed himself in the politics of mid-eighteenth-century Britain, talking his way into the British Museum to check the footnotes in the great study by Sir Lewis Namier. Like all who followed in Namier's footsteps, Brewer was awed by his thoroughness. Yet he also found himself fundamentally at odds with Namier's emphasis on political elites and his denial of the importance of ideas and ideologies in politics. This was to provide the thrust behind what became Brewer's PhD and first book.

But first, Brewer spent a year at Harvard. Here, he attended lectures by such illuminati as Stanley Cavell (on Wittgenstein) and John Rawls (the theory of justice). Under the tutelage of that outstanding scholar of Puritan New England, Bernard Bailyn, he wrote a paper about the early history of publishing and patronage. He remembers being disconcerted at first to discover that his American counterparts did not necessarily share his particular interests and preoccupations. History, as understood in Cambridge, Massachusetts, was different from – and in some ways more radical than – what Brewer had been taught in that other Cambridge back home. As he studied the past from what was (to him) a new perspective, he began to realize that history, like any other intellectual discipline, was itself 'situated' in its own space and time.

The year 1968 was a dramatic period for a young man to get to know the US for the first time. The Vietnam War was looming large, as were racial issues and the sexual revolution. Chicago, hosting the Democratic Convention that summer, erupted in riot and the year ended with Richard Nixon being elected to the White House. For a while, student protest brought Harvard to a close, like so many American universities, and Brewer went along to the football stadium with thousands of others to witness what was in effect a giant attempt to revive the democratic traditions of the New England Town Meeting. Looking back, Brewer regards 1968 as a caesura, a moment – rather like 1789 – when the history of previous decades had to be rewritten. At the time, however, as he tried to make sense of the exciting turmoil going on around him, he simply presumed that this was what America was always like. He readily resonded to the 'can-do' optimism of the USA, even if it sometimes perplexed him, and he knew that, one day, he would have to return to the States. But not until he had Namier nailed.

Party Ideology and Popular Politics at the Accession of George III , published in 1976, arose out of Brewer's PhD and was a conscious assault on the Namier school with its anti-theoretical bias and contempt for equality. Namier himself, an émigré from Central Europe, had understandably detested the political dogmatism he saw on the continent and admired the British ruling class for what he believed had always been its non-ideological pragmatism. But Brewer sought to demonstrate the importance of ideas and arguments in politics, and insisted that even in the eighteenth century, often regarded as an era of oligarchical complacency, political principles were in fact vigorously debated. And not just by the political elite, either. To Brewer, commercialised, popular, mass culture played a part in political decision-making, then as now, and warranted serious historical analysis.

It was an insight Brewer shared with many among his generation as old-fashioned political history came to be enriched, and perhaps ousted, by the new social (and often socialist) history of *Annales* and such writers as Edward Thompson, Eric Hobsbawm, Christopher Hill and Rodney Hilton. Never, however, a Marxist historian in the sense of seeing economic forces at the root of social change, Brewer drew more on the insights available from social and cultural anthropology and the work of Natalie Davis, Jack Goody, Max Gluckman and Victor Turner.

Above all, Brewer found himself in the court of that prince among patrons, J.H. Plumb. Jack Plumb was almost single-handedly responsible for the revival of interest in the social and cultural history of the eighteenth century, not least because of his insistence on writing (and lecturing) in language non-experts could understand and enjoy. He was Brewer's thesis supervisor, though they did not see much of each other and, as Brewer recalls, their relationship began with an almighty row about something or other and remained uneasy. But Plumb, an energetic networker as we would say nowadays, greatly helped promote the careers of the galaxy of young stars who emerged around his orbit, among them not only Brewer but also Roy Porter, Simon Schama, Linda Colley and David Cannadine.

Did the Plumb 'babes' think of themselves as a group? Perhaps not, though Brewer has always been a close friend of Schama (and is joint dedicatee of Schama's book about Rembrandt), and he still grieves over the premature death of that over-energized supernova, Roy Porter, whom he had known since undergraduate days.

A combination of Brewer's talent and Plumb's connections led Brewer to professorships at Yale and Harvard, and a flood of solo and collegiate publications. There were articles on Bute and Burke, a book (with John Styles) on the ungovernability of the English and another (with Plumb and Neil McKendrick) on the emergence of consumerism. Brewer's interest in cultural history emerged strongly when he was at Yale in the late 1970s and was able to work in the Yale Center for British Art, rubbing shoulders with people like the Hogarth specialist Ronald Paulson. Nevertheless, he retained his interest in political history. Thus, *The Sinews of Power*, Brewer's book about the relationship between war, finance and the formation of the eighteenth-century English 'state', was written while at Harvard (where he had professorships of both history and literature). Then, in 1987, Brewer went to California as Director of UCLA's Center for Seventeenth and Eighteenth Century Studies.

He came to love Los Angeles. Its crude commercialism, vibrant optimism and vigorous cultural life seemed to feed off one another, Brewer felt, rather as they had done in eighteenth-century England. It was the same kind of brash excitement that must have characterized Renaissance Florence, too, where brutal politics, big money and daring art were equally flaunted. For a few years in the 1990s, Brewer and his wife – the historian Stella Tillyard – were based in Florence where, as Professor of Cultural History at the European University Institute, he supervised the postgraduate research of some of the finest young minds in the new Europe (and tried to keep up with his daughter's increasingly idiomatic Italian). By now very much the peripatetic cosmopolitan he had aspired to become when a teenager, Brewer continued to read widely outside his 'field' and was at home with intellectual developments and debates on the continent. But he remained resolutely loyal to British history, producing articles – and a trio of co-edited books arising from a three-year UCLA project – on the complex relationships between culture, commerce and consumption in seventeenth- and eighteenth-century Britain. What we like to think of as 'high' culture, Brewer consistently tried to show, does not become culture unless people choose to finance, promote and patronize it.

This was the central message of the book for which Brewer is best known and which appeared in 1997. *The Pleasures of the Imagination* contains a series of London-based chapters on publishing and printing, painting and art, theatre and music, goes on to explore culture in the provinces, and ends with speculation about the role of culture in the emerging idea of British nationhood as a whole. If you read the book, your strongest memory will probably be of Brewer's vivid vignettes of persons, places and events, some well-known (Vauxhall Gardens, *The Beggar's Opera*, Garrick, Reynolds), others less so (the diarist Anna Larpent, the Newcastle engraver Thomas Bewick). The arts in Hanoverian England, Brewer suggests, were less courtly and more commercial than on the continent, partly no doubt because of the incompetence or penury of the monarchy but also as a concomitant to the vigorous, commercially-based urban life that sprang up alongside the industrial revolution.

Today, as we look back to the arts in eighteenth-century England, we tend to construct a smooth and genteel picture of high cultural competence, elegantly highlighted by the occasional presence of genius. Yet Brewer regards this as a nostalgic reverie and will have none of it. At the time, he says, things felt much rougher, lumpier, with a thousand noisy elements constantly jostling for attention. Artists were regarded as craftsmen, paid hands with a job to do. 'Sensibility' was deemed to lie not so much with those who produced culture as with those who consumed it. Thus, Brewer is concerned not with making an aesthetic assessment of Hogarth, Handel, Haydn and the rest but to discover the part these and countless others played in helping to create the exuberant, multifaceted culture of their day. It is faintly ironic, and perhaps comforting, to realize that many of today's anxieties about the arts ('dumbing-down' of the media, deleterious impact of sex and violence in the arts,

commodification of culture) were prefigured in an age whose
cultural highlights we have now come to revere.

The Pleasures of the Imagination was mostly written in
Florence and London. But the lure of America took Brewer
across the Atlantic once again, initially to that hothouse of
intensive learning, the University of Chicago, then back to Los
Angeles where, firmly ensconced at Cal Tech, he now holds
one of those Elysian chairs that are the envy of lesser mortals.
He and Stella and the children are all frequent flyers, with
homes in Oxford and Italy as well as California. But, says
Brewer, America frankly gives him facilities that would be
unattainable elsewhere: the Getty and the Huntington on his
doorstep, opportunities for consultancy work (for example,
for the Arts Institute in Detroit, which has one of the finest and
least known museums in all of North America) – and, above
all, serious time for research and writing. Learned historical
papers flow from his pen on power and patronage, culture
and commerce, sentiment and sensibility. He also evinces a
growing interest in the nature of history itself, what history
is or should be about, the latest and most innovative ways
of trying to write about it, and how to bring it to a wider
audience. Much of this comes together in his latest book, a
slim volume, disarmingly easy to read at a sitting or two, yet
packed with layers of meaning.

On the face of it, *A Sentimental Murder* is what it says it is: a
rollicking good yarn about 'Love and Madness in Eighteenth-
Century England'. In 1779, Martha Ray, the long-term mistress
of the First Lord of the Admiralty, the Earl of Sandwich, was
shot dead by a distressed young man evidently in love with
her. Aristocrats and government ministers have had mistresses
before and since, and murders by unrequited lovers are not
unknown to history. So what is special about this event?

Brewer's main concern is not with pinning down the precise
historical truth about this particular murder but, rather, with
its wider ramifications. How did people get to know about

it, how was it reported, what did people at the time believe about the three characters involved and how did the story play to later generations? In a sequence of Russian-doll-like chapters, he uncovers his deeper purpose subject by subject. Thus, a section about the press in eighteenth-century Britain leads Brewer to consider the 'sentimental' framework within which such stories were recounted. As readers lapped up the juicy gossip of Martha's murder, they were encouraged to try and share the emotions – the *sentiments* – of each of the three emblematic protagonists, the Earl, the Mistress and the Murderer. As it happens, Sandwich was a notorious libertine, Martha a singer and her killer a failed soldier-cum-prelate, all of which provided the tabloid press of the day – and Brewer and his readers today – with further fun. We hear about the war in America and encounter Boswell and John Wilkes, while Brewer goes on to consider the extraordinary subsequent career, in 'history' and 'fiction' (but which is which?) of this multilayered story.

Brewer acknowledges that *A Sentimental Murder* is frankly experimental, a 'micro-history', somewhat in the tradition of Natalie Davis or Carlo Ginzburg perhaps, aimed to show that much can be revealed about the past by teasing out the wider (and in Brewer's case, later) reverberations of an apparently inconsequential personal saga. He acknowledges, too, the influence of his wife's work, how in *Aristocrats*, for example, Stella Tillyard drew on material about people's private lives and linked it to the better-known public face of history. All this is a long way from the craft Brewer was taught at Cambridge where most of the historians he encountered regarded their subject as a record of events based on 'facts' that were 'out there' waiting to be identified and assessed by agreed processes of objective scholarship. Nowadays, says Brewer, historians are more aware of the subjectivity of the observer, the interaction between what happened and whoever happens to be describing it. To Brewer, intellectual endeavour is essentially speculative, open-ended, concerned not with 'closure' but with the constantly shifting margins of understanding.

Perhaps this is one reason why John Brewer eschews the role of public pundit. A high-profile US-based British intellectual, he would be a gift to the American media. But Brewer says he finds it cheap to criticize what's wrong in public affairs unless you also have better alternatives to propose. He searches for an apt metaphor and finds one in art connoisseurship. 'It's always easier to prove a painting isn't by Leonardo', he says, 'than to prove that it is.' This leads him to tell me the saga of Leonardo's *La Belle Ferroniere*. The painting was about to be sold by its owners, the American millionaire Harry Hahn and his wife, to the Kansas City Art Institute in the 1920s when the British expert Sir Joseph Duveen proclaimed it a mere copy. The genuine Leonardo, said Duveen, was the one in the Louvre. The sale was abruptly halted, the value of the painting plummeted and the Hahns decided to sue. The trial lasted nearly a decade, cost millions and raised every imaginable question about New World enterprise and Old World snobbery, art, authenticity, money and the art market. It's a great story. Let's hope Brewer finds time to write it up some day.

EPILOGUE

John Brewer writes:

There are times when every historian's life is dominated by a grand project, a major work which requires years of research and writing. But sometimes there are pauses, moments of reflection perhaps, or times before you move off in another direction. In the year or more since I spoke with Daniel, I've been exploring a lot of different avenues of research, without fully committing myself to any one of them, though they all, in one way or another, are concerned with either the nature of historical writing or with the world of the visual arts. The first grows out of issues that I touched on but did not develop in my last book, *A Sentimental Murder*, and which also connect to my interest in Italian *microstoria*. I'm interested in thinking about the issue of scale in historical writing. Under the influence of literary criticism this has usually been posed as a question of narration – grand narratives versus small incidents – but I want to think about it visually and spatially, in terms I adapt from landscape theory, as 'prospect' and 'refuge' history. I do so in part because I'm interested in how issues of closeness and distance affect how we understand and appreciate historical writing. (Here I've been inspired by the brilliant work on eighteenth-century historical writing by Mark Salber Phillips.) I've also been trying to connect Italian neo-realist film (for example Roberto Rossellini's *Paisa*), which uses different ways of representing 'the real' to certain forms of historical writing which are, of course, concerned to do the same thing.

In the world of the visual arts, I am still working on the case of the two versions of Leonardo's *La Belle Ferroniere*. The Duveen archive at the Getty is full of materials about the case of Duveen versus Hahn, including extraordinary books of newspaper cuttings which show it to have been one of the most widely publicized art trials of the twentieth century. But equally fascinating is the subsequent history of the Hahn's *Belle Ferroniere* – its travels seeking authentication in Europe; its periodic exhibition, and the attempts to sell the picture that persist today. I hope eventually to write the history of the picture rather than a history of the trial about its authenticity.

Simon Schama

Simon Schama studied history at Cambridge University where, from 1966 to 1976, he was Fellow of Christ's College. From 1976 to 1980 he was Fellow and Tutor in Modern History at Brasenose College, Oxford. From 1980 to 1993 he was Professor of History, Mellon Professor of the Social Sciences and William Kenan Professor of the Humanities at Harvard University, and Senior Associate of the Center for European Studies. He has also taught at the Ecole des Hautes Etudes en Sciences Sociales in Paris. He is currently University Professor in the Department of Art History and Archaeology at Columbia University.

His many award-winning publications include: *Patriots and Liberators: Revolution in the Netherlands 1780–1813* (1977) which won the Wolfson Prize for History; *Citizens: A Chronicle of the French Revolution* (1989) for which he received the major non-fiction prize in the UK, the NCR Prize; and *Landscape and Memory* (1995), the winner of the W.H. Smith Literary Award and the student-voted Lionel Trilling Prize at Columbia.

Simon Schama has been a regular contributor to the *New Republic*; the *New York Review of Books*; the *Guardian*, and since 1994, art and cultural critic for the *New Yorker*, winning a National Magazine Award for his art criticism in 1996. His criticism has been published in Dutch as *Kunstzaken* (1998) and in Spanish (2002) as *Confesiones y Encargos*. His books have been translated into eleven languages. He has received a literature award from the National Academy of Arts and Letters; and in 2001 was made a Commander of the British Empire in the Queen's Birthday Honours List.

His television work as writer and presenter for the BBC includes *Art of the Western World, Rembrandt: The Public Gaze and the Private Eye,* a five-part series based on *Landscape and Memory,* and most recently an award-winning 15-part *History of Britain* which drew four million viewers in the UK and was shown in the United States on the History Channel.

PRINCIPAL PUBLISHED BOOKS

Patriots and Liberators: Revolution in the Netherlands 1780–1813 (1977)

Two Rothschilds and the Land of Israel (1979)

The Embarrassment of Riches: An Interpretation of Dutch Culture in the Golden Age (1987)

Citizens: A Chronicle of the French Revolution (1989)

Dead Certainties: Unwarranted Speculations (1991)

Landscape and Memory (1995)

Rembrandt's Eyes (1999)

A History of Britain Volume 1: The Edge of the World (2000)

A History of Britain Volume 2: The British Wars (2001)

A History of Britain Volume 3: The Fate of the Empire (2002)

Hang-Ups: A Collection of Essays on Art (2004)

Rough Crossings: Britain, the Slaves and the American Revolution (2005)

PROFILE, July 2004

I have just read, or re-read, some six thousand pages of history. Not all of Simon Schama's published *oeuvre;* but most of most of his books. Not that there are that many of them. But several are journeyings across vast cultural landscapes, Grand Tours of the mind. You embark upon *The Embarrassment of Riches,*

Citizens, Landscape and Memory or *Rembrandt's Eyes* in the
spirit of old-time travellers boarding the Trans-Siberian or
Orient Express. These are Big Books. Reading, as Roy Porter
famously pointed out, can be bad for your health and (how
shall I put this delicately?) my lap is just recovering from
having supported, day after day, some 2.5 concentrated kilos
of Schama's *Rembrandt* in hardback. I did wonder at one
point whether it might not be safer to chain the book up like
a medieval bible and read it standing up.

Size, of course, is not everything and other authors have
produced a sequence of doorstops. But few have Schama's
capacity to clamp personal experience and prodigious
scholarship to so glittering a literary imagination. His writings
are packed with evocative detail: rich fruitcakes crammed with
raisins, currants, nuts and glacé cherries all mulled in brandy
sauce. Too rich for their own good? It is sometimes easy to
forget where the journey is supposed to be taking you. But,
as in any Grand Tour, the byways are as absorbing as the
route map. And it's always worth persevering, for Schama's
cascades of intellectual bonhomie ensure that he is invariably
a stimulating guide: even if you feel temporarily lost in the
woods, you sense he will get you there in the end.

Schama was born in February 1945, a few hours before the
destruction of Dresden. His parents were typical products of
East End Jewry: poor immigrant by background, keen to taste
the enticing offerings of Northwest London suburbia and to
improve their prospects and those of their offspring. Simon
went to school at Haberdashers' and remembers himself as
a noisy, clever adolescent; an observant Jew, serious Zionist
and committed CND leftie. He was torn between English and
History (he says he still is). Perhaps his love of language and
literature came from his father, evidently something of an
actor *manqué*, who read Dickens aloud to the family. When
the family fortunes made one of their periodic downturns,
Mrs Schama would round on her husband, upbraid him as

a latter-day Micawber and proclaim they were all headed for
the workhouse. Simon, whose historico-literary imagination
was already on heat, would think: 'Oh God; it's Newgate and
gruel for me!' At his first attempt to get into Cambridge, he
was so nervous he passed out during the European History
exam and had to be fanned back into consciousness. Years
later, he recounted this episode to Quentin Skinner. 'I know,'
smiled Skinner; 'I was the invigilator!'

In due course, Schama went up to Christ's where he fell
under the influence of the abrasive but irresistible Jack Plumb.
After a starred First in Part II, Schama soon became a multi-
tasking junior don required to teach everything from Thomas
Aquinas to Thomas Jefferson. He also moonlighted on the
Sunday Times' new colour supplement, where he was let loose
on a project called 'A Thousand Makers of the 20th Century'.
He loved it. Not for the last time, he admits, the 'naughty
journalist in me' struggled mightily with the serious historian.
Meanwhile, at Cambridge, Schama was being pressed to find
a research topic. He had been reading about the expansionism
of post-Revolutionary France (not to mention the recent Soviet
invasion of Czechoslovakia). What happens when a little state,
with its own proud history, culture and identity, is overrun
by a newer, ideologically-driven bigger one? Around this
time, Schama caught a series of lectures about those fading
polities of the eighteenth century: Genoa, Poland, Venice and
Holland. It was to the Netherlands that he was to turn for his
first book.

Patriots and Liberators was ten years in the making and
chronicles the decline of the once wealthy Dutch Republic
under the onslaught of Napoleonic France. It also pre-echoes
much in Schama's later writing. He notes the crude and wilful
stereotyping of the Dutch, a topic that forms the gateway
to *The Embarrassment of Riches*. He focuses on the tragedy
of a traditional culture trying not to fall apart under almost
impossible provocation – rather as, in *Citizens*, he was to

evince unfashionable empathy for the hard-pressed French aristocracy. If *Patriots and Liberators* gave signs of themes to come, chronologically it represented the conclusion to much Schama was to write later. It was as though he had started with a death scene, and then proceeded to study the life. Thus, both *The Embarrassment* and *Rembrandt* explore the origins of that rich Dutch culture that was later to be so brutally trampled underfoot, while *Citizens* draws the reader into the early years of the French Revolution before the advent of Napoleon.

It was a further decade before the appearance of *The Embarrassment of Riches* (people lamented that, of all the top Plumb students, those least likely to get books published were Schama and Roy Porter!). *The Embarrassment* was preceded by a real embarrassment. Schama was awakened one night to be told that Victor de Rothschild's vast and priceless family archive, temporarily lodged at Christ's for Simon to catalogue, had been flooded by a ruptured heating pipe. His vivid description of this near-calamity crosses the Story of Noah with a scene from *Titanic* as he and a few heroic friends desperately baled water. Eventually, by harnessing nothing more hi-tech than mountains of blotting paper, much of the archive was saved, Victor was gracious and understanding – and Simon produced a book about the Rothschilds and Israel.

Water abounds, too, in *The Embarrassment of Riches*: as threat, promise, opportunity, symbol. An interpretation of Dutch culture in the Golden Age, the book invites the reader to step through the formal mirror of all those genre paintings and to wander with Schama as omni-observant guide through the cities, streets, homes and taverns, and along the canals and across the bridges, of seventeenth-century Holland, bumping into the cultural furniture en route. Schama's writing is imaginative, allusive somewhat in the *Annales* style, a resonant text constantly nourished by well-chosen illustrations as our historian-cum-journalist-cum-littérateur assumes the additional role of demystifier of art and image. One sometimes senses

the ghost of Rembrandt by his side. The Dutch, within their
undulating frontiers, found themselves almost accidentally a
people of great wealth; and Schama is illuminating about the
way they would enjoy, and portray, the pleasures of good food,
drink, clothing, sex and smoking. He has much to say, too,
about Calvinism, abstention and guilt. The Dutch virtually
invented themselves as a nation, he suggests, their unifying
characteristic this central conflict – encapsulated in his title
– between self-indulgence and self-denial.

By now, Schama had left Cambridge (and Oxford where
he had been a Fellow at Brasenose in the late 1970s) to take
up a Chair at Harvard. *Citizens*, his French Revolution book
timed for the 1989 bicentenary, was a product of his Harvard
years. Written as a kind of nineteenth-century chronicle,
a homage to Carlyle, Michelet et al., it carries the reader
effortlessly from the Bastille to Beaumarchais, Rousseau to
Robespierre, Voltaire to the Vendée. We soar above Versailles
with the Montgolfiers, flee to Varennes with the King and
watch close by as appalling terror is inflicted and suffered.
If this great Hugo-esque chronicle has a thesis, it is that the
quality of life for ordinary people in France was improving
during the years preceding 1789 and that the Revolution, far
from speeding up reform, impeded it. The rural poor, Schama
shows, gained little; fat cats got fatter. He is scathing about the
bloodcurdling rhetoric of the revolutionary leaders, too: they
were rash geologists gouging out great holes in the volcano
of political discourse and then purporting surprise and shock
when seismic violence erupted.

Many gave *Citizens* a warm welcome as evidence of the
long-awaited return to narrative history. But it also attracted
criticism, even close friends seeing it as evidence that the
former *Annaliste* had deserted the socialism of his youth and,
seduced by American wealth, sided with the *ancien régime*. To
his chagrin, Schama saw himself described in *Le Monde* as a
Reaganite. He claims to have been surprised and shocked at

such reactions. If so, he must surely have known the controversy his next book would elicit.

Schama doesn't call *Dead Certainties* a history book as such but 'a work of the imagination that chronicles historical events'. The events in question are two deaths: that of General Wolfe on the Heights of Abraham in 1759 and the murder of the physician and property speculator George Parkman in Boston in 1849. Both men died, but there the certainties end; hence Schama's subtitle, 'Unwarranted Speculations'. The death of Wolfe became the subject of a painting by Benjamin West so celebrated, copied and emulated ('Death of Chatham', 'Death of Nelson') that it became almost impossible to recapture the real man or event. As for Parkman, was he really murdered by the Harvard Professor who was pronounced guilty? Or by the janitor who found parts of his corpse? Wolfe after death became transfigured into quasi-divinity, while Parkman descended from Boston Brahmin to a bunch of bones. Schama links the two stories with the figure of Parkman's nephew, the historian Francis Parkman who, eschewing the sophisticated attractions of Europe, became preoccupied with the quest for the authentic origins of America. He visited and revisited the Heights of Abraham, believing the epic Anglo-French battle had been a pivotal moment in not only European but American history. Towards the end of his life, as the neurasthenic, ailing Parkman struggled to set down his thoughts about Wolfe, the two merge, historian and subject, both of them figures of fortitude and perseverance, determined against the odds to ascend the heights that duty demands.

Don't all historians, as they enter the spirit of their subject matter, come to identify with it to some degree? Doesn't all history contain an element of speculation? Yes, of course, says Schama; there is inevitably a teasing gap separating what actually happened from how it is subsequently narrated or (in Wolfe's case, literally) portrayed. *Dead Certainties* is an attempt to illustrate ways that gap can come to be filled. It is a daring, risky book, nowhere more so than in its opening pages, a memoir of the Battle of Quebec by a foot soldier who was present – an inspired passage of fiction which predictably ruffled the territorial susceptibilities of anxious novelists and earnest historians alike.

Schama cheerfully caught the brickbats and threw them back, moving on to a work that, according to taste, is arguably his most inspired and/or bewildering. By the time *Landscape and Memory* was published in 1995, Schama had taken up his present post at Columbia and established an enviable reputation as a brilliant and compulsive communicator. He regularly packed lecture halls with doting students eager to learn from his legendary torrent of ideas (a Columbia student report said he 'cuddles up to his fame as though it were a fluffy teddy bear'), and was increasingly courted by the media. Schama's early TV appearances reveal a highly energized, somewhat restless presenter (usually bearded) whose entire body reaches out to share with the viewer his latest enthusiasms. These enthusiasms continued to proliferate. Keen to develop his interest in the relationship between history and the historian, Schama investigated how far myth and memory might be incorporated into historical narrative. Art and image fascinated him, too; he contemplated returning to an earlier pet project about Rembrandt, while his art and culture pieces for the *New Yorker* won a prestigious National Magazine Award. Everyone was talking about the 'environment', Schama noticed – but few seemed to realize that the environment itself had a history.

Landscape and Memory brought much of this together. Open it anywhere and you are guaranteed a vivid story about woods, trees, gardens, greenery, rivers, fountains, rocks or mountains. Maybe it's the Nazis and the forests you alight upon, or Robin Hood, the Greenwood and the English oak. Perhaps it's Mount Rushmore (and the woman who wanted Susan B. Anthony's face up there), or Louis XIV's fountains or the mythic qualities attributed to the Thames, the Tiber or the Nile. There's not a dull page, from the personal peregrinations into the Polish forestlands with which he opens to the final Arcadian tranquillity of Thoreau, while Schama's intellectual exuberance is counterpointed by a cornucopia of evocative illustrations. What emerges as you work through this dense but rewarding knot garden of a book is that the landscape is not something 'out there' threatened by the depredations of humankind but has itself been moulded by our collective memory. To Schama, culture and nature are not in antithesis; each creates the other.

Balance in all things: that is a theme in much of his writing. Thus, the *ancien régime* was of course corrupt; but don't go to the other extreme and exonerate all the Revolutionaries. Of course we are in danger of ruining landscapes; but let's remember we also helped create them. And so it is, too, in *Rembrandt's Eyes*. Schama is a paid-up member of the new school of art historians and fully acknowledges the importance of context. But he knows his deep-textured portrayals of Rembrandt's world cannot in themselves explain the *Night Watch*. Schama wants to edge the pendulum back a degree or two and re-examine the purely artistic impulses that projected Rembrandt from craftsman to genius. He finds a link in Rembrandt's anxiety to become a second Rubens. At times, the book reads like a double biography as Rembrandt emulates everything his idol did, even buying a house from the family that had sold Rubens his. But *Rembrandt* is also packed with thick description of one masterpiece after another as Schama unpicks the messages embedded on the famous canvases (all superbly reproduced). His language is rich, dark and luxuriant when appropriate, or pert, lively, cocky, demotic. A Rubens *Judith* shows the murderess with 'spectacularly bared kiss-me-and-die breasts'. Later, Rembrandt paints himself 'godlike, enthroned, mantled in lustrous gold, staring down presumptuous mortals, his lips pursed, a suggestion of lordly amusement playing about his eyes'. Eyes that reveal or conceal, that are dark unseeing coals – or engines of fiery Old Testament judgement.

Schama's output was by now exceptionally wide-ranging. But if there was one area he wasn't particularly associated with, it was the one he was invited to make a BBC television series about: the history of Britain. Perhaps his very distance from the subject was a recommendation; also, he had already done quite a bit of TV and was renowned for his ability to integrate story and image. It was some time, however, before he was persuaded. Not only would a British history project be a steep intellectual mountain to climb. He would have to take substantial time off from Columbia, and his young family must be enabled to accompany him to Britain for the duration.

In the event, *A History of Britain* was a greater success than anyone anticipated. Schama was very much a hands-on presenter, helping decide subject matter and locations, sitting in on editing sessions and of course attending shoots and writing and speaking all his own scripts. His trio of accompanying books went on to notch up sales of a million, almost unprecedented for serious works of historical scholarship. Beginning (as on TV) in the Orkneys and ending with Orwell and Churchill, these eminently readable, impeccably researched volumes have become as indispensable to today's history-conscious home as were Churchill's own a few generations ago.

Press reports tell of a new £3 million multi-book-and-TV deal. Schama wears his celebrity lightly and talks with undiminished energy and enthusiasm about future dragons he plans to turn into teddy bears. *Rough Crossings*, four stories about the Anglo-American relationship, will tell of former black slaves who came to England after the Revolutionary war, an armed dispute in the 1840s over whether British or American actors were better Shakespeareans, the simultaneous aesthetic pronouncements of Oscar Wilde in the Wild West and Whistler in the drawing rooms of London, and Churchill's heart attack in the White House in late 1941. Then there's a project examining various artistic masterpieces and the pressures, threats and conflicts to which their creators were subjected. Then maybe a book about Hawaii ...

As he approaches 60, it is safe to say that Mr and Mrs Schama's boy is in no imminent danger of having to subsist on gruel.

Niall Ferguson

BIOGRAPHY

Niall Ferguson, MA, D.Phil., is Laurence A. Tisch Professor of History at Harvard University. He is also a Senior Research Fellow at Jesus College, Oxford University, and a Senior Fellow at the Hoover Institution, Stanford University.

Born in Glasgow in 1964, he was a Demy at Magdalen College and graduated with First Class Honours in 1985. After two years as a Hanseatic Scholar in Hamburg and Berlin, he took up a Research Fellowship at Christ's College, Cambridge, in 1989, subsequently moving to a Lectureship at Peterhouse. He returned to Oxford in 1992 to become Fellow and Tutor in Modern History at Jesus College, a post he held until 2000, when he was appointed Professor of Political and Financial History at Oxford. Two years later he left for the United States to take up the Herzog Chair in Financial History at the Stern Business School, New York University, before moving to Harvard in 2004.

His first book, *Paper and Iron: Hamburg Business and German Politics in the Era of Inflation, 1897–1927* (1995), was shortlisted for the *History Today* Book of the Year award, while the collection of essays he edited, *Virtual History: Alternatives and Counterfactuals* (1997), was a UK bestseller and subsequently published in the United States, Germany, Spain and elsewhere.

In 1998 he published to international critical acclaim *The Pity of War: Explaining World War One* and *The World's*

Banker: The History of the House of Rothschild. The latter won the Wadsworth Prize for Business History and was also shortlisted for the Jewish Quarterly/Wingate Literary Award and the American National Jewish Book Award. In 2001 he published *The Cash Nexus: Money and Power in the Modern World, 1700–2000*, following a year as Houblon-Norman Fellow at the Bank of England.

He is a regular contributor to television and radio on both sides of the Atlantic. In 2003 he wrote and presented a six-part history of the British Empire for Channel 4, the UK terrestrial broadcaster. The accompanying book, *Empire: The Rise and Demise of the British World Order and the Lessons for Global Power*, was a bestseller in both Britain and the United States. The sequel, *Colossus: The Rise and Fall of the American Empire*, was published in 2004. His latest book is *The War of the World: History's Age of Hatred, 1914–1989*, a global history of World War II, published in September 2006, and broadcast as a six-part series presented by Ferguson in 2006 for Channel 4 Television.

A prolific commentator on contemporary politics and economics, Niall Ferguson writes and reviews regularly for the British and American press. He is a weekly columnist for the *LA Times*. In 2004 *Time* magazine named him as one of the world's 100 most influential people.

He and his wife Susan have three children. They divide their time between the US and the UK.

PRINCIPAL PUBLISHED BOOKS

Paper and Iron: Hamburg Business and German Politics in the Era of Inflation, 1897–1927 (1995)
Virtual History: Alternatives and Counterfactuals (ed.) (1997)
The Pity of War: Explaining World War One (1998)
The House of Rothschild (2 vols) (1998–99)

The Cash Nexus: Money and Power in the Modern World, 1700–2000
  (2001)
*Empire: The Rise and Fall of the British World Order and the Lessons
  for Global Power* (2003)
Colossus: The Rise and Fall of the American Empire (2004)
The War of the World: History's Age of Hatred, 1914–1989 (2006)

PROFILE, October 2004

John Ferguson, Niall's paternal grandfather, was one of the
lucky ones. He fought in the trenches in World War I and
survived to live out his days to their normal span. His other
grandfather, a journalist with literary leanings, spent much of
World War II fighting in India and Burma. Great-aunt Aggie
had emigrated to Canada, while Uncle Ian worked in India,
Africa and the Gulf. As for Niall's father, a Glasgow doctor,
he whisked his family off to do good works in Kenya for a
couple of years in the 1960s. You don't have to look far to
find out why Niall Ferguson has written so powerfully about
war and empire; the subjects are in his blood.

This summer, just 40 years of age, Ferguson became Professor
of International History at Harvard. Not that being a Professor
was anything new. In 2000, he became Professor of Political
and Financial History at Oxford and two years later took up
the Herzog Chair of Financial History at New York University's
Stern Business School. Books and articles have continued to
pour off his computer, while he has also become a skilled TV
presenter and journalist (his wife was one-time editor of the
Sunday Express). Today, Niall Ferguson is one of the most
prominent historians of his generation. He is also one of the
more controversial, a convinced neo-conservative arguing, for
example, in favour of more assertive American imperialism.
Some academic critics ask if he is still really a historian.

Niall Ferguson came from an ambitious, middle-class
Scottish family which, while free-thinking almost to the point

of atheism, was deeply imbued with an almost Calvinist ethos of hard work and self-improvement. Education, particularly in the 'hard' sciences, was understood to provide the best route up the social ladder from the mines and shipyards to bourgeois respectability and thence perhaps to England or the colonies. Niall's earliest memories include the magic of those two childhood years in Nairobi. When the family returned to Glasgow, Dr Ferguson resumed his medical practice. Was it a source of disappointment that the son didn't follow in his father's footsteps and instead, encouraged by excellent teaching at the Glasgow Academy, became an avid reader of literature and edged towards the 'soft' subject of history? Possibly. But Niall's wise parents gave him every encouragement. After all, what the boy was best at was maths.

At 17, Niall went up to Oxford with a History scholarship to Magdalen. At 18, after a pretty dissolute first year, he was nearly back in Glasgow. Not that he wasn't active. He tried, with variable success, the Union, journalism, politics, acting, playing double bass in a jazz quintet ('the thing I enjoyed most about being an undergraduate') and somehow also found time to write the requisite history essays. Then, one night, he suddenly decided he was wasting his time. This Damascan moment occurred while Niall was sitting on a toadstool smoking a hookah – playing the Caterpillar in a student production of *Alice in Wonderland*. After the performance, he went back to his rooms and resolved to pull out of all his extracurricular activities and settle down to the one thing he was any good at, which was history.

He had also retained his flair for maths and found himself captivated by economic history and the statistics these entailed, two things that were anathema to most of his contemporaries. A stage adaptation of Karl Kraus' *Last Days of Mankind* convinced Ferguson he must learn German and for a while he thought of researching German satirical literature. Still regarded by the Oxford sobersides as something of a wild Glaswegian, he was sent to consult Norman Stone, recently arrived from Cambridge. Stone sensibly persuaded his young compatriot to focus on something more specific, perhaps involving 'number-crunching'. As Ferguson soon discovered, numbers don't come much bigger than those of the German hyperinflation of 1923–24 when millions of marks scarcely bought a loaf of bread. He had found his focus. In due course, a Hanseatic scholarship took Ferguson to Hamburg (the 'Glasgow of Germany') to research a D.Phil. about business and politics in the years preceding and just after World War I.

The German hyperinflation was hardly virgin territory. Many historians saw it as an inevitable product of the punitive post-Versailles policies of the victorious powers and argued that the social instability it caused helped prepare the way for Nazism. More recently, revisionists had thought the hyperinflation less onerous and more functional, the result of Weimar politicians trying to manoeuvre their way out of unpayable war reparations. Who was right? Neither, said Ferguson, in what later became *Paper and Iron*, his first book. To Ferguson, the roots of the Great Inflation were to be found not in the settlement following World War I but in the economically expansionist policies of the Wilhelmine era that preceded it.

It was a bold approach by a young historian, new to his topic, robustly challenging both the existing orthodoxy and the revisionist heterodoxy on a topic packed with political resonance. Never a man to seek refuge behind the shield of academic jargon, Ferguson states his arguments and conclusions with transparent clarity just in case anyone should miss them. For those not entirely at home with the statistical correlations between industrial output, unemployment rates and the rise of wholesale and retail prices, Ferguson sweetens the pill of his dense archival research with the seductive facility of an expert storyteller: a nice marriage between his boyhood love of novels and of maths. Thus, an early chapter begins with the launch of the latest proud product of the Hamburg shipyards; nearly 400 pages and countless economic graphs and statistics later, Ferguson paints a poignant parallel as, in the early days of Nazism, two little boats slip unceremoniously out of Hamburg harbour bound for London bearing the library of Aby Warburg – the *fons et origo* of London University's Warburg Institute. The Warburg family play an important part in *Paper and Iron*, particularly the banker Max Warburg. A chance meeting with Max's son Eric Warburg led Ferguson to Max's papers and thereby into the whole world of German-Jewish banking history, a topic that was later to move centre stage in his work.

One of the questions raised in *Paper and Iron* is whether, had other policies been adopted, the Great Inflation could have been avoided. Ferguson's preparedness to confront the 'ifs' of history is a recurrent theme in his writing: in order to understand what *did* happen in the past, he became convinced, you must also examine what might have happened but *didn't*. A few years later, he edited a volume of 'Virtual History' in which John Adamson suggested how history might have unfolded if Charles I had avoided civil war, Jonathan Clark imagined there had been no American Revolution, Andrew Roberts that Hitler invaded England in 1940, Michael Burleigh that the Nazis defeated the Soviet Union. Ferguson's own contribution was a piece arguing that Britain could have avoided going to war in 1914. He also composed a 90-page introduction setting out the intellectual value of the 'counterfactual'. From our vantage point, he says, we can see how things worked out. But to understand the past from the perspective of those who experienced it, we must consider the alternatives that people at the time actually considered. Ferguson is fiercely critical of historians (mostly Marxists in his view) who see the past as determined by demonstrable rules of cause and effect. History, he says, is not a science following iron laws of causation. But then nor, he points out, is science nowadays. Just as scientists have had to come to terms with relativity, uncertainty, entropy and chaos theory, so historians should re-embrace the idea of contingency. This is not to say that events occur at random; simply that the old causal models were too ironclad, too dependent on what we know about later outcomes. Ferguson proposes a new 'chaostory' – the 'chaos' approach to history.

The book was intended as something of a manifesto. Some critics read the contributions – not least Ferguson's own – as wish-fulfilments by predominantly conservative intellectuals venting their regret at the turns history had in fact taken. Ferguson had known the risks involved in publication of such a book. But he had long nurtured a desire to reach a wider public than the merely academic. A Research Fellowship at Christ's, Cambridge, brought him into daily contact with Jack Plumb under whose encouragement Ferguson continued to hone his literary style and pester London's literary and feature editors to let him write for their papers. If historians like A.J.P. Taylor, and Plumb himself to some extent, had become known to a nationwide public, why couldn't he? And why (the young Thatcherite asked) shouldn't historians sell their talents and make money like anyone else? With *Virtual History*, Ferguson had a book that would display his name in airport outlets. It was not to be his last.

It was Ferguson's unusual combination of skills that led George Weidenfeld, over lunch at the Garrick, to suggest that he undertake a history of the Rothschilds. It seems the Rothschild family had agreed to open up their vast archive if the right historian could be found. The aim was to publish in time for the 1998 bicentenary of the establishment of N.M. Rothschild in London, already looming a mere half-dozen years away. By now, Ferguson was a Fellow and Tutor in Modern History at Jesus College, Oxford, and Weidenfeld felt he'd found his man: a rising young academic who was at home among arcane nineteenth-century German archives, revelled in the minutiae

of economic and financial history, yet also commanded the
literary skills of the thrusting journalist.

The project presented Ferguson with a formidable mountain
to climb, one he couldn't have undertaken without the aid
of an army of intellectual sherpas, among them some of his
brightest students who joined him on the trail during university
vacations. The result, *The House of Rothschild*, is probably
Ferguson's most important scholarly achievement and the
work he is most proud of. On the face of it, mightn't a 1,000-
page account of a banking family seem a little esoteric to your
average reader raised on 'mainstream' nineteenth-century
political, diplomatic, social or cultural history? Not at all,
Ferguson insists (almost incredulous at the question). For a
start, he has an epic story to tell, of a family of Frankfurt Jews
who moved out of the ghetto in the later eighteenth century and
within a generation or two had become among the wealthiest
people in the world. The book is thus a case study in the history
of German Jewry, leading from the Enlightenment world of
Lessing and Moses Mendelssohn, through the emancipation
of the nineteenth century towards the horrors of Nazism and
beyond. But it's far more than that. The Rothschilds played a
vital part in the creation of the modern financial markets and
what we would nowadays call 'globalization'; they were more
influential, indeed, than most nation states – many of which
they virtually financed. No country could pursue fiscal policy,
no war be prosecuted, without reference to the Rothschilds.

Niall Ferguson is not the first to highlight the links between
war and high finance: think of Shaw's *Major Barbara*,
Eisenhower on the 'military-industrial complex' or the antiwar
rhetoric of the New Left in the 1960s. But Ferguson's take is
somewhat different. If not actually 'approving' of war, he is an
avowed advocate of international capitalism; the connections
between them were to dominate his next two works, *The Pity
of War* and *The Cash Nexus*.

Ferguson was already on record as believing that the *real* pity of the Great War was that it occurred at all. He now argued not only that the British could (and should) have kept out but also that they didn't really 'win'. En route to this genuinely piteous conclusion he punctures a lot of myths: that the Germans were 'militaristic', that the British war effort was sustained by popular enthusiasm, that the British soldiery stuck at it because of the patriotic propaganda (and belief in German 'atrocities') they had been fed, that they were shocked and unnerved at the killing, and that the collective memory of the Great War, distilled through the work of poets and painters, was one of unmitigated horror. Ferguson confronts us instead with a war in which men fought and faced death (including their own) from a mixture of motives, including the deep, dark truth that many *enjoyed* it.

What if Britain had tried to prevent the diplomatic tensions of August 1914 from escalating into war and had kept out of any ensuing conflict? Suppose Germany had defeated France, and maybe Russia, in 1916? A triumphant Kaiser might have dominated the continent for a while and established a European union not unlike that which – half a century and another global apocalypse later – occurred anyway. Meanwhile, Britain's international power and influence would have remained largely intact, while Hitler would have eked out his life as an unknown painter and Lenin would probably have continued his utopian scribbles in Zurich.

Good, 'bat-swinging' stuff, in Ferguson's words – and an approach to the past that is caustically parodied and precisely targeted by Alan Bennett in his recent play *The History Boys*. But Ferguson is absolutely serious about the importance of war as a principal driving force of history. In *The Cash Nexus* (researched during a Fellowship at the Bank of England), he tries to draw together the complex relationships between money, politics and conflict that had been illustrated in previous books. What lies behind the processes of historical change? Does economic growth bring about democracy – or does democracy promote prosperity? Is there *any* causal link between the two? Do either (or both) lead to greater international power and influence? As Ferguson tries to penetrate the engines of change, he directs us towards the development of such crucial institutions as a national debt, a central bank to fund it, a parliament to authorize taxes and a bureaucracy to collect them. Such achievements, he finds, have all been nurtured by the economic exigencies of war. Like a good general, Ferguson leads the reader confidently through often difficult terrain, much of it more theoretical (and statistical) than conventionally historical. We encounter the growing cost of political parties, the rise of economic 'globalization' – and the countervailing tendency of nations to fragment into ethnically based substates, frequently through civil war. Ferguson surveys American dominance of the post-Cold War world and has some fun at the expense of those, like Paul Kennedy, who had earlier predicted the decline of both global superpowers. Is the USA in decline, overstretched? Not at all, says Ferguson, a confirmed Americophile (writing during the run-up to the election of George W. Bush). To Ferguson, the USA is *under*stretched, and he ends *The Cash Nexus* with a robust plea for the one nation with the resources to 'make the world a better place' to have the guts to do so.

Some of these themes reappear in two of Ferguson's most recent books and their TV tie-ins. *Empire* argued the economic motives and merits of British imperialism, while *Colossus* showed that America, too, has had an empire in all but name. Ferguson acknowledges that appalling things were done in the course of British imperial history, but argues that these should not blind us to more benign, long-term legacies of 'Anglobalization', such as the widespread adoption of liberal capitalist economies, the English language, representative democracy, personal freedom and the rule of law. And America? An 'Empire in denial' is how Ferguson sums up a story characterized by systematic expansion across a continent followed by a century of world-wide military intervention. His book is subtitled 'The Rise and Fall of the American Empire' and it is the fall that worries him. All this was guaranteed to shock American traditionalists to whom the 'E' word is unmentionable, while liberals flinch at Ferguson's repeated advocacy of worldwide US interventionism on a scale, and over a timescale, far beyond anything the Bush administration would contemplate.

Ferguson is unrepentant. As a historian he takes the long view. The problem with a modern republic like the USA, he says, is that it can't make decisions beyond the short time-frame of the electoral process. Never mind. One day America will wake up to its worldwide responsibilities. After all, he adds teasingly, it took Rome some 400 years before Caesar crossed the Rubicon and transformed a weak republic into a powerful empire. So maybe America is half-way there!

EPILOGUE

Niall Ferguson is currently writing a life of Siegmund Warburg and is beginning the research for a biography of Henry Kissinger.

Laurence Rees

BIOGRAPHY

Laurence is Creative Director of BBC Television History programmes and was also, for a number of years, editor of *Timewatch*, the BBC's Historical Documentary strand (the equivalent in Britain to *American Experience* in the United States). Under his editorship *Timewatch* won a host of awards including three Emmys.

As an Executive Producer of historical programmes he has been responsible for series on a wide variety of historical topics from Michael Wood's *Alexander the Great* and *Conquistadors* (both co-productions with PBS) to the BBC2 reality history series about Captain Cook, *The Ship*. He also previously worked as the BBC's Executive Producer on *The Great War and the Shaping of the Twentieth Century*. More recently, as Creative Director of BBC History, he oversaw the final series of Simon Schama's *A History of Britain*.

He is best known, however, for the four documentary series on World War II which he has written and produced. He wrote and produced the six-part series *The Nazis: A Warning from History* which first transmitted on BBC TV in 1997 and was subsequently sold to more than 30 countries. The series won him a myriad of awards, including a George Foster Peabody Award, a BANFF festival award, an IDA award and gained him the most prestigious award a British television producer can win – a British Academy of Film and Television Arts award. He followed that series with *War of the Century* (1999), a four-part examination of the Hitler–Stalin conflict, and the two-part *Horror in the East* (2000) about the war against Japan. Most recently he wrote and produced *Auschwitz: The Nazis and the 'Final Solution'* for BBC Television and PBS.

He was educated a Solihull School and the University of Oxford. In July 2005 he received an Honorary Doctorate from the University of Sheffield for services to television and history.

PRINCIPAL PUBLISHED BOOKS

Selling Politics (1992)
The Nazis: A Warning from History (1997)
War of the Century (1999)
Horror in the East (2001)
Auschwitz: The Nazis and the 'Final Solution' (2005)

PROFILE, February 2005

Is this the man who launched a thousand Hitler programmes? Well, no, actually, and Laurence Rees confesses to being a little tired of being labelled the *fons et origo* of the supposed 'Hitler Wave' on television. For a start, he says, there isn't a Hitler Wave. Last year (and he has the figures), 89 per cent of BBC history output was not about World War II, Hitler, the Holocaust, and so on. Rather, the most frequently aired and popular programmes were about the history of Britain and of the Ancient World, or industrial and technological history. If there has been a 'Hitler Wave' on television, it would seem to be on the wane and, Rees suspects, will diminish further once this year's 60th anniversaries have come and gone and the period gradually moves out of living memory.

Nonetheless, the most distinctive projects for which Rees has been responsible are a quartet of multi-programme TV series about the horrors of World War II: *The Nazis: A Warning from*

History; *War of the Century* (about the Nazi–Soviet conflict); *Horror in the East* (the Japanese war and atrocities); and now, *Auschwitz: The Nazis and the 'Final Solution'*. These have helped bring to millions in Britain and around the world a greater understanding of the appalling barbarism and suffering incurred by the war.

Laurence Rees was born in Ayr in 1957, but when he was a small child the family moved to Birmingham where his father, a BBC TV producer, took up a post at the Pebble Mill production centre. Among Laurence's early memories is the excitement of being taken into his father's TV studios and being allowed to sit with the vision mixer, twiddle the knobs and change the lighting and camera angles. Those were the days of the 11-plus, which Laurence not only failed, but failed badly (interestingly, for a future TV producer, it seems he had poor 'spacial awareness skills'). His parents retained their faith in the boy, however, dug deep into their pockets and sent him to Solihull School (a minor public school) where Laurence began to flower. Influenced, perhaps, by his mother who was an actress, he enjoyed participating in school plays. He also read widely, especially in history. In the run-up to O Level, a teacher pointed out that he was including material in his essays that was not from the official textbook. Laurence thought this a rebuke: it was intended as a compliment.

His father died when Laurence was still a schoolboy, but his mother helped nurse him through his A Levels and thence to Oxford where Laurence read a mix-and-match degree including elements of History, Philosophy and Law. He also resumed his career as an amateur actor, somewhat to the consternation of Mrs Rees (who had obviously absorbed the advice proffered to Mrs Worthington); why not become a lawyer, she suggested – pointing out that barristers, like actors, can dress up and show off but usually make a lot more money. In the event, Laurence deserted acting for directing which felt much closer to his natural *métier*. From Oxford, he entered the BBC's

General Traineeship Scheme where his first assignment was as a researcher on *Nationwide*. Here he absorbed a variety of television skills, but it was a painful baptism. Typically, Laurence would be told to track down an interviewee who was apparently indispensable to the programme, only to discover, on finding the person first thing the next morning, that the story had 'moved on' and his labours had been in vain. He failed to understand how something could be of absorbing interest one day and of none the next. Laurence, his report stated after a three-month stint, 'has no journalistic ability and is often hysterical'.

News, clearly, was not his natural habitat. He soon found himself in documentaries where the longer timescale was altogether more congenial, and thence to *That's Life* where he learned much from Esther Rantzen, who not only presented but also produced these highly professional shows. It was Rantzen who taught him the useful maxim that when making TV programmes, assume your audience has 'minimum information and maximum intelligence'. Rees returned to documentaries and by the age of 25 was producing his first history programme: a richly theatrical documentary about Noel Coward that intercut interviews, archive material and location footage with liberal excerpts from Coward's own films and recordings.

The Coward programme doubtless represented filial homage of a kind. But it also gave notice of Rees' meticulous yet inventive use of television as a medium for programmes about recent history (he followed it with a documentary about the abortive 'Groundnuts' scheme, one of the great failures of the Attlee regime). At that time, there hadn't been that much history on television, he says, looking back. What about such legendary BBC triumphs as A.J.P. Taylor's history lectures or Kenneth Clark's *Civilisation* series? It seems that such programmes achieved pretty low viewing figures, notwithstanding popular mythology to the contrary. As a representative of the new generation of producers – and inspired by such rare but shining precedents as Jeremy Isaacs' series *The World At War* – Rees wanted to bring serious history to large audiences.

British Betrayal did just that. It also nearly cost Rees his job. The film dealt with the forced repatriation at the end of the war of émigré Cossacks and Yugoslavs, many of them anti-Soviet refugees, by the British authorities in Austria, despite the knowledge that most would be exterminated on their return. The story of this mass deportation had first been revealed by the historian Nikolai Tolstoy, who also identified the former Brigadier Toby Low, by then Lord Aldington, as the man in charge. The embattled Aldington sued for libel and, while never seriously discrediting the story, won his case. Later, with a high Establishment wind behind him, Aldington tried to get Laurence Rees sacked for revisiting the same territory.

Rees had been brought up in the shadow of the war. His father had served in the RAF and an uncle had been lost in the Battle of the Atlantic, and Rees knew, as all his generation knew, that the Nazis had been the epitome of mindless evil. Then he began to meet some. While working on *British Betrayal* he had encountered a Russian Cossack who had defected to the Germans and become a Nazi officer. He was one of those forcibly returned to the Soviet Union after the war; he had been transported to Siberia where, improbably, he had survived. This impressive, reflective man certainly didn't come across as 'Nazis' were supposed to do. Nor did Goebbels' personal attaché, whom Rees met when producing a series about political propaganda. On the contrary, he proved to be a man of charm and intelligence, clearly relishing the opportunity of revisiting Goebbels' old villa in Lanke on the edge of Berlin and regaling Rees and his camera crew with fond memories of the wonderful dances, parties and film shows that used to take place here. 'Paradise', he beamed when asked how he looked back on those days. Men such as these were not the kind of Nazis that Rees had been taught about.

Such encounters perplexed Rees and led him to want to understand – and try to explain in televisual terms – the mentality of people who had ordered and enacted (and endured) the almost unimaginable atrocities of war. *The Nazis: A Warning from History* was transmitted in 1997 and won Rees a BAFTA award; *War of the Century* and *Horror in the East* followed soon afterwards. The latest is the Auschwitz series. These projects have not been dry academic exercises. But nor have they been aimed at the ghoulish or voyeuristic or resorted to simple moralising. Working closely with historians of the calibre of Ian Kershaw, Rees has created a body of work that is carefully structured and impeccably researched, incorporating vivid archive material from a wide array of sources. Most remarkable, perhaps, are the interviews he has filmed. Rees is one of the few people – perhaps the only one – who has met and interviewed at length not only hundreds of people who suffered from the barbarities of World War II right across the globe but also, crucially, many of the perpetrators. Few academic historians would normally have the aptitude, training or resources to garner data of this kind. All this has given Rees a comparative, cross-cultural perspective on the horrors of the war that no academic could match.

'When I went into these projects,' says Rees, 'I suppose I thought I would come across people who were obviously "evil" in some sense, or at least different from the rest of us.' He recalls his many encounters with gnarled old men and women in North and South America, Western and Eastern Europe, Russia and Japan. What often most struck Rees about them, even those with a dreadful war record, was their sheer normality. None turned out to be the monsters of picture-book history. Many ex-Nazis, if not finding the Third Reich 'Paradise', had clearly believed in and admired a political system that had given them work, status and dignity. None resorted to the cliché that they were 'just obeying orders'(though some veterans of Stalin's Russia did, understandably enough). Nor did Rees encounter torrents of apology or guilt or, for that matter, much vestigial pride or defiance. Rather, most of those interviewed tried to describe the context of the time and explained that what they did was more or less what anyone would have done in similar circumstances. German concentration-camp guards told him this, as did Russians and Japanese who had murdered prisoners – and Allied pilots who had lightened their planes by carpet-bombing undefended city centres. This was what you did, people told Rees. I wasn't a criminal. On the contrary, I was a good, law-abiding citizen in trying times doing what I had to do, what we all did. The details varied, but the refrain was always the same: 'If you'd been there, you'd have done the same.'

Rees came to realize that most people tend to conform to what psychologists call the 'situational ethic'. When the situation changes (or the law, or the identity of those in charge), most of us adapt our behaviour easily enough to conform to the new ethic. One old Japanese soldier recalled participating in a gang rape of a Chinese woman; to him, this was not so much a sexual experience as a way of confirming acceptance by the group. Rees interviewed a German, a fervent member of the Hitler Youth when a teenager, who had fought the Soviets on the Eastern Front, embraced Communism when his part of Germany had been incorporated into the GDR and was now, after reunification, a committed capitalist running a thriving business. A Japanese interviewee who had routinely bayoneted Chinese prisoners in the name of the Emperor was later, as a Chinese POW, praised by his captors for writing the longest and most accurate prisoner confessions – thus moving seamlessly from best murderer to best prisoner. Rees came to think that the real social misfits are not so much those we consider 'criminals' but, on the contrary, those few who oppose the 'situational ethic' at the time. Hitler was one such; so were members of the Resistance. It was a sobering discovery.

Rees was lucky with his timing. Doubly so, perhaps. The collapse of Communism gave him and his team untrammelled access to people and places across the whole of Eastern Europe and Russia. Broadcasting authorities helped provide archive footage never shown before, while ordinary people felt free to give honest interviews, no longer constrained by the Party line. But Rees was lucky in another sense too. Many of those he interviewed had hitherto talked very little about the war years, preferring to get on with their lives in the postwar world. But, as often happens, old age loosened the tongue as countless elderly interviewees, after half a century of reticence, found a kind of catharsis in telling the future about the past.

Laurence Rees is best known for his films about the horrors of war, but his contribution to televising history is far more extensive. In addition to the many programmes he has himself written and produced, he has been Editor of *Reputations* (which he created) and *Timewatch* (which he ran for ten years) and Executive Producer of such programmes as Michael Wood's *Alexander the Great* and *Conquistadors* and the Captain Cook series, *The Ship*. His most important contribution has arguably been his role in developing mass-audience programmes such as *Pyramid*, a film that educated by stealth (in the best Reithian tradition) by combining elements of drama with vivid computer-generated imagery (CGI).

Pyramid reached over 11 million viewers, the largest audience ever achieved by any BBC history programme. Moreover, the audience profile revealed that it had brought in an appreciably younger audience than was normal for history programmes. *Pyramid* launched a whole new genre of TV history programmes – *Coliseum*, *Pompeii*, a forthcoming film about Genghis Khan. In *Auschwitz*, Rees decided to make discreet and limited use of both CGI and dramatization. He now has the title of Creative Director, BBC History Programmes, a position that gives him editorial control over the entire historical waterfront. But Rees is also one of the very few people in his position to have continued to write and produce his own programmes from time to time; when I met him he was still editing *Auschwitz*.

The exigencies of television production demand that material be ruthlessly tightened, edited, and some would say simplified. But Rees remains at heart a serious historian. He has written books to accompany each of his major series about World War II, including a substantial research-based work to accompany *Auschwitz*. The uncut tapes and transcripts of the interviews from his *Nazis* series have been deposited in the library at the University of Sheffield (where the series consultant, Ian Kershaw, is Professor of Modern History). Rees expresses the hope that all his filmed interview material might eventually be made available to scholars. He talks warmly of his collaborations with academic historians, a partnership that in other hands might not necessarily be mutually reinforcing.

The goodwill is evidently reciprocated. Ian Kershaw recalls the way that Rees, from the start, drew him into all aspects of the planning and devising of *The Nazis: A Warning from History*, and invited him to check and criticize not only the scripts but also the film rushes. To Kershaw, a vivid sequence of someone describing to camera what it had felt like killing women and children on that very spot can convey a message more movingly and starkly than acres of print. Rees once said publicly that he thought Kershaw could have made a first-class TV producer – doubtless damaging Sir Ian's standing among his stuffier academic colleagues!

Academic and media history are both subject to vicissitudes of fashion, but the swings in TV history move more rapidly. Here, crucially, it's partly a question of how the material is presented – and to whom. Hence the importance of *Pyramid* and its mass-audience successors, programmes that, while not cheapening the serious research on which they are based, can encourage younger viewers to develop the habit of watching history programmes. With luck, TV history may be moving on from the tired clichés of echo-laden drumbeats and shadowy, unfocused men wielding slow-motion weaponry. As for subject matter, the supposed 'Hitler Wave' of recent years may be on the way out, and once audiences are eventually sated with Schama and Starkey or Adam Hart-Davis, British and technological history will doubtless be edged from the top of the pile. Part of Rees' job is to anticipate what will come next. He talks with enthusiasm about a forthcoming Hart-Davis series (*What The Past Did For Us*) that includes episodes on old favourites like Egypt and Rome, but also stakes out less familiar histories such as those of Mesopotamia, the Aztecs, China and India. Wouldn't it be wonderful, he muses, if some of these wider histories became the next TV chic? If anyone has the power to make it so, it is Laurence Rees.

EPILOGUE

Laurence Rees writes:

Since the article was published the Auschwitz series has transmitted in more than a dozen countries and the accompanying book has sold well both in Britain and the rest of Europe. In July 2005 I was awarded an Honorary Doctorate by the University of Sheffield for services to History and Television and gave the annual Holocaust Public Lecture for the Holocaust Educational Trust at the House of Lords. I think those are the most important things that have happened to me since Daniel wrote his piece!

Jeremy Black

BIOGRAPHY

Jeremy Black was born in London in 1955. After graduating with a starred First from Cambridge, he undertook research at Oxford and has subsequently been Professor of History at the universities of Durham and (since 1996) Exeter. Editor of *Archives* and a Council member of the Royal Historical Association, Black is a prolific lecturer and writer, the author of (to date) some 60 books. Many concern aspects of eighteenth-century British, European and American political, diplomatic and military history. But he has also broadened his perspective, both temporally and geographically, and published on the history of the press, cartography, warfare, culture and on the nature and uses of history itself.

PRINCIPAL PUBLISHED BOOKS

British Foreign Policy in the Age of Walpole (1985)
Europe in the Eighteenth Century (1990)
Culloden and the '45 (1990)
The Rise of the European Powers 1679–1793 (1990)
A Military Revolution? Military Change and European Society 1550–1800 (1991)
War for America: The Fight for Independence 1775–1783 (1991)
The British Abroad: The Grand Tour in the Eighteenth Century (1992)
History of the British Isles (1996)
Maps and History: Constructing Images of the Past (1997)

War and the World: Military Power and the Fate of Continents: 1450–2000 (1998)

European Warfare, 1453–1815 (1999)

Studying History (with Donald M. MacRaild) (2000)

European Warfare, 1815–2000 (2001)

The English Press: 1621–1861 (2001)

Eighteenth-Century Britain (2001)

Nineteenth-Century Britain (with Donald M. MacRaild) (2002)

European International Relations, 1648–1815 (2002)

War: An Illustrated World History (2003)

France and the Grand Tour (2003)

The British Seaborne Empire (2004)

Using History (2005)

Introduction to Global Military History, 1775 to the Present Day (2005)

The Age of Total War, 1860–1945 (2006)

George III: America's Last King (2006)

Altered States: America Since the Sixties (2006)

PROFILE, April 2005

When I first came to know Jeremy Black, he was in his late thirties and already widely recognized for two things: his expertise on eighteenth-century British and European history, and his extraordinary industriousness. Jeremy's ambition, nicely symmetrical for one steeped in Enlightenment rationality, was to have authored 40 books by the time he turned 40. Today, I'm afraid, he has things completely out of phase: approaching 50, the Professor of History at Exeter already has some 60 books to his credit.

For once in these essays, I cannot claim to have read all of my interviewee's books; I suspect only Black himself has read everything he has written. But I have sampled a good deal and learned a lot about Hanoverian politics, diplomacy and culture, the history of the press, maps, warfare and much else. As I did so, it rapidly became clear that the criticism of Black – that he merely 'turns out one damn book after another' – is far from just, though the often mundane titles of his gigantic bibliography can seem to merge, diverge and re-form like oil blobs on a watery surface. Some of the books are, in effect, extended versions of earlier academic papers; others are heavyweight monographs or, latterly, synoptic *tours d'horizon*. All historical writing, including his own, says Black disarmingly, must be understood as no more than an interim report. Of course, he acknowledges, there are differences and maybe inconsistencies between an early book and a later one on, say, the Grand Tour or the development of the English press (topics he has recently revisited). That's because he himself is older, hopefully wiser, and has researched new sources. History permits of no 'master narrative', Black asserts, and no publication is definitive or even necessarily that particular author's own last word on a subject. Are there borrowings in his books from earlier publications? Why not, if the point, or the example, is a good one and the new book takes the subject further?

Jeremy Black is the product of a hard-working, socially mobile Northwest London family; today, his sister works with a top entertainment agency while his brother is in real estate. Like Simon Schama, Black attended Haberdashers' Aske's School and went on to read History at Cambridge where, he recalls, he at first found intellectual standards rather lower than those he was used to at 'Habs'. At Cambridge, Black continued to revel in the joys of public debate, a skill he had first honed at school, and in time came to value the personal and intellectual tutelage available to a bright undergraduate. He still speaks with affection of his Director of Studies at Queens', Jonathan Riley-Smith, though the admiration did not extend to his becoming a fellow-medievalist.

A starred First led to postgraduate work at Oxford and then a lectureship at Durham, where Black completed his doctorate

(and first book): a study of British foreign policy in the age
of Walpole. Foreign policy, he insisted then and has insisted
ever since, cannot be understood in isolation from domestic
policy, or vice versa. This may be obvious to us today as, for
example, we note the links between George W. Bush's domestic
constituency and the war in Iraq. But Black recalls that, when
he was beginning his career, historians routinely ignored this
interconnectedness, a profound gulf separating those who
studied, say, the diplomacy or warfare of the Napoleonic or
Crimean wars from those who wrote about the growth of the
franchise or of cities. From the start, Black liked to question
whatever he took to be the received wisdom. He thought of
himself as something of an intellectual loner, a maverick.
As a debater, he prided himself on his ability to understand
the other side's arguments; he had a recurrent fantasy as an
undergraduate that he would go into an exam room and,
instead of answering the requisite number of questions, would
take just one and give it a number of alternative answers.

He still sees himself as a maverick, an intellectual irritant.
Thus, Black is critical of much TV history for presenting what
he sees as too simple and one-dimensional an interpretation
of great and complex events. If he had his way (and he is an
excellent but under-used broadcaster), he would encourage
producers to present the same range of alternative views about
the past as their colleagues in news or documentaries do about
contemporary affairs. In much the same spirit, Black begins his
recently published *Rethinking Military History* with a (highly
plausible) list of what he sees as the theoretical inadequacies
underlying much military history as currently practised: it tends
to concentrate too much on Europe and the West and is too
preoccupied with state-versus-state conflicts, too concentrated
on weapons technology and too inclined to separate naval from
land conflict. As always, Black is making a plea for a broader,
more multifaceted perspective than is commonly adopted.
In addition, he has never been shy of entering territory that

other historians might think of as their specialist preserve. He doesn't expect to be loved for this kind of approach; self-confessed mavericks rarely are by the rest of the herd. But he does sometimes feel under-appreciated. 'I don't set out to irritate people, or try to show that I am better than everybody else', says this most self-aware of historians. 'But I clearly do irritate people by thinking for myself.'

Surprisingly, perhaps, for an author distinguished by such superabundant productivity, Black was something of a slow starter. He was 30, and well into his career at Durham, before his first books began to roll off the presses. The startling truth, therefore, is that he has produced 60 books in 20 years. Meanwhile, this three-books-a-year man has risen steadily up the academic ladder (Black is an excellent lecturer and was made Professor of History at Durham before taking up his Chair in Exeter), travels widely, especially to the USA where he has lectured in 35 states, pours out articles and reviews, sits on a variety of academic and editorial boards (including that of *History Today*), and was appointed MBE for advising the Royal Mail on the historical topics to adopt for its Millennium stamps. Yet if you read any of Black's more important books and pursue his sources and references, you get the impression of a scholar steeped in archival research, a man happiest when working his assiduous way through the kind of arcanae made available to him in the Manuscript Room at the British Library.

How – and why – has Black produced so much? The 'why', he laughs, doubtless goes back to deep insecurities dating from childhood; which of us, after all, really knows why we are driven to do what we do? 'I get depressed about my own abilities', Black acknowledges with remarkable frankness. But he also knows that he is brighter than most people; perhaps he has an inner need to demonstrate this. In addition, of course, authorship helps boost the Black family income. When I asked whether he had ever considered (or been offered) a post in

London, his instant response was that he could never afford to live in the capital – unless, he mused, one of his books became a bestseller.

As for how he writes, there are both mundane elements and surprising ones. Most obviously, Jeremy Black works ferociously hard. When he is not at home writing or at the university lecturing, he is most likely to be found working methodically through a mountain of untapped historical documents in one of the world's great research libraries. Like most high-achievers, Black regards time as a scarce and valuable commodity to be used with care. After a day's research at the British Library, he can be seen huddled in a corner in the train back to Exeter tightening a draft, correcting proofs, preparing a lecture or catching up with a book he has agreed to review. All this you might have guessed. What is more unexpected, perhaps, is that, in this hi-tech age of ours, Jeremy Black doesn't use a computer or email and doesn't drive; all his books and articles are handwritten. He must love writing, I suggest coyly. Of course, or he wouldn't do so much of it. But at the end of a full day of it, Black confesses, he is exhausted and his body 'incredibly tense'.

The results, as he is the first to admit, are variable. A lot of Black's *oeuvre* consists of essentially straightforward narrative history illustrated by a mass of precisely sourced instances. His tables of contents can be predictable and his language lacking in metaphor, while many chapters and even books seem merely to stop rather than conclude. You often sense that Black is in a hurry to set down the results of that day's researches before going on to the next. Not that he is incapable of stylish and even touching prose. Some of his introductions are elegantly calibrated essays setting up the detailed study that is to follow. Thus, *The British Seaborne Empire*, another recent publication, establishes itself from the outset as a major counterpart to the works of Boxer (on the Dutch and Portuguese empires) and Parry (on the Spanish) as

Black proceeds to lay out, in a few virtuoso and highly readable pages, the unusually wide geographical and temporal limits he thinks his subject warrants. The British imperial experience, he suggests – in the face of much current historiography, which he feels is disproportionately obsessed with India – was for a great deal of its time essentially maritime. There is much robust, analytical writing here. But it soon gives way to a densely written chronological account packed with a catalogue of meticulously researched facts delivered in sometimes pedestrian language. Here, as elsewhere, Black seems reluctant to incorporate all his thoroughly researched richesse into an arc of argument, to draw inferences, to reach conclusions.

At root, I suspect, is Black's profound belief, going back to the way he himself was trained, that people should be enabled to reach their own conclusions on the basis of the sources consulted and evidence adduced. He is sceptical of what he calls 'history in the bath': historians (or books) proclaiming overarching theories and principles about the nature or causes of historical change, often on the basis of skimpy archival research. To Black, history should above all be a journey, not necessarily an arrival.

His own journey continues apace as new books appear, or are planned, on a raft of subjects, many of them already familiar. But Black's intellectual restlessness and his preternatural suspicion of facile questions or easy answers have led him of late to venture far beyond the more familiar narratives of eighteenth-century Britain, continental Europe and North America. Today, his purview is much wider, the world his oyster and the twentieth century his new pearl. In *The British Seaborne Empire*, Black (unlike Boxer or Parry) brings the story up to date, dealing with the Falklands War and going on to consider such current issues as Gibraltar, immigration and economic globalization. Other recent titles tell a similar story: *The World in the Twentieth Century*; *War: An Illustrated World History*; *World War Two: A Military History*; *Visions of the World: A*

History of Maps and *The World in the Twentieth Century*.
Jeremy Black has navigated an unimaginable distance beyond
his initial harbour in Walpole's England. These latest voyages
have led him to encounter new hazards. For example, Black,
ever the conscientious archivist and a reasonably accomplished
linguist in the main European languages (at least for research
purposes), now finds himself having to draw on other people's
translations of, for example, Arabic or Chinese sources.

Black's teenage children recently suggested their dad develop
a hobby. Would reading James Bond books count? In *The
Politics of James Bond*, Black analysed the novels and films as
reflections of the political anxieties of the West during the Cold
War years. The book was evidently great fun to research (and
the children doubtless approved); Black refers to it as one of
his 'lollipop' projects. But he did encounter some difficulties in
trying to persuade the Inland Revenue that all those Bond books
and videos he brought home one Christmastide amounted to
a legitimate tax-deductible expense!

As Black approaches his sixth decade he claims to be cutting
back on his writing commitments somewhat. But ask him about
new projects and he replies with the vivacity of a youngster
at the outset of his career. Black is like a gifted postgraduate
student, endowed with formidable intellectual energy yet
uncertain of his powers and parameters, constantly stretching
and testing them in full view of a cartel-like profession which,
he senses uneasily, regards him as something of an outsider.
Before 2005 is out, Black will have published a textbook giving
a global perspective to the history of warfare from 1775 to
the present, plus a study of English culture in the eighteenth
century in which he emphasizes the rich divisions it contained.
He also has a book in the works called *Using History* in which
he considers the shifts that occur in the ways people regard
the past and asks what causes them. His answers could cause
a flutter or two in the academic dovecotes. To Black, trends
pioneered in the intellectual world such as *Annales* history

or postmodernism are far less influential than, say, popular representations of history on film and TV, or such forces in the outside world as the postwar achievement of independence by new countries and their attendant need to provide national histories. In each of these books, as so often in his writing, Black is at pains to eschew cut-and-dried interpretations, preferring to let his evidence suggest range and diversity.

What will this high-achieving *Ewige Student* be doing over the next five or ten years? Doubtless lecturing in America's remaining 15 states – maybe living in one of them? – and, he hopes, writing on subjects that at present he doesn't know that much about. Unlike many of today's academic historians, Black is not a man to trim and hone the minutiae in his particular 'field'. Perfectionism on a tiny scale is not his *métier* and he is fond of quoting Voltaire to the effect that 'the best is the enemy of the good'. Black would rather be good at lots of things than the best in only one. He is not omniscient and doesn't pretend or plan to be. We are unlikely to see a book about religious history, say, or Ancient Greece. When a Texas bookshop, awed by his presence in town a few years ago, put out a display of his wares, he had to point out gently that the volume on Ancient Sumerian Poetry was by another Jeremy Black! Our Jeremy is essentially a modernist. Not only because the (more or less) modern world happens to be his 'field', but also because he is mindful of the vital lessons he feels the past has for the present.

Take, for example, the growing emphasis in his recent work on military and world history. As distant parts of the globe engage with each other more and more, Black feels it is increasingly important for people in the West to know about cultures other than their own. Most warfare in the modern world has not directly involved Western powers, he points out, despite what you read in most books of military history (and in the newspapers). Now, however, with the US acting as an 'expeditionary state' across the world, Black feels it is becoming urgent for historians to demonstrate that no nation, however powerful, has been able to impose its values upon another simply by force of superior weaponry. Concepts such as victory and defeat, suffering and loss, have varied and continue to vary from one culture to another. Thus, the US might have believed it 'won' the 2003 war in Iraq but many Iraqis self-evidently did not; America regarded the human cost of the war as acceptably low while to Iraqis it was shockingly high.

Sceptical of ideologies of all kinds, Black still has what he thinks of as a 'debater's view of history', instinctively looking for alternative views, evidence that challenges the conventional wisdom. Does this make him a cynic? Far from it. To Jeremy Black, the study of history can help inculcate a profound sense of that most valuable commodity, 'humane scepticism'. Voltaire couldn't have put it better.

Norman Davies

BIOGRAPHY

Norman Davies was born in Lancashire and educated at Magdalen College, Oxford, where he was much influenced and encouraged by A.J.P. Taylor. Davies travelled extensively in his 20s, settling eventually in Krakow where he acquired a Polish wife and a PhD. For many years, Davies taught at London University's School of Slavonic and East European Studies (where he was Professor from 1985–1996), and he has made many appearances as guest professor at universities in North America, the Far East and many countries of Europe – especially Poland, where he continues to be regarded as the nation's outstanding historian.

PRINCIPAL PUBLISHED BOOKS

God's Playground: A History of Poland (1981; revised two-vol. edn, 2005)

Heart of Europe: The Past in Poland's Present (1984)

Europe: A History (1996)

The Isles: A History (1999)

Microcosm: Portrait of a Central European City (with Roger Moorhouse) (2003)

Rising '44: The Battle for Warsaw (2004)

PROFILE, July 2005

What led Norman Davies to his lifelong interest in Poland? An accident, it seems. At the height of the Cold War, he and a bunch of student friends decided to go by train to Moscow but the USSR embassy wouldn't grant visas. Dejected, they checked the map to see how far their tickets would take them before reaching the Soviet border. The last stop would be Warsaw. Very well, they thought, and went off to see the Poles. Would they give visas? Certainly, said a cheery official – adding *sotto voce* that it was a pleasure helping people who'd been rejected by the Russians!

Some forty-odd years on, Oxford University Press have just reissued a revised edition of Davies' two-volume history of Poland, *God's Playground*, bringing the story up to date. Or nearly up to date. We were meeting on the day of the Pope's funeral and Davies had flown back the night before from an emotional, crowd-packed Krakow. If there's ever a third edition, he would like to include an assessment of the impact and legacy of the 'greatest Pole' of modern times, John Paul II.

One of Davies' earlier books is dedicated to the memory of a grandfather who, he says, was 'English by birth, Welsh by conviction, Lancastrian by choice, British by chance'. It is a revealing formulation by a man whose writings constantly remind us of the surging cultural eddies and undercurrents that criss-cross the map of history (and in many ways his own history).

Norman Davies was born and raised in Bolton, and the first foreign language he encountered was Welsh when the family motored across to the Conway coast for a summer holiday. Norman's strong-minded, Nonconformist mother gave the boy a sense of pride in achievement and he discovered early prowess on the soccer field. His boyhood hero was his uncle, Donny Davies, a sporting legend-turned-journalist. Norman sailed through his schoolwork, showing particular talent in geography and languages, but he gained admission to Magdalen College, Oxford, on a History Exhibition, after a gap year in France.

At Magdalen, the *genius loci* was the formidably gifted and preternaturally provocative A.J.P. Taylor. Taylor was a fellow-Lancastrian and, like Davies perhaps, felt himself to be something of an outsider in the hallowed halls of Oxford. He had an impish streak and, like many famous dons whose work reaches out to an audience beyond the purely academic, could be waspish to colleagues while being kindness itself to his students. All this Davies observed and absorbed. But when it came to choosing a special subject, he didn't follow Taylor into the History of Central Europe but turned instead to Italy and the age of Dante. A few months before Finals, his Dante notes were stolen and, to make matters worse, he had a viva at which he revealed his ignorance about Chartism. As Davies left the room, he heard a plummy voice pronounce: 'We can't possibly give a First to a chap who doesn't know about the Chartists!'

For a while, Davies taught French and history at St Paul's School. His most vivid memory is of being painfully ribbed by 'effete' southern colleagues for preferring the round ball to the ovoid after leading the boys on the soccer field. One summer, he extended his linguistic skills further by taking an intensive Russian course in Cambridge. This enabled Davies to leave St Paul's for the University of Sussex, where he did an MA in Russian Studies and thence, on a British Council grant, to Poland. Here, Davies went native, staying on in Krakow, marrying a Polish wife and relishing late-night conversations with a doughty father-in-law who recalled fighting in the Polish-Soviet war of 1919–20, a ferocious episode in which the resurgent Poles defeated the new Soviet Republic and which was airbrushed from the textbooks during the Communist years.

By his late twenties, Davies had travelled extensively, both geographically and intellectually. Yet his mother was not entirely wrong in asking him, with increasing anxiety, what it was all going to lead to and when he was going to come home and get a proper job. On a trip to Britain, Davies visited

Taylor, who had remained a friend and guru. What did he advise? Taylor's answer was pithy and to the point: 'Get your first book published!' Davies returned to Krakow and began to turn his researches on the Polish-Soviet war into what eventually appeared as *White Eagle, Red Star* – written not in Poland, but back in Oxford, where he had been given a one-year Fellowship at St Antony's. The book was well received (and gave Davies a considerable samizdat reputation among Polish intellectuals). Published in 1972, it led to a lectureship under Hugh Seton-Watson at London University's School of Slavonic Studies. A 'proper' job at last!

From obscurity in Krakow, Davies found himself catapulted to the forefront of those in the West with expertise on the Communist world. Before long, he was approached by Oxford University Press with a proposal to undertake a major history of Poland. *God's Playground* became the first of Davies' trademark Big Books. Like all of them, it begins with a lengthy statement of intent in which a number of perceived impediments are revealingly kicked aside. Davies says he doesn't expect Polish officialdom to vouchsafe his work any attention, while ordinary Poles who get to hear about it will probably be disappointed by the objective way he deals with such emotion-laden topics as Polish nationalism. Throughout, Davies eschews simple formulations ('It would be nice to have a theory; but I do not have one'). Indeed, the very idea of 'Poland' has varied through the ages. Again and again, Davies documents the establishment, overturning, dismemberment, abolition or resurrection of the Polish state, Volume I ending with the partition of Poland in 1795 and its disappearance from the map. As for 'Polish society', says Davies, this 'has never encompassed the same collection of people at any two successive moments in time'. *God's Playground* is thus about a country, culture and nation that have only rarely overlapped. But if the tapestry is frayed and tattered, in Davies' hands it becomes one of the richest.

By a curious piece of serendipity, the book was published in 1981, a day after General Jaruzelski brought out the tanks, guaranteeing Davies maximum exposure in the West. At the time, of course, the book was not available in Poland. Today, Davies is probably the best-known historian of Poland in Poland, where *God's Playground* enjoys wide circulation – a fact mentioned in the new edition, which is thus the only book I know that is part of its own narrative.

In all his writings about Poland, Davies is at pains to emphasize that its history and people have always been profoundly integrated with the destinies of the rest of Europe. Poland is not simply (as many still think) an isolated, faraway land in the East that was once Nazi and then Communist. On the contrary, insists Davies, it lies at the very 'Heart of Europe', the title he gave his next book. Powerful monarchs left their mark on the wider world (Jan Sobieski defeated the Ottomans at the gates of Vienna, Augustus the Strong built Baroque Dresden) while artists such as Chopin and Mickiewicz were merely the most celebrated members of Poland's large intellectual diaspora in nineteenth-century Paris. Such pan-European links are not only essential to the understanding of Poland but also provide the Westerner's best introduction to the country. When I first visited a few years ago, I went armed with Davies' *Heart of Europe* and found it an excellent companion, an ingenious book that starts with the mid-1980s and, chapter by chapter, works its way backwards in time. Davies' premise is that you cannot understand the present and recent past unless you understand what it came out of. Modern Polish Catholicism, Communism, unionism ('Solidarity') and literary culture all had their pre-echoes in the more distant Polish and European past.

In time, Davies came to apply this kind of thinking to a far larger canvas. *Europe: A History* is a massive but eminently readable work in which Davies wields not only the telescope, providing a survey of 2,000-odd years of history, but also the

microscope. It is the detail, perhaps, rather than the overall
tour d'horizon, that impresses most, especially the 'capsules'
– boxes a page or more in length about the origin, meaning and
historical reverberation of words and concepts we probably
know but can't quite place. There are over 300 of these, from
'Abkhazia' to 'Zeus'. *Europe* is a brilliant and in some ways
quirky book. Chapters have catch-all Latin titles, and maps
are fitted to the page by placing Portugal at the top. When the
mood takes him, Davies will devote precious space to a lengthy
summary of *Don Giovanni* (including musical quotations) or
stanzas in Russian from Pushkin. Of Augustus the Strong, a
militant monarch alleged to have fathered 300 illegitimate
children, Davies says he 'would have been a great king if
only his political ventures had been half as well aimed as his
spermatozoa' (adding that 'spoil-sports estimate his progeny
at eight'!).

At times, *Europe* reads almost like a rebuke against more
narrow-minded specialists who, as Davies says in another
typically pointed introduction, wouldn't dare assay anything
comparable. It's the queen bees, he says, not the workers, who
bring order to the hive; there'd be no honey if the workers
took over completely! Such comments are not best placed to
garner universal approval and affection. But then, Davies is
no stranger to controversy. Back in the mid-1980s, Stanford
University promised and then withdrew the offer of a lucrative
and prestigious Chair for reasons never precisely specified.
A lengthy and wounding judicial process revealed that some
had objected to a chapter in *God's Playground* on Polish
Jewry where Davies had argued that in pre-Nazi times not
all Poles were anti-Semitic and that the discrimination Polish
Jews experienced was not exceptional. After the Nazi takeover,
ordinary Poles were no more able to help the Jews in their
midst than most Jews were able to do anything to help Poles. A
Polish slave doctor in Auschwitz, wrote Davies, could no more
be judged by the morality of free people in normal times than

a Jewish informer who sought to save his life by denouncing his fellows. Extreme circumstances produce extreme behaviour. On the sensitive subject of Auschwitz, Davies pointed out that for many years it had been erroneously portrayed in the West as a death camp only for Jews, while Poles during the Communist period had been led to believe its victims were mainly Polish. Inevitably, perhaps, this kind of writing aroused criticism. Davies was an anti-Semite, it was said – doubtless an unfair accusation.

When *Europe* was published, the same critics circled overhead waiting to swoop. Errors of fact were discovered (inevitable in a book of such scope and ambition) and new evidence sought for Davies' alleged softness towards Polish anti-Semites and Nazi collaborators. For his part, Davies pointed out that 'critics from more fortunate countries' do not always realize how a totalitarian regime – and by that he meant not only Hitler's regime but also Stalin's – 'drives everyone in its power to varying degrees of complicity'. As the almost unimaginable horrors of the Holocaust unfolded and people across Europe forced to comply, responses ranged from the heights of heroism to the depths of depravity. News of what was happening was initially met in Britain and America with incredulity; indeed, it was a good half-century before historians fully came to terms with what had gone on at Auschwitz. But Western refusal to believe was just as great about Stalin's mass murders, insists Davies. Stalin, after all, was 'our ally' and, in any case, the monstrous brutalities of his regime were mostly perpetrated far from the Western gaze.

Europe had its share of hostile notices, particularly in America. But in general it was widely welcomed, became a bestseller and enabled Davies to quit academe and devote himself entirely to writing. Buoyed by its success, Davies followed *Europe* by producing another huge work, *The Isles*, in which he applied his accumulated historiographical attitudes and skills to his homeland. As a young man, he had noticed that by 'British' history people mostly meant southern 'English' history. A Lancastrian with Welsh blood in his veins, he found this sloppy, much as he did when people spoke of 'Russia' when they meant the Soviet Union. *The Isles* is an attempt to reinstate the history of Scotland, Ireland and Wales into that of – what? Britain? The British Isles? The United Kingdom? None of the current words or phrases will do. This is the message of both the title and content of *The Isles*. As in *Europe*, Davies makes it clear that cultures are generally more enduring than states and that political boundaries and allegiances are inherently impermanent. What we now think of as 'the UK' is a fairly recent fabrication and one that, in his view, is unlikely to last much longer in its present form.

The road to *The Isles* was long and arduous, and it was with some relief that Davies returned to the subject of Poland. In *Microcosm* (co-authored with his research assistant Roger Moorhouse), Davies examines the history of the Silesian city on the Oder that the Germans called Breslau and is now the Polish city of Wroclaw. Situated at the intersection of the German, Czech and Slavic worlds, it was at one time governed by the Hungarian king Matyas Corvinus, invaded by Swedish armies under Lennert Torstenson and was the temporary home at the outset of the Thirty Years' War to the fleeing Bohemian 'Winter King' and his Stuart wife. For much of the eighteenth and nineteenth centuries, it was under German rule and many upwardly mobile Silesians migrated westwards, to Munich, Frankfurt and Berlin. But Breslau also became a renowned cultural capital on its own account, so that by the 1890s it was experiencing something of a reverse cultural exodus. This was the city of the painter Adolf Menzel, the historian Theodor Mommsen and the playwright Gerhart Hauptmann. Max Bruch conducted here, while it was to mark an honorary degree in Breslau that Brahms wrote his 'Academic Festival Overture'.

The book considers in some detail the city's triumphs and tortures in the nineteenth and twentieth centuries. An account

of the appalling sufferings of Poles caught in the Soviet net
after 1945 and desperate to flee westwards is preceded by
an equally harrowing description of the often sadistic cruelty
meted out by Poles to ethnic Germans whom they summarily
expelled. In 1945–47, some 6 million desperate human beings
were tramping westwards, from the USSR to Poland and from
Poland into Germany. Such facts are too little known in the
West, Davies feels, as are those of the Warsaw uprising, the
subject of his most recent book, *Rising '44*. This is a vivid
account of one of the most brutal episodes in the war in which
the Nazis systematically tried to destroy the Polish capital and
all who defended it, while Soviet troops, relaxing across the
Vistula, did nothing, knowing that the whole of Poland would
soon fall into their hands.

As we emerge from a season of sixtieth anniversaries marking
the end of the War in Europe, it is easy to imagine that 'we'
bore the brunt. In the UK, we rightly celebrate the Battle of
Britain, the Normandy landings, Churchill and VE Day. But, as
Davies emphasizes, the sheer scale, suffering and destructiveness
of the war in Central and Eastern Europe dwarfs anything
experienced in the West. This will be a central theme of a short
(by his standards!) book Davies is currently undertaking about
World War II in which he intends to write about 'all the things
that British and Americans don't understand about the war'.
He also plans to write a book about 'Vanished Kingdoms'.
People have always assumed that whatever prevails in the
present is likely to be permanent. Not so, says Davies, as he
contemplates chronicling the rise and fall of the kingdom of
Strathclyde, Andorra, Sicily, Sardinia, Provence, Burgundy,
Galicia, the Grand Duchy of Lithuania, and that spectacular
example of a once-mighty state that disappeared in a puff of
utterly unanticipated smoke – the Soviet Union. Oh, and also
a chapter about New Amsterdam that Davies hopes will be
the prelude to a history of the United States. Let's hope he also

leaves time to write what I'm sure would be a big, readable,
irritating and brilliant book about the late Pope.

POSTSCRIPT

Daniel Snowman writes:

After publication of this article, Norman Davies expressed
reservations about two things I had written. At one point, I said
that many still often thought of Poland as 'an isolated, far away
land in the East that was once Nazi and then Communist' while
Davies (I wrote) was at pains to argue that, on the contrary,
it lay at the very 'Heart of Europe'. What I said was accurate
enough, I think, as far as it went. But Davies explained, in
a letter published in the next edition of *History Today*, that
Poland had never been 'Nazi'.

'There were no Polish Nazis,' wrote Davies in his letter to the
Editor. 'There was no Polish branch of the Nazi Party. In 1939–45,
there were no Polish armed forces under German command, and,
unlike almost every other German-occupied country, there were no
Polish volunteer divisions in the Waffen SS. Despite what one often
hears, there were no "Polish concentration camps", and there was
no collaborationist Government, as in Vichy France or in Norway.
Since wartime Poland was forcibly annexed either to the Greater
Reich or to the USSR, there was never any question of a Polish
Quisling. Indeed, there were very few Polish collaborators of any
sort. As concerns the Holocaust, which was largely perpetrated
in the German zone of occupation, the SS chose to recruit Jewish
police to control the main Ghettos and non-Polish auxiliaries to
guard the camps and the transports.
  'What there was in wartime Poland was the largest resistance
movement in Europe: a multi-ethnic population whose different
elements were targeted both by Nazi programmes of "racial
reconstruction" and by Soviet "social engineering": and a death-
toll, inflicted by the Soviets as well as by the Nazis, where the
Jewish victims were actually outnumbered by non-Jewish victims.
The true outlines of this tragedy can only be comprehended once
one realises that the largest cohort of civilian losses among the

so-called "Russian war dead" (now put at 27 million) does not refer to ethnic Russians but to "citizens of the USSR": and that a large part of those often involuntary Soviet civilians were made up of the Polish, Jewish, Lithuanian, Belarusian, and Ukrainian inhabitants of eastern Poland.

'The principal source of these difficulties, I think, lies in the inability of British and Americans to think of the Second World War in Europe in any terms other than those of a simple conflict between ourselves and the German enemy. We forget that Stalin's regime killed more people than Hitler's: that Stalin was Hitler's partner when we went to war in 1939 over Poland: and that later in the War our Polish ally was attacked and dismembered (with our connivance) by our Soviet ally. As a result, we should not be perpetuating the stereotype of a non-existent "Nazi Poland", but talking instead of an Allied Poland torn apart by its Nazi and Soviet neighbours.'

Davies also had reservations concerning the way I concluded what I thought to be a carefully balanced consideration of his discussion of the treatment of Polish Jewry during the war. In a chapter in *God's Playground*, Davies had argued that in pre-Nazi times not all Poles were anti-Semitic and that the discrimination Polish Jews experienced was not exceptional. After the Nazi takeover, he said, ordinary Poles were no more able to help the Jews in their midst than most Jews were able to do anything to help Poles. On the sensitive subject of Auschwitz, Davies pointed out that for many years it had been erroneously portrayed in the West as a death camp only for Jews, while Poles during the Communist period had been led to believe its victims were mainly Polish. 'Inevitably, perhaps,' I wrote, 'this kind of writing aroused criticism. Davies was an anti-Semite, it was said – doubtless an unfair accusation.'

Davies told me later that, to the best of his knowledge, no one had ever called him an anti-Semite, certainly not in public or in print, and I am sure he is right. But the suggestion has certainly been there in occasional hostile reviews and lay, at least according to some accounts, beneath the withdrawal of his offer of a Chair at Stanford. Davies acknowledges he *has* sometimes been openly accused, in the context of Polish-Jewish relations, of being 'pro-Polish' or 'Polonophile' – the implication being (as he himself puts it) that pro-Polishness is not acceptable, whilst pro-Jewishness is.

One of the central planks of much of Davies' writing, as my article showed, has been to remind readers of the almost unimaginable suffering incurred by the war on Eastern European, mostly non-Jewish people. This is not, he emphasizes, to downplay the horrors caused by Nazism and anti-Semitism; merely to redress the historiographical balance. I understood and appreciated that. But while researching Davies and his work before meeting and writing about him, I read a great deal about him and came across a number of hostile reviews of his work, especially by (mostly Jewish American) writers accusing him of equating the suffering of non-Jewish Poles with what they regarded as the unique enormity of the Holocaust. Davies does not equate. But he does juxtapose. And in doing so, as I'm sure he knew, he was bound to incur the disfavour of those to whom the paramount facts about the war were German aggression and Jewish suffering.

John Morrill

BIOGRAPHY

John Morrill is Professor of British and Irish History at the University of Cambridge and is a Fellow (and sometime Vice-Master and Acting Master) of Selwyn College. He has written and edited 19 books and is a prolific author of essays on many aspects of Early Modern history, especially the political and religious history of the Revolution of the mid-seventeenth century and the tense relations between the peoples of Britain and Ireland. He has a special fascination with Oliver Cromwell, serving as President of the Cromwell Association from 1989 to 1999, and he has written extensively on him, including a full biography in the new *Oxford Dictionary of National Biography* (for which he wrote twelve other lives and for which he served as Consultant Editor with overall responsibility for the 6,000 men and women whose fortieth birthday fell in the seventeenth century).

John Morrill was educated at Altrincham Grammar School and at Trinity College Oxford, staying on there as a Fellow (1970–74) after completing his D.Phil. He was a Lecturer at the University of Stirling where his interest was kindled in the historical relationship between Norman and Celt, Lowland and Highland. He moved to Cambridge in 1975 and has taught there for more than 30 years. Above all, he has now supervised more than 100 graduate students, nearly half of whom now work in universities and research libraries in all five continents, and he has served as external examiner in twelve universities in all parts of the UK and Ireland and he has examined 150 PhD theses from 37 universities. In recent years he has been very actively concerned as a Consultant in several Irish Universities and in Finland on the development of collaborative research cultures in the Humanities. From 1999 to 2004, he was a member of the Arts and Humanities Research Board of the UK. He was elected a Fellow of the British Academy in 1996, and has served on its Council, as Chair of the Communications and Activities Committee and as its Vice-President, 2000–02. Other public duties include a period as President of the Cambridge Branch of the Historical Association and a member of its Council, an eight-year stint on the Council of the Royal Historical Society (four as Vice-President) and three years as Deputy Director of the interdisciplinary Centre for Research in the Arts, Social Sciences and Humanities in Cambridge. Outside academic life, John Morrill is a husband, a father of four daughters, a grandfather, a lover of classical music, football and cricket, something of a connoisseur of malt whiskies, and what time is left over he devotes to his duties as a permanent married deacon in the Roman Catholic Church (ordained 1996).

PRINCIPAL PUBLISHED BOOKS

The Revolt of the Provinces: Conservatives and Radicals in the English Civil War 1630–1650 (1976)

Revolt in the Provinces: The English People and the Tragedies of War 1630–1648 (a recast and extended version, 1999)

The Nature of the English Revolution (1993)

Oliver Cromwell and the English Revolution (1990)

The British Problem: State Formation in the Atlantic Archipelago (with Brendan Bradshaw) (1996)

The Oxford Illustrated History of Tudor and Stuart Britain (1996)

Uneasy Lies the Head that Wears a Crown: Dynastic Crises in Tudor and Stewart Britain and Ireland, 1504–1746 (2005)

PROFILE, October 2005

The Professor of British and Irish History at the University of Cambridge turned up sporting a splendid 'Guinness'-emblazoned tie. It was a hot, sticky summer's evening and John Morrill had spent much of the day working on the Ford Lectures he is to deliver in Oxford next year. But, in the best traditions of the God-fearing Puritans he and I were shortly to discuss, we decided to work first before allowing ourselves the pleasures of a nearby hostelry.

One of the leading authorities on the Civil War and its participants, John Morrill is an expansive and exuberant conversationalist who gives the impression of being on almost personal terms with many of the seventeenth-century figures he writes about. He hasn't produced many Big Books (and has abandoned some). Rather, Morrill's most important work has often taken the form of scholarly articles and papers, alongside an impressive record as prime mover, editor and/or co-author of major collaborative works. He is the master of intellectual collegiality, of the engaging summary, the trenchant argument, the revisionist review, the compact biography.

Morrill was born in 1946 'within the sound of the roar of Old Trafford' and raised and educated in Altrincham. His parents were practising Anglicans (his father was head of a local Church of England primary school) and John grew up appropriately devout. An early interest in history was nearly extinguished by poor teaching soon after he entered grammar school; he came fourteenth in history but top in geography and for a while might have specialized in geography but for the fact that he wasn't much good at drawing maps. In the end, chaps won out over maps as a far better teacher, Norman Dore, recognized the boy's potential and inspired him with a love of the past and, in particular, the importance of local and county history and of the Civil War – themes that have informed Morrill's work ever since. After triumphing at O and A Level, it was to Dore's old Oxford college, Trinity, that Morrill headed in 1963. Here, he encountered the Tudor historian John Cooper, whom he gratefully recalls as a truly magnificent (and demanding) teacher, an academic skill Morrill still regards as profoundly under-appreciated. Oxford was packed with Civil War expertise when Morrill was up. Hugh Trevor-Roper, at the time Regius Professor, spotted the young man's potential and gave him support and encouragement. Christopher Hill was there, too. Morrill went to Hill's lectures and, although instinctively unsympathetic towards his Marxist historiography, took Hill's writings as a comfort blanket on a revision retreat during the run-up to Finals.

Morrill's religious upbringing had produced a rather serious-minded, ethically driven young man whose contribution to the radical 1960s led him not to CND or the hippy trail but to social work; 'I felt I had to give something back', is how he explains it now, recalling how he began to think of himself as a future prison governor. For a second time, Morrill was nearly lost to history until, at the urgent intervention of Cooper, he was persuaded to stay in the academic world, his tutor's earnest arguments reinforced, Morrill recalls hazily but happily, by generous drafts of Scotch.

Morrill retained his social conscience (he did voluntary work in the probation service for many years). But he stayed on at Oxford to do a D.Phil., remaining at Trinity with a Research Fellowship until leaving in 1974 for a post at the University of Stirling. At Stirling, Morrill found, like many a young don, that he had to lecture on all sorts of topics including some on which he felt he scarcely knew more than did his audiences. The one thing no Sassenach was allowed to teach was Scottish history. Morrill found Stirling tough but immensely enjoyable, with a bunch of congenial colleagues (including Richard Evans and the Africanist Robin Law with whom he shared a historiography course) and a home in Bridge of Allan on the edge of the Highlands. But a year later,

Morrill was lured to Selwyn College, Cambridge, where he has remained ever since.

In many ways a conservative figure, John Morrill gives the impression of being happiest in familiar territory. Deeply devoted to Cheshire and to his parents (his father died a year ago and his mother is still alive), he met his wife when still an undergraduate; John and Frances are now grandparents and have lived for the past 30 years in Cambridge. Some might see Morrill as something of an institutional figure, too. He has sat and served on fistfuls of academic committees, been external examiner and promotions or awards assessor for dozens of universities, Acting Master of his college (Selwyn), Editor of the *Historical Journal*, Editor or Editorial Consultant for several substantial history series, and latterly Consultant Editor for the 6,000-odd seventeenth-century lives in the *Oxford Dictionary of National Biography*. Morrill was President of the Cromwell Association in the 1990s, and is a Fellow of the British Academy (Vice-President in 2001–03) and of the Royal Historical Society whose online British history bibliography he edited. He has also supervised the work of over 100 postgraduate students (the 'New Morrill Army', his colleagues have dubbed them). And, it has to be said, for virtually his entire career, Morrill has toiled in more or less the same intellectual vineyard. His first book, based on his D.Phil. research, was a study of government and society during the Civil War in his home county of Cheshire, while recent publications still include essays and collaborative projects on Civil War history, including a dozen contributions to the *DNB*, among them almost book-length essays on Oliver Cromwell and (as co-author) Charles I. John Morrill is, among historians, the professionals' professional.

Yet examine the man and his work more closely and it becomes evident that this catalogue of stability, localism and good works is only part of the story. Even before he left Oxford, Morrill was giving indications of things to come. Trevor-Roper invited him to give some faculty lectures reflecting on seventeenth-century history. Morrill, building on his Cheshire research, challenged orthodox Civil War historiography by arguing that local tensions and preoccupations were often more important than national issues or abstruse constitutional principles. All over the country, ordinary people often reacted to the Civil War with incomprehension rather than with principled anger, their primary worry being that issues that didn't concern them might intrude and threaten their way of life.

This was brave stuff to present at a time when the Civil War was widely interpreted as the more or less inevitable outcome of long-term ideological or economic forces. Morrill, in contrast, became increasingly convinced that it was the messy, the contingent, that characterized the past rather than the neat and tidy, the cut and dried. The Civil War was not simply a war of convinced Royalists and Parliamentarians, Cavaliers versus Roundheads, but of a complete spectrum of troubled, uncertain people struggling to come to terms with troubled, uncertain times. Morrill's convictions were strengthened when his researches uncovered a group of people who, though treated as committed Royalists, were really the victims of feuds among Parliamentarians. All this helped lead to his next book, *The Revolt of the Provinces*, initially published as part of a series edited by Geoffrey Elton. Elton was often notoriously abrasive towards colleagues (and was heartily disliked by Morrill's mentors John Cooper and Hugh Trevor-Roper). But he could also be generous towards juniors, Morrill recalls, though he did order Morrill to edit out a fifth of his text before the book could be published. In his panic to do the right thing, Morrill cut his final chapter – the one that, in effect, gave the book its title (the book was later filled out and republished, with a subtle shift of title, as *Revolt in the Provinces*).

By now, at 30, Morrill's view of the Civil War was becoming clear. Charles I believed in the rule of law and in his right to impose it; he certainly waged war with a greater concern for the rule of law than his Parliamentary opponents. But, partly as a consequence, he became so short of resources that his movement collapsed into complete anarchy and plunder. By contrast, the Parliamentarians were more prepared to set aside the laws and liberties they claimed to be defending – with the result that they could produce the men and money required to win the war. Both sides struggled to win men and resources, regarding anyone who was not with them as an enemy. But if the belligerents painted a picture of a polarized and committed population, the reality included widespread antiwar sentiment (the 'Clubmen' and others) and, Morrill insisted, large numbers of people living in the provinces away from the great Royalist or Parliamentarian strongholds whose concerns were local and who were not strongly committed to one side or the other. If so many people feared anarchy and war, Morrill asked, why did it happen – and what did the people who didn't want it do about it? Thus, it was not so much the political or military aspects of the Civil War period that came to concern him so much as the psychological. What was it like being the people at the time?

Another, related, aspect of Morrill's thinking began to push itself to the forefront around this time. During his twenties, and for all his abiding reverence for his parents, he had found himself increasingly at odds with the Anglicanism in which he had been raised. Then, gradually, he came to embrace Roman Catholicism and in 1977 was converted. Morrill's personal odyssey did not transform his historiography in the sense of leading him towards a simplistically 'Catholic' view of the past. Indeed, he has written extensively about Puritans and Puritanism and noticeably little about (for example) Elizabethan recusants, the Catholic wives of the Stuart kings or Restoration-era anti-popery. But the fact that this is a man who takes religious ideas seriously has undoubtedly enriched his view of the men and women of the seventeenth century. In 1984, Morrill gave a paper to the Royal Historical Society that concluded with a splendid flourish. Were the English

civil wars (as it was then common to argue) the world's first
'Revolution'? No, said Morrill, they were the world's last
great wars of religion. Once again, Morrill had hit upon a
deeply unfashionable interpretation of history. At the time,
it was routine for self-consciously modern-minded historians
to see the Civil War through the supposed self-interest of its
various participants, virtually dismissing their religious beliefs
as a smokescreen. Morrill, by contrast, urged the integrity of
religious belief. If those who fought said they did so in the
name of God and Christ and quoted the Bible as authority,
he argued, historians should pay them the compliment of
believing they meant what they said.

Morrill has written a great deal about the religious psychology
of those who fought in the civil wars, especially Cromwell
– a man who, for the first 40 of his 58 years, lived in almost
total obscurity. Yet Cromwell is someone whose mind and
personality Morrill feels he has really come to know. He has
found that the very gaps in the record of Cromwell's early life
can be almost as revealing as the few things we do know. For
example, in an early letter written when Cromwell was still
living in Huntingdon, he reproves a certain Mr Storie for not
subscribing to a 'lecturer' (that is, a preacher) called Wells.
Morrill decided to hunt down anything he could about Storie
and Wells. Wells, it transpired, was a preacher from across the
Ouse while Storie was a prominent cloth merchant involved in
a decision about whether to use a recent bequest to endow a
new 'lectureship'. One link led to another, enabling Morrill to
cast new light on Cromwell's move from Huntingdon to St Ives
and to establish a chain linking him to the patronage network
of the Earl of Warwick, the greatest of the 'establishment
Puritans' of the pre-Civil War era. Morrill has developed a
nose for this kind of historical sleuthing. He enjoys pondering
the strings or straws of history that seem to lead nowhere but
which, when tugged hard and intelligently, can lead to new
revelations. Sometimes, he says (in another metaphor of the

kind Cromwell would have approved of), our ignorance about the past arises not so much from the silence of the sources as from the deafness of the historian.

Morrill is struck by the fact that what we loosely call the Civil War has in fact no single, universally accepted title. We can all agree on the 'Norman Conquest', the 'Reformation' or the 'French Revolution'. But what of the 'English' (or 'British'?) Civil War (or 'wars' or 'Revolution')? How does Scotland fit into this? And what of the Irish dimension? All of which has led Morrill to reflect on the historical background of the nation state in which British people live today, with its current mouthful of a title: the 'United Kingdom of Great Britain and Northern Ireland'. No simple or single word or phrase will do, for present or past, because (except briefly and controversially under Cromwell) the people of these islands have never been fully integrated into a single state. Morrill has taken time off from sleuthing and string-pulling to contemplate a longer and larger tapestry: the switchback state formation of what, for want of a better term, he has dubbed 'the Atlantic Archipelago'.

In a devastating analysis of centuries of dynastic accidents and upsets, Morrill shows how the so-called continuity of the so-called British monarchy has been no such thing but has swung hither and thither as a result of treachery, war, whim, sickness and the unpredictable repercussions of individual birth and death. These reflections have led him to raise some challenging counterfactual hypotheses – for example, that the marriage of Mary Queen of Scots to King Francis II of France might easily have produced a son (had Francis not died at the age of 18) who would have inherited and perhaps united both thrones. If you have difficulty imagining the repercussions of a Franco-Scottish state, such a union was no more improbable, suggests Morrill, than the actual linking of the English crown 150 years later to that of a Hanoverian duchy. Morrill has trenchant things to say, too, about Scottish independence, which, he points out, was there for the taking on several occasions. When the monarchy was abolished in England and Ireland in 1649, Scotland had an opportunity to go its own way but chose to throw in its lot with its southern neighbours. And the Jacobite rebellions of 1715 and 1745 were fought by Scots to reinstate the Stuarts as monarchs not of Scotland but of Britain. No wonder Morrill was discouraged from teaching Scottish history at Stirling!

As Morrill approaches 60, he says he plans to be less of an 'educational manager' and to produce more history. The Ford Lectures will feature a series of pivotal 'moments' during the Civil War, including a lecture on the Putney debates, another on Scottish self-identity and reactions to regicide, and a third on what amounted to ethnic cleansing in Ireland. Morrill is also nursing book-length projects on the two principal trajectories he has pursued over the years: the 'mind' of those who fought the Civil War, and the unstable nature of the emerging English/ British state over time. Thus, he is contemplating a volume about Cromwell and the Bible (the only book we know for sure that Cromwell read), a study of the formation of the British state system in Tudor and Stuart times, and a book about the changing physical and mental frontiers of Britain from pre-Norman times to the present with chapters on attitudes to law, language, religion and national or ethnic identity.

Is there any thread unifying these ambitious projects? Perhaps it is his emphasis on the inchoate, the uncertain, the contingent, the game of chance and happenstance that is history – and life. An appropriately un-Puritan reflection, we agreed, on which to adjourn for a couple of beers and a bite.

EPILOGUE

John Morrill writes:

After a decade of 'running things', I decided in 2004 to return principally to research and writing. In 2006, I have been invited to deliver the Ford Lectures in Oxford and have chosen to speak on the subject of 'Living with Revolution: The Peoples of Britain and Ireland 1647–1661'. I intend to publish these in 2007. I am also working on a series of projects relating to Cromwell's religious psychology and on what I call 'the creation of a British state system but not a British state' across the Early Modern period. I have also been commissioned, with John Saward and Michael Tomko, to edit an 850-page selection of spiritual writings by English Catholics since 1500, which will be entitled *Truly I believe*.